DISPATCHES FROM NOVA SCOTIA DURING THE COVID-19 PANDEMIC

STAY THE BLAZES HOME

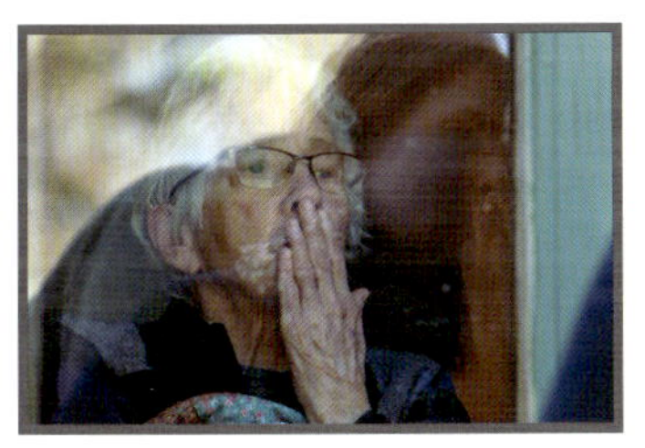

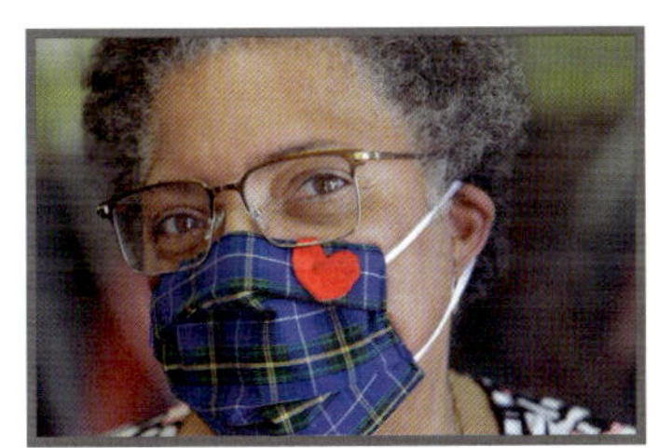

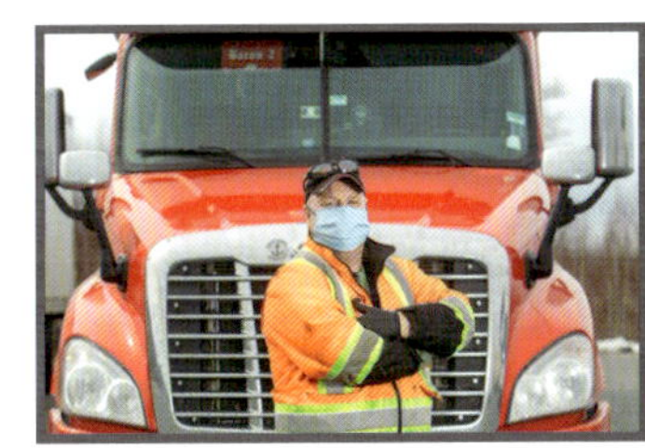

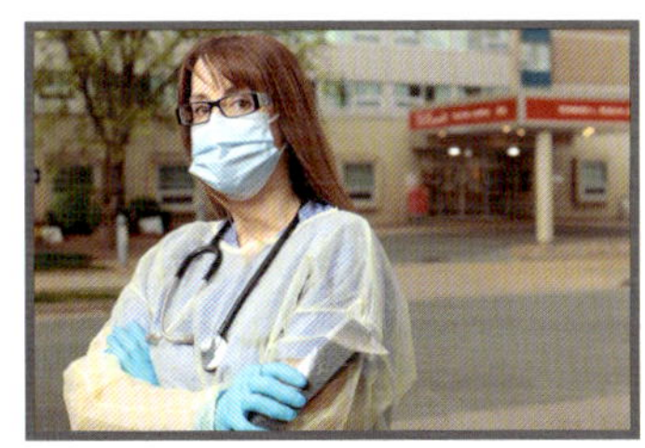

LEN WAGG

Foreword by *DR. ROBERT STRANG*

Afterword by *THE HONOURABLE STEPHEN MCNEIL*

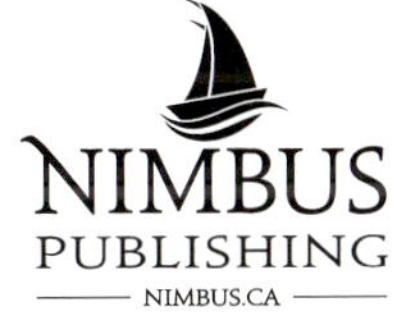

NIMBUS PUBLISHING
NIMBUS.CA

Nimbus Publishing Limited
3660 Strawberry Hill Street, Halifax, NS, B3K 5A9
(902) 455-4286 nimbus.ca

Printed and bound in Canada

NB1558

Editor: Angela Mombourquette
Design: Jenn Embree

Library and Archives Canada Cataloguing in Publication

Title: Stay the blazes home : Nova Scotia and the COVID-19 pandemic / by Len Wagg.
Names: Wagg, Len, photographer.
Identifiers: Canadiana 20200229001 | ISBN 9781771089432 (softcover)
Subjects: LCSH: Nova Scotia—Social conditions—21st century—Pictorial works.
Classification: LCC FC2312 .W335 2020 | DDC 971.6/050222—dc23

Canada

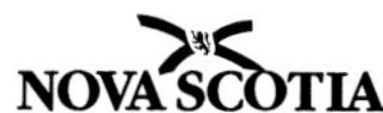

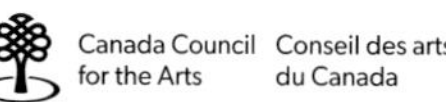

Nimbus Publishing acknowledges the financial support for its publishing activities from the Government of Canada, the Canada Council for the Arts, and from the Province of Nova Scotia. We are pleased to work in partnership with the Province of Nova Scotia to develop and promote our creative industries for the benefit of all Nova Scotians.

Spring 2020 was a dark time for Nova Scotians.

On April 18–19, a gunman went on a rampage that began in Portapique, NS; before it ended, he had taken twenty-two lives. On April 29, a Nova Scotia–based Royal Canadian Air Force Cyclone helicopter crashed off the coast of Greece, killing all six members on board. On May 6, three-year-old Dylan Ehler of Truro went missing; he still has not been found. And on May 17, Capt. Jennifer Casey of Halifax died when the Snowbirds aircraft she was in crashed after takeoff in Kamloops, BC. The flight had been part of a cross-country tour known as Operation Inspiration, which was meant to lift the spirits of Canadians during the COVID-19 pandemic.

And, of course, between March and July, COVID-19 took the lives of sixty-five Nova Scotians.

Nothing I can say in these pages can come close to honouring each and every one of those lives.

This book is dedicated to the memory of all those Nova Scotians lost.

TABLE OF CONTENTS

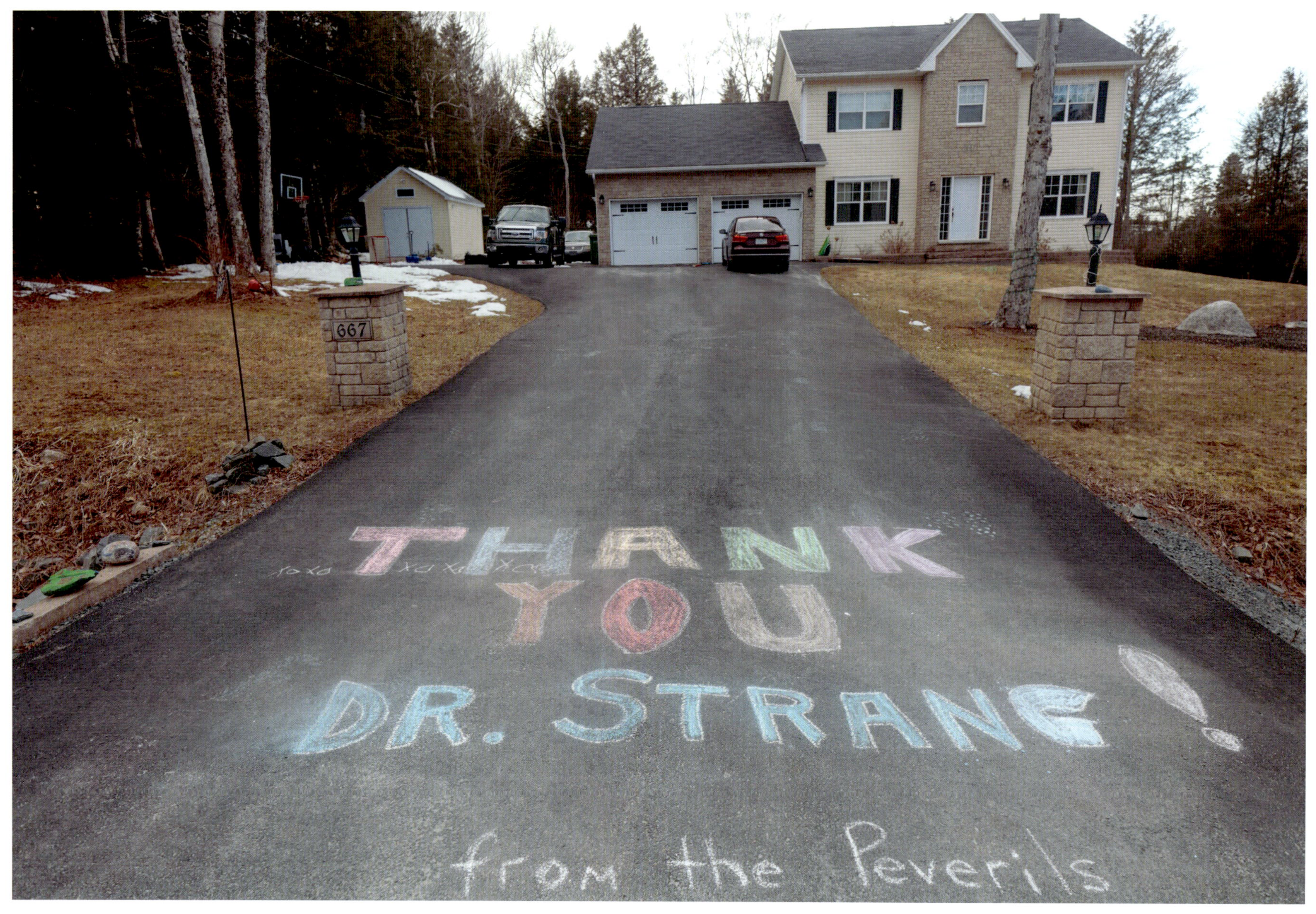

A family in Dr. Robert Strang's neighbourhood posted this message of support in chalk, thanking him for the long hours he has put in coordinating the province's COVID-19 response.

FOREWORD

In January 2020, when I and other Canadian public health leaders began to discuss the reports of an outbreak of severe respiratory illness in Wuhan City, China, we were aware of the pandemic potential of a new respiratory virus—but none of us could have predicted what the coming months would bring.

We had no real model to go by. Many of us had been involved in the 2009 H1N1 pandemic, but that had had much less impact because it was a new strain of a known virus—influenza—and a vaccine was available in time for the second wave. The 1918–19 influenza pandemic had happened under such different societal conditions that it was not able to help us predict in detail the possible impacts of this COVID-19 pandemic. Our federal/provincial/territorial pandemic plans provided a good starting point for the early planning of how to manage COVID-19's arrival in Canada, and continue to guide the health-care system's response, but this pandemic's deep and complex impacts across society have proven to be unprecedented, immensely challenging, and, for me, deeply humbling.

At a personal level, the first wave of COVID-19 has been difficult, and has brought countless long days, challenging decisions, and a feeling of tremendous responsibility. However, these challenges have been balanced by the many Nova Scotians who have reached out to me to say thank you, to provide encouragement, and to offer their prayers.

Professionally, it has been humbling to see the care and dedication of people throughout Nova Scotia's health-care system and within our communities who have worked tirelessly to keep us safe and healthy and to provide essential services for all.

I know that many Nova Scotians have been greatly impacted by COVID-19 and the necessary control measures—most significantly the sixty-five families who lost a loved one to COVID-19. At the same time, Nova Scotians have witnessed countless examples of people and families going to great lengths to take care of one another.

It is my great hope that such caring and compassion can be the ongoing legacy of COVID-19.

Thank you, Len Wagg, for capturing this historic time for all of us.

Dr. Robert Strang
CHIEF MEDICAL OFFICER OF HEALTH, NOVA SCOTIA

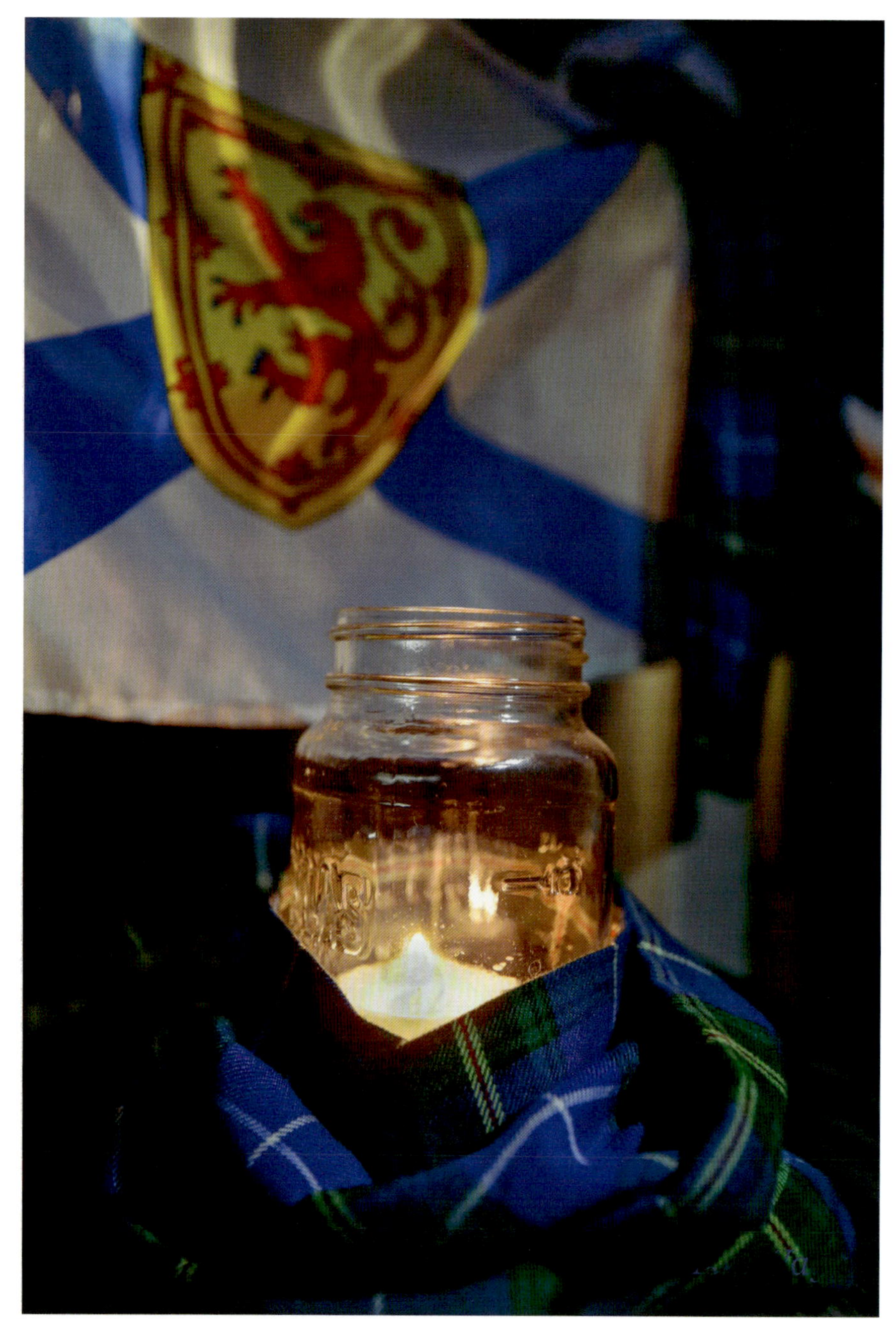

INTRODUCTION

The COVID-19 pandemic, like so many other things that affect Nova Scotians, began a long way away.

In early January 2020 our nightly newscasts mentioned a new respiratory disease that was affecting people in Wuhan, China. Later that month the news reported that the entire province of Hubei, with a population of 58 million, had been locked down to avoid the spread of this new coronavirus.

As February turned to March, thoughts of a trip down south were still on some people's minds, but the possibility of international travel soon came to an end as the WHO declared a global pandemic and Canadians were advised to avoid non-essential travel outside of Canada.

We watched with growing anxiety as Nova Scotians, in places all across the globe, scrambled to get home.

When they did, they found that stores, like those across North America, were experiencing shortages of toilet paper, hand sanitizer, and disinfecting wipes. (Months later, we are still trying to figure out why there was such a run on toilet paper!)

A provincial state of emergency was declared; schools and non-essential businesses were closed; airlines virtually shut down. With all this, the economic impact started to become apparent.

While people isolated at home, front-line and essential workers carried on, driving down empty streets or riding buses and ferries for free en route to work. We quickly came to understand that many people in the lowest-paying jobs were truly essential—truckers, grocery clerks, those working in home care. Large grocery-store chains implemented incentive-pay programs for the workers who were responsible for keeping stores open. Ad campaigns thanking health-care workers, truckers, and farmers popped up on television and social media.

Like millions of Canadians and thousands of Nova Scotians, I watched Prime Minister Justin Trudeau—and later Premier Stephen McNeil and Nova Scotia's chief medical officer of health, Dr. Robert Strang—present daily updates on the COVID-19 situation, and I began to wonder where we would be in the weeks, months, and years following this pandemic.

When I saw social media posts with stories and photos from the Nova Scotia Archives referencing the influenza pandemic of 1918, I began to wonder how future generations would see this pandemic. Where would the images of this unprecedented time come from? After the Facebook posts and tweets went away, what would remain as a snapshot of life during COVID-19?

Terrilee Bulger, the general manager and co-owner of Nimbus Publishing, wondered as well. Within days in March we had an outline, and my search for those images and stories began.

One problem became immediately apparent: How could I photograph people without going near them? How could I do interviews without breaking Public Health's social distancing orders? I resolved to find a way.

I didn't do it alone. I had help from other photographers, like Paul Darrow, who had started with me in the newspaper world decades ago. Paul found pictures in his Cole Harbour neighbourhood in Halifax. Steve Wadden in Sydney covered the socially-distanced wedding of a couple near him. Photographer Nicola Davison captured the boredom-breakers in her Dartmouth community. Tim Krochak, newly laid off from his newspaper job, contributed images of daily life during the pandemic. Importantly, Nimbus Publishing put out a call on social media asking you—Nova Scotians—to submit your images of what life was like under lockdown. You came through in a big way, and your images have been included on these pages to help tell the whole story from Port Hawkesbury to Parrsboro to Salmon River.

As COVID-19 arrived in Nova Scotia, the stories became apparent. Heather Thomson, of Pictou County, found solace in music, so she started the Ultimate Online Nova Scotia Kitchen Party (COVID19 Edition), which grew to more than a quarter of a million members. "Caremongering" groups started up all across Nova Scotia, where people found ways to reach out and help others in need. Older Nova Scotians learned how to use Zoom and FaceTime, and younger people learned the value of puzzles and time at home with family.

Father Simon Lobo delivered his Easter Mass to an empty Halifax church, but to sixteen thousand viewers online. As his colleague, Father Alex Colautti, noted, "it's not the darkness that defines the limits of darkness, it's the light that defines the darkness."

That light shone brighter through the actions of Crystal Blair, who worked every day to make sure long-haul truckers were fed when restaurants were closed. It shone through the actions of acute-care nurse Andrea Jenkins, who suited up daily and headed to the epicentre of the Nova Scotia pandemic—the Northwood long-term care facility in Halifax—to care for those who were sick and dying. It shone through the kindness of Mariah Kearney, whose business was in trouble, but who came up with an idea that went viral and raised over $100,000 for charities dealing with the fallout from the pandemic. It shone in the words of Charlene Chiddenton as she told me, through tears, about the last time she saw her father, who died from COVID-19.

As I listened to these stories, it became more and more obvious that the pandemic would have a long-lasting effect on all of us. How incredibly lucky we are to live in an empathetic and caring place like Canada—and more specifically, in Nova Scotia.

Of course, the rules about things like distancing and mask-wearing in public were a moving target as the science around the pandemic evolved. These stories represent the state of things when I spoke with people, mostly in May, June, and July.

While the spring of 2020 will be remembered as the time we stayed home, watched Netflix, shopped online, and did lots of home cooking, it will also be remembered as the time we cooked for neighbours, shopped online for people who could not afford what they needed, and sang to connect with those we couldn't meet with in person.

I could go on, but I won't.

As I quickly realized as I sat or stood six feet away from my interview subjects, my arm stuck out as far as possible as I recorded their voices, this is not my story.

It's theirs.

A TIMELINE OF COVID-19 IN NOVA SCOTIA

DECEMBER 31, 2019 ≈ The World Health Organization is alerted to several cases of pneumonia in Wuhan, China, caused by a virus that does not match any other known virus.

JANUARY 7, 2020 ≈ Chinese researchers identify a new coronavirus (COVID-19) behind the illness.

JANUARY 15 ≈ The Public Health Agency of Canada activates the Emergency Operation Centre to support Canada's response to COVID-19.

JANUARY 22 ≈ Canada implements screening requirements related to COVID-19 for travellers returning from China to major airports in Montreal, Toronto, and Vancouver.

JANUARY 25 ≈ Canada confirms its first case of COVID-19 (in Toronto).

JANUARY 30 ≈ The World Health Organization declares the outbreak of COVID-19 a public health event of international concern (PHEIC).

FEBRUARY 9 ≈ Canada expands COVID-19 screening requirements for travellers returning from affected areas to ten airports across six provinces.

FEBRUARY 28 ≈ Nova Scotia advises anyone traveling from "an affected area" to closely monitor their health for fourteen days after their arrival in Canada.

MARCH 9 ≈ Canada confirms its first death related to COVID-19. Nova Scotia reports no cases.

MARCH 11 ≈ The World Health Organization declares the global outbreak of COVID-19 a pandemic.

MARCH 13 ≈ Canada advises citizens to avoid all non-essential travel outside of Canada until further notice. Nova Scotia's chief medical officer of health, Dr. Robert Strang, encourages "individuals, employers, and community organizations" to limit social gatherings to "no more than 150 people."

MARCH 15 ≈ Nova Scotia reports its first three presumptive cases of COVID-19 and the province implements additional measures under the Health Protection Act, including closing long-term care facilities to visitors, closing public schools for two weeks following March Break, and closing regulated daycares.

MARCH 16 ≈ Canada advises travellers entering Canada to self-isolate for fourteen days.

MARCH 18 ≈ Canada implements a ban on foreign nationals from all countries, except the United States, from entering Canada. The Canada–US border closes to all non-essential travel, and international passenger flight arrivals are redirected to four airports in Calgary, Vancouver, Toronto, and Montreal.

MARCH 19 ≈ Personal service and fitness establishments in Nova Scotia, such as hair salons, barbershops, spas, nail salons, body art establishments, and gyms are ordered to shut down. Restaurants are restricted to take-out and delivery only. University students from Nova Scotia who are still living in residences are told to go home to provide space for social distancing for students from outside the province who are not able to travel.

MARCH 21 ≈ Nova Scotia restricts hospital visitors.

MARCH 22 ≈ Nova Scotia declares a provincial state of emergency. Residents are told not to leave the province and to only leave home for essential items and services. Provincial parks, beaches, and tourist attractions are closed. Social gatherings of more than five people are prohibited, and police are authorized to enforce orders around gathering limits and social distancing under the Health Protection Act.

MARCH 30 ≈ All public schools and licensed childcare providers in Nova Scotia are ordered to remain closed until at least May 1.

APRIL 2 ≈ Canada surpasses ten thousand confirmed cases of COVID-19.

APRIL 3 ≈ Premier Stephen McNeil, in response to reports of a rise in attendance at provincial parks and beaches, tells Nova Scotians to "stay the blazes home." The phrase takes off on social media, inspiring numerous memes, stickers, songs, posters, beer labels, T-shirts... and books.

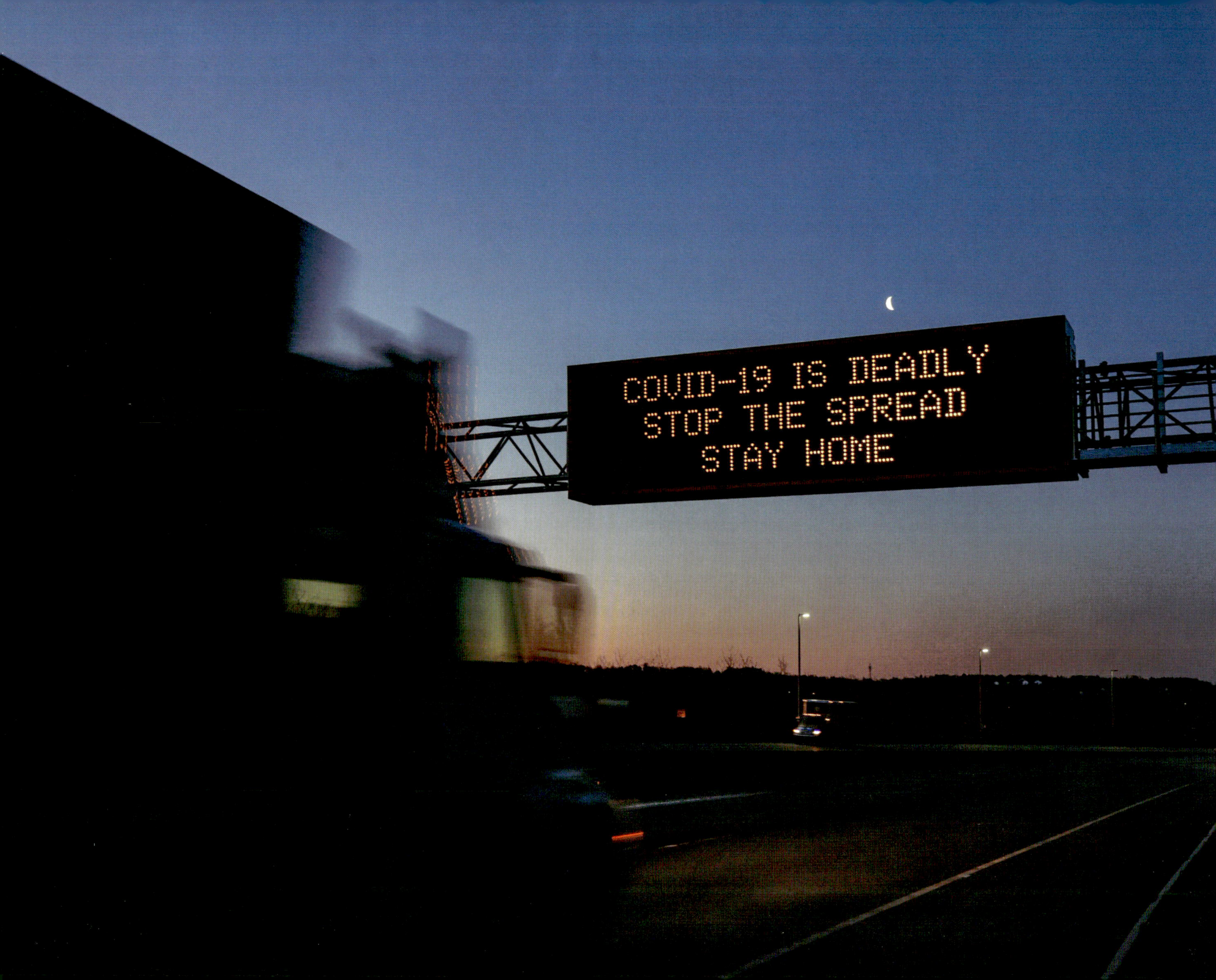
COVID-19 IS DEADLY
STOP THE SPREAD
STAY HOME

Part One: LOCKDOWN

An overhead sign on Highway 118 in Dartmouth displays an ominous warning during the early days of the pandemic.

AN EERIE EMPTINESS

As the COVID-19 pandemic began to take hold in Nova Scotia in mid-March 2020, schools, businesses, and restaurants closed down. When the provincial state of emergency was declared on March 22, Nova Scotians were asked to leave home only for essential items and services. The result was eerily empty streets all across the province.

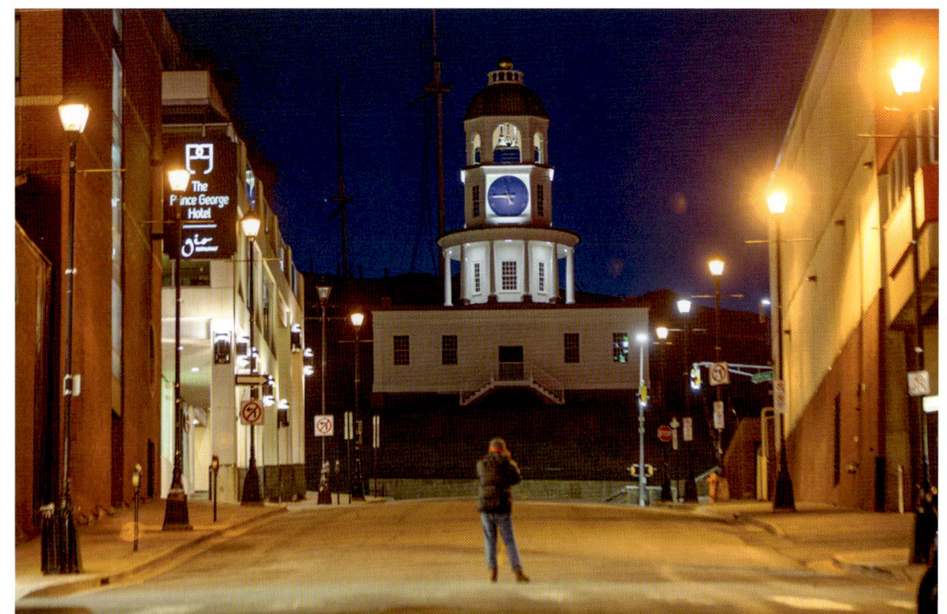

TOP LEFT: *Images that had been impossible to capture due to traffic suddenly became possible during the pandemic, like this shot of the Old Town Clock looking up Carmichael St. in Halifax.*

BOTTOM LEFT: *Halifax's Grand Parade—usually a busy spot with patrons of the local bar district milling about—sits empty on an April evening.*

BOTTOM RIGHT: *Billboards advertise since-cancelled shows at Neptune Theatre in Halifax.*

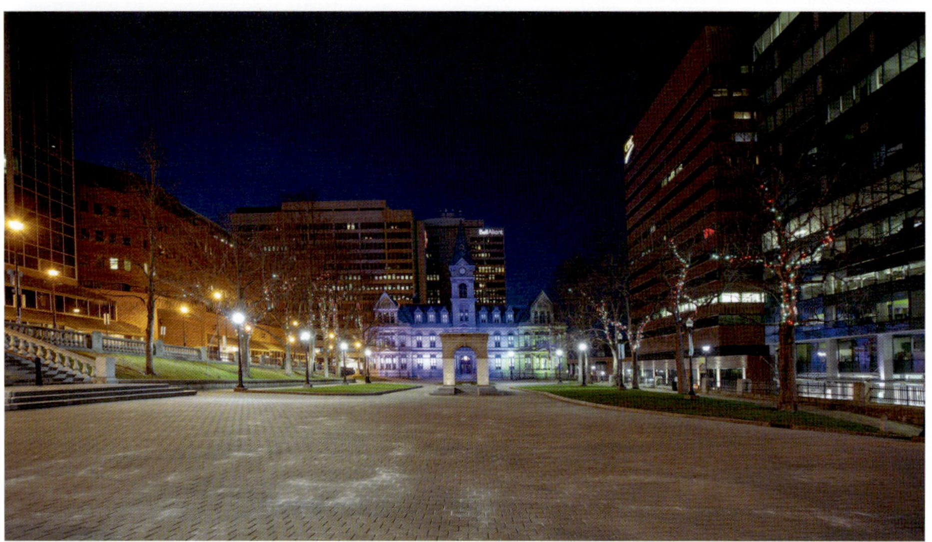

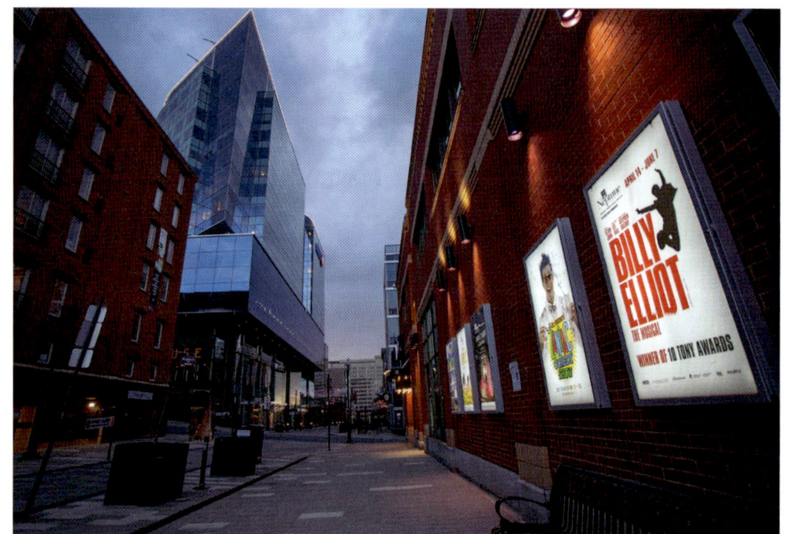

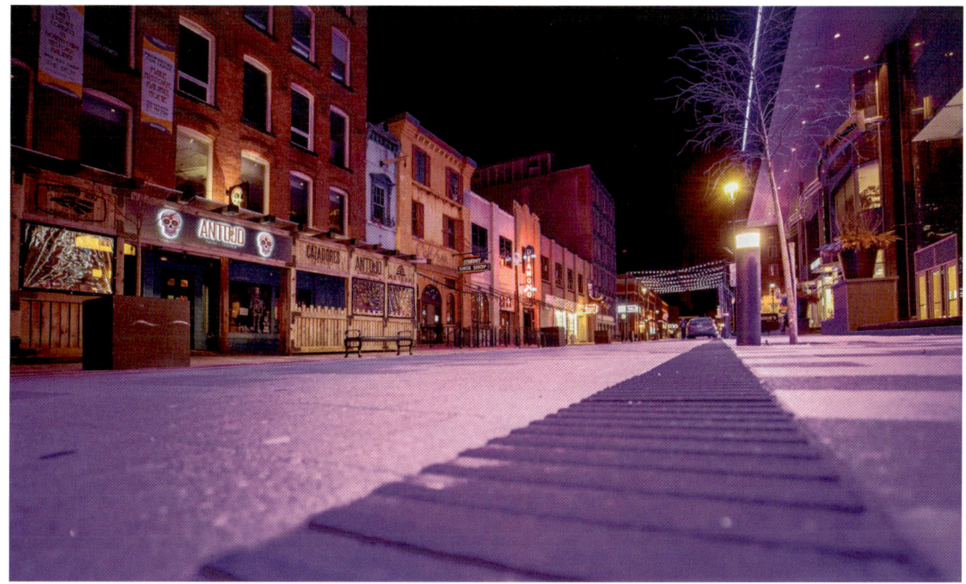

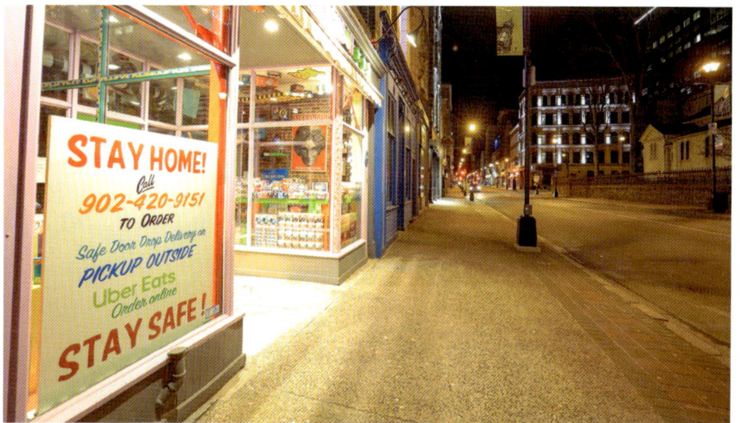

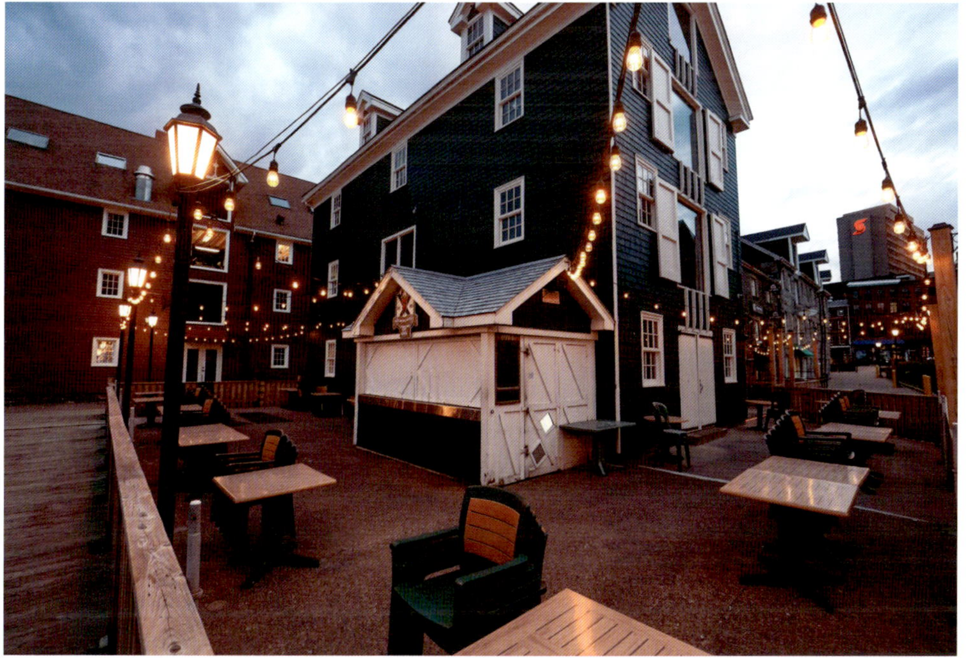

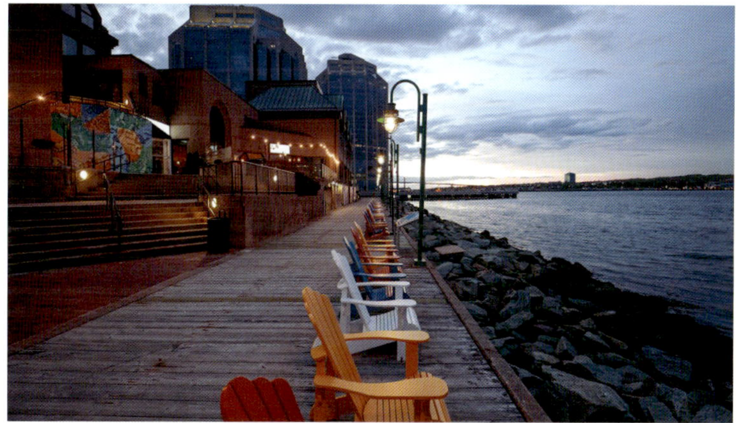

TOP LEFT: *Halifax's usually bustling Argyle St. bar district.*

TOP RIGHT: *Retail businesses like Freak Lunchbox, a candy store on Barrington St. in Halifax, found creative ways that included home delivery and roadside pickup to serve their customers.*

BOTTOM LEFT: *Empty sidewalks and tables at The Lower Deck pub on the Halifax waterfront.*

BOTTOM RIGHT: *These Adirondack chairs are usually filled with tourists enjoying the sights and sounds of Halifax Harbour.*

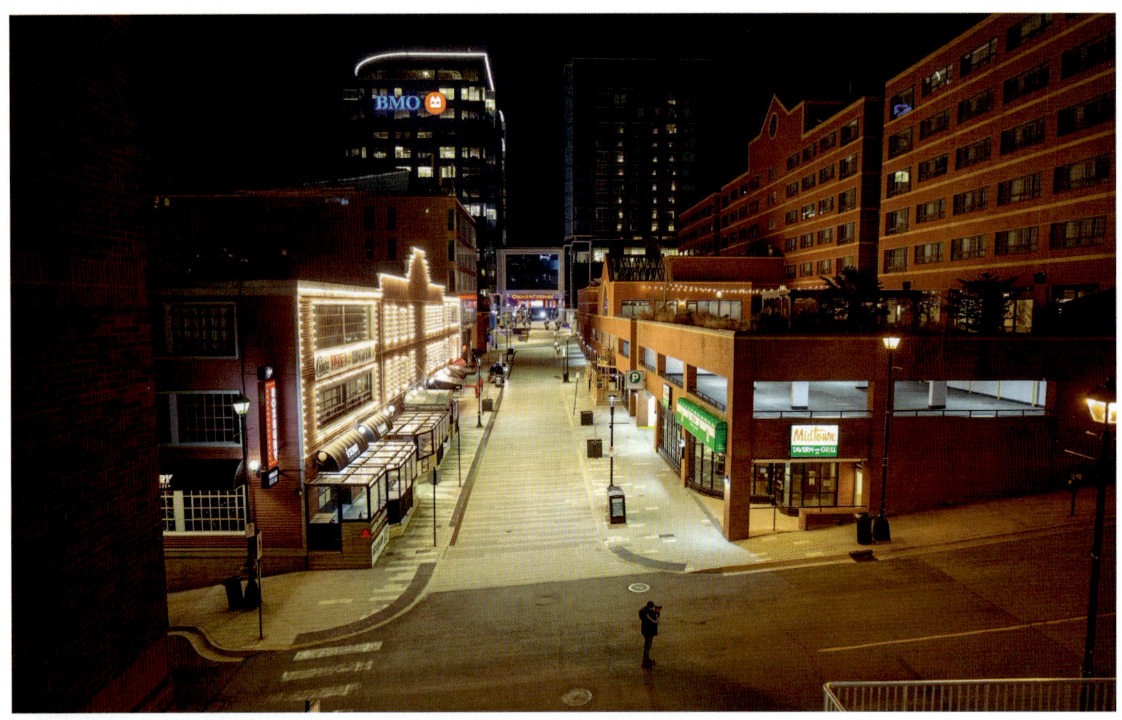

TOP LEFT: *No cars, no taxis, no groups of people chatting and smoking outside the establishments on Halifax's Grafton St. The popular bar and hotel area was empty except for the presence of another photographer.*

BOTTOM LEFT: *The traffic lights continued to change even though there were few vehicles on Halifax's Hollis St.*

BOTTOM RIGHT: *A March rush hour in Halifax.*

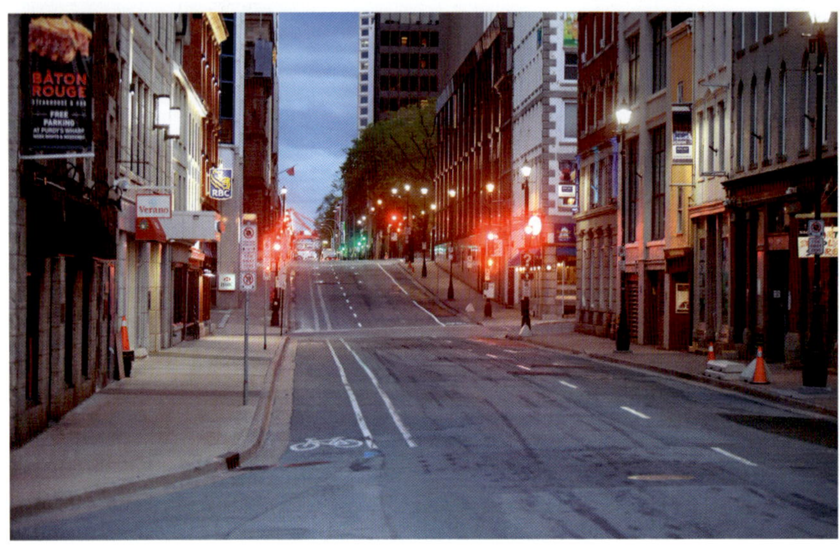

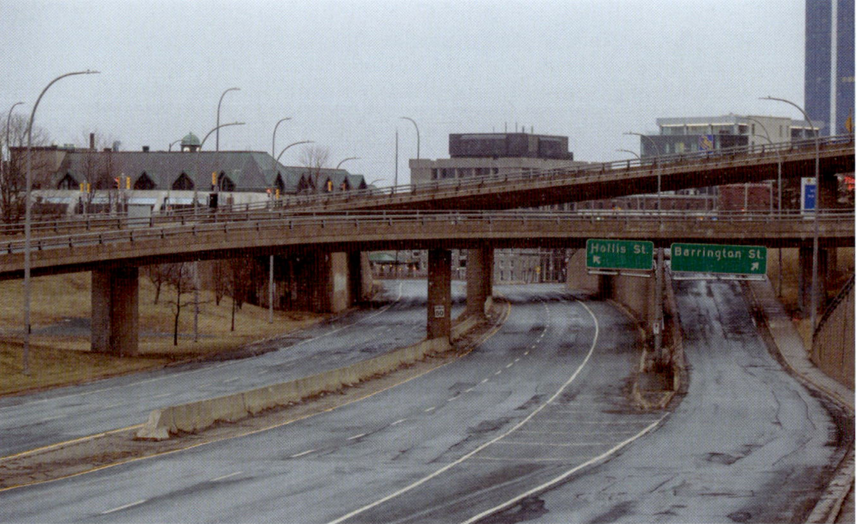

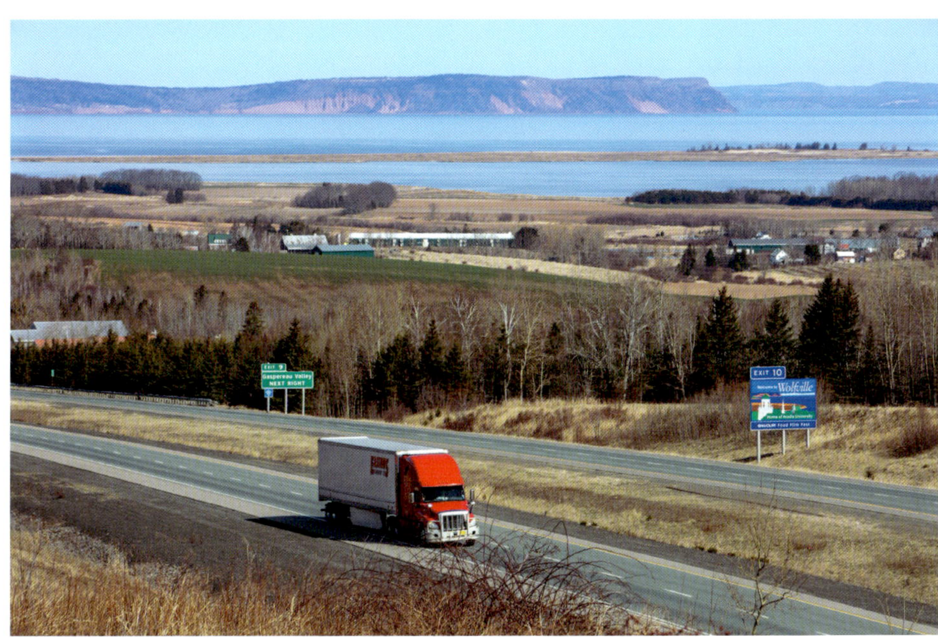

TOP LEFT: *Nova Scotia's 100-series highways, like the 101 near Avonport shown here, had very little traffic other than transport trucks in early April.*

BOTTOM LEFT: *The deserted main artery of the Cogswell Interchange in Halifax's downtown core.*

BOTTOM RIGHT: *Freddie Wilson has been waving at cars from this overpass on Highway 101 for decades—so long the overpass was actually named after him. In an encouraging sign of "normal" life, Freddie was spotted in late April at his favourite spot.*

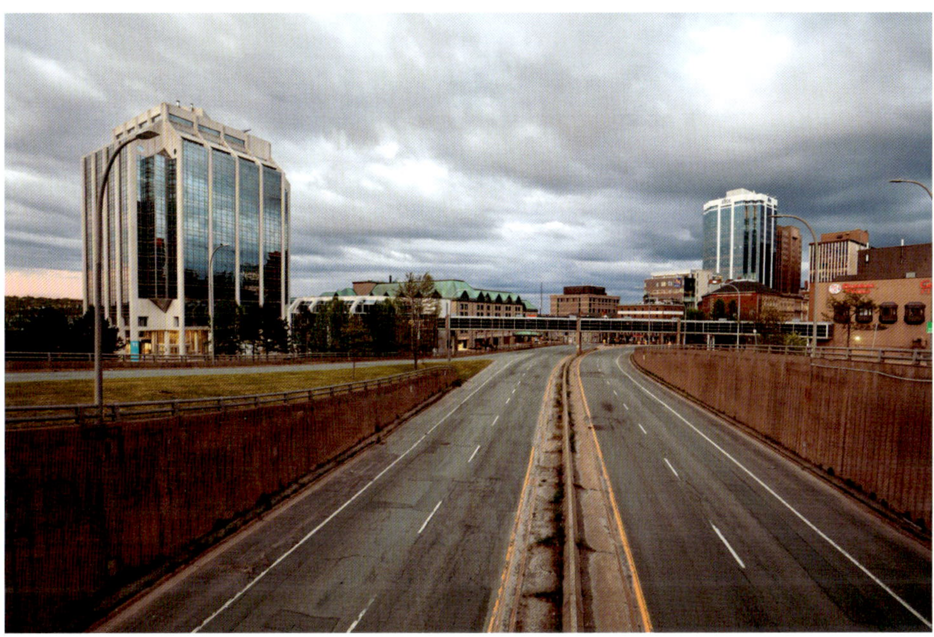

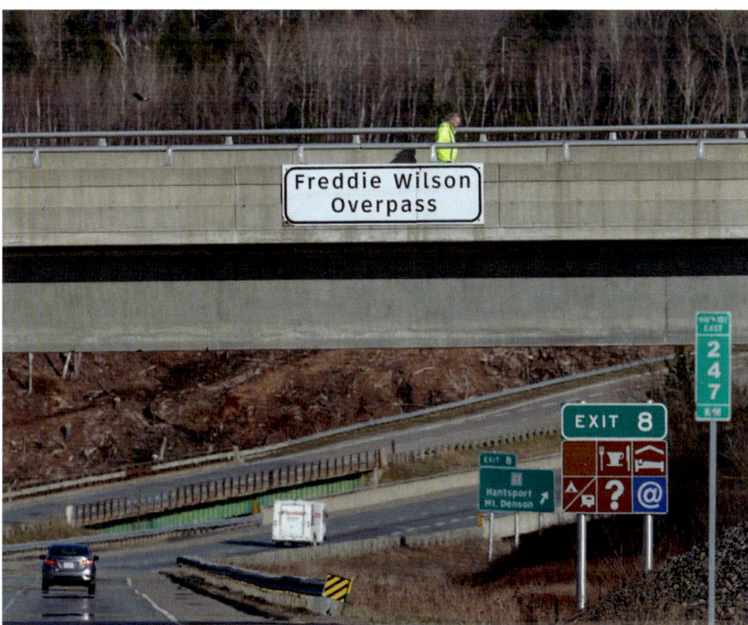

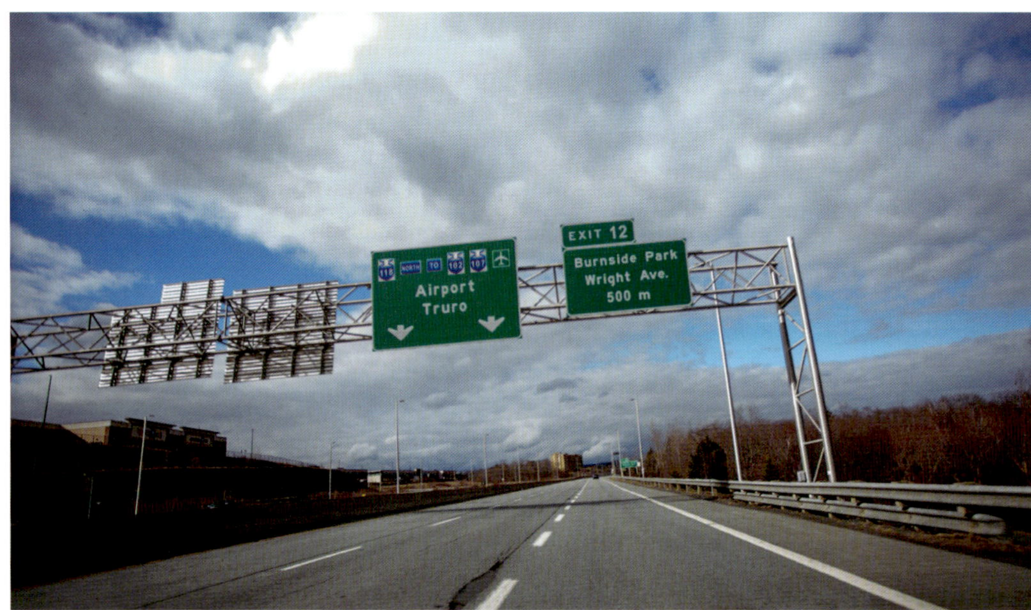

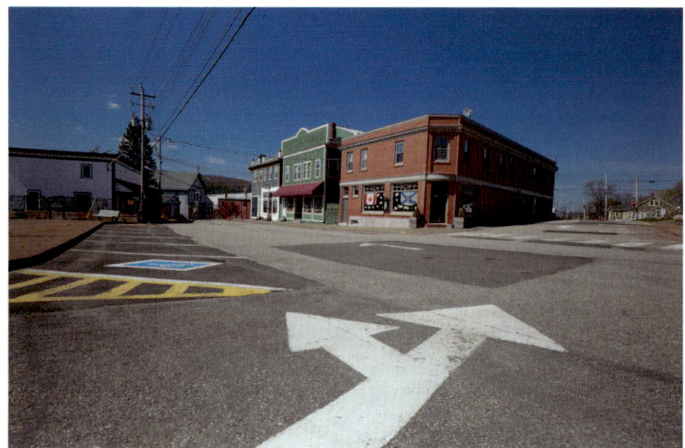

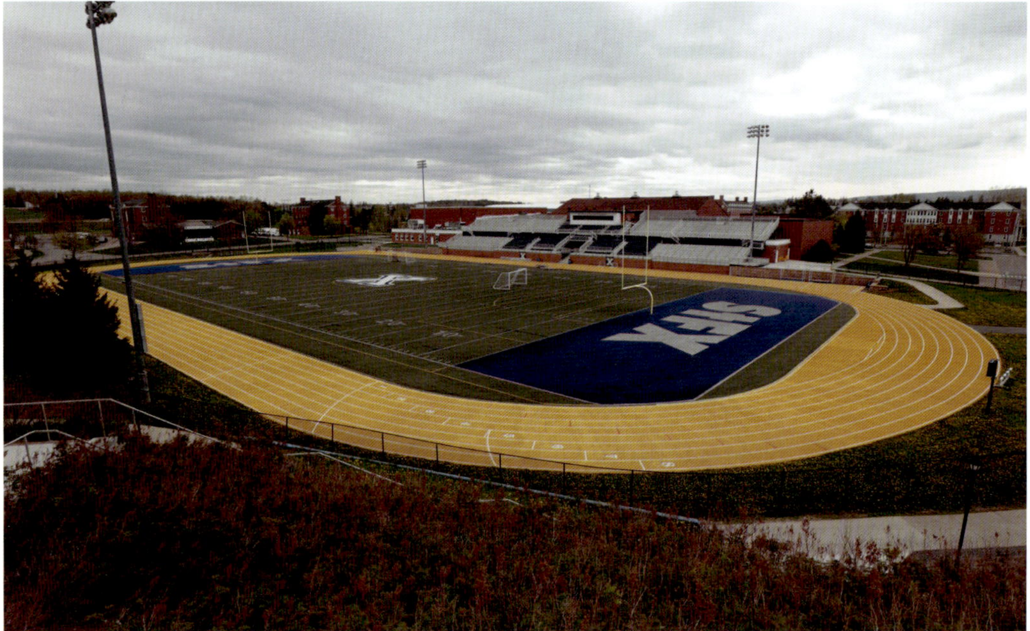

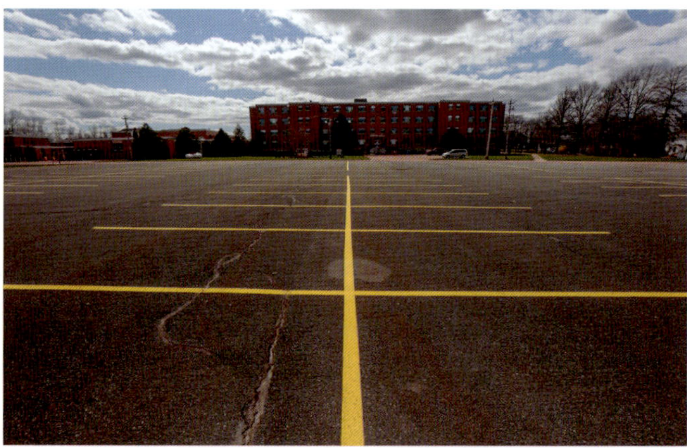

TOP LEFT: *Highway 118, on the outskirts of Dartmouth, with none of the usual traffic.*

TOP RIGHT: *St. George St. in Annapolis Royal on a sunny April afternoon.*

BOTTOM RIGHT: *Students at the Nova Scotia Community College in Truro finished their year online.*

BOTTOM LEFT: *The sports field at St. Francis Xavier University in Antigonish—typically a busy spot in early spring.*

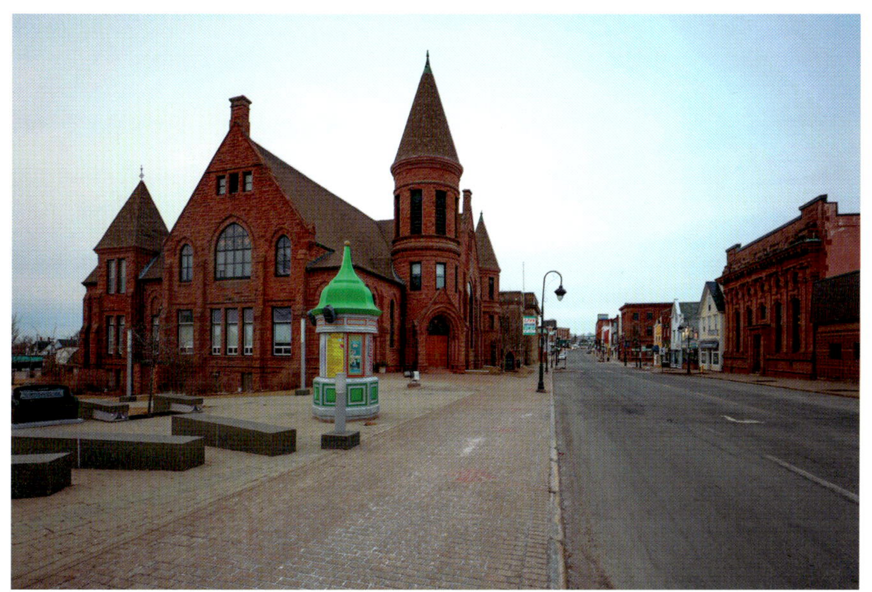

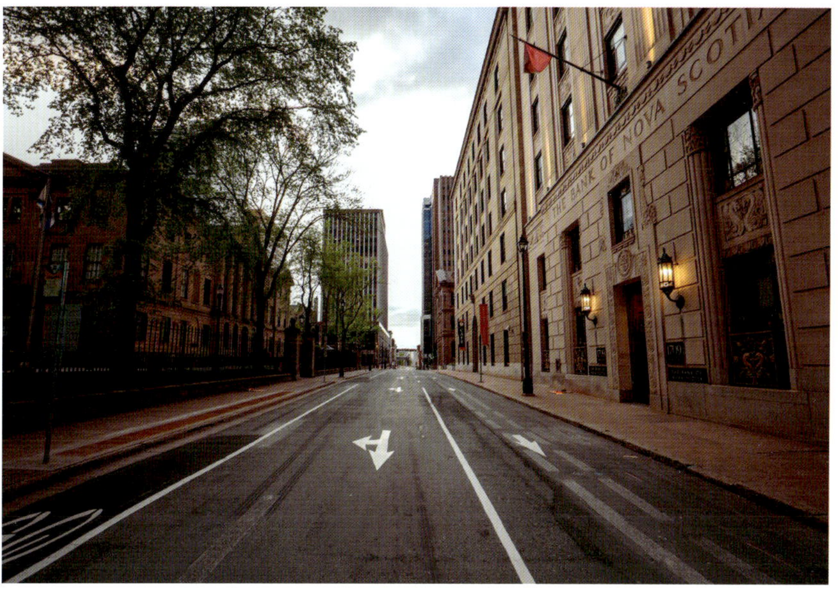

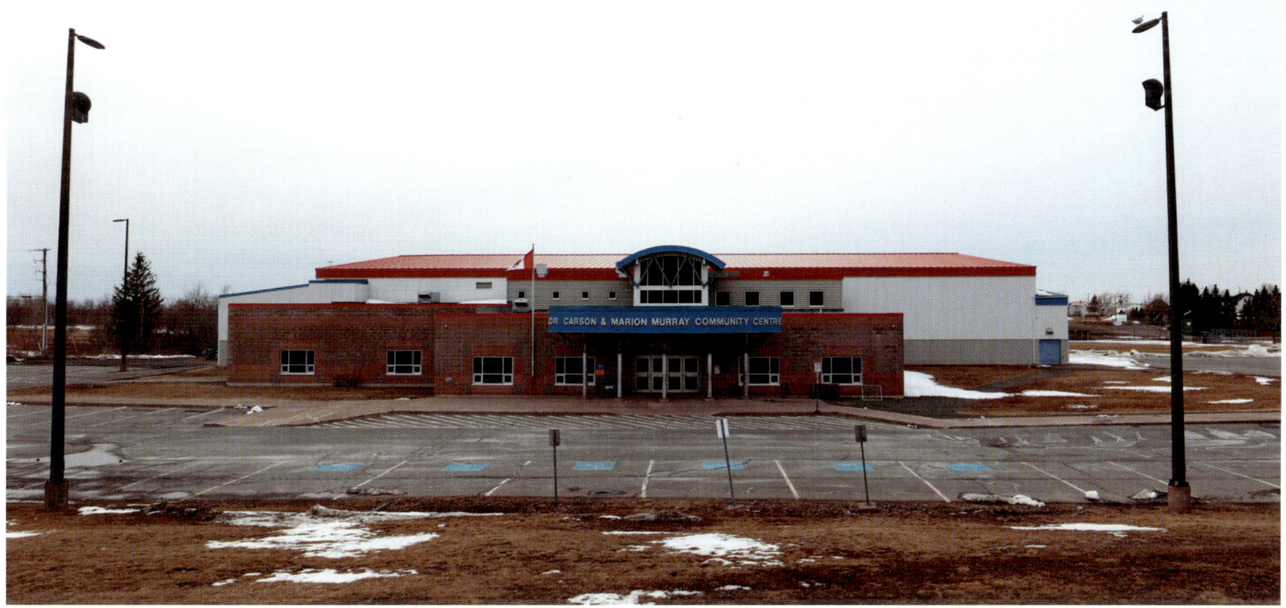

TOP LEFT: *Victoria Park and Highway 6 in downtown Amherst are deserted in late March 2020.*

TOP RIGHT: *Another view of Hollis St., Halifax.*

BOTTOM: *Skating, hockey, and community get-togethers all came to a halt at the Dr. Carson & Marion Murray Community Centre in Springhill.*

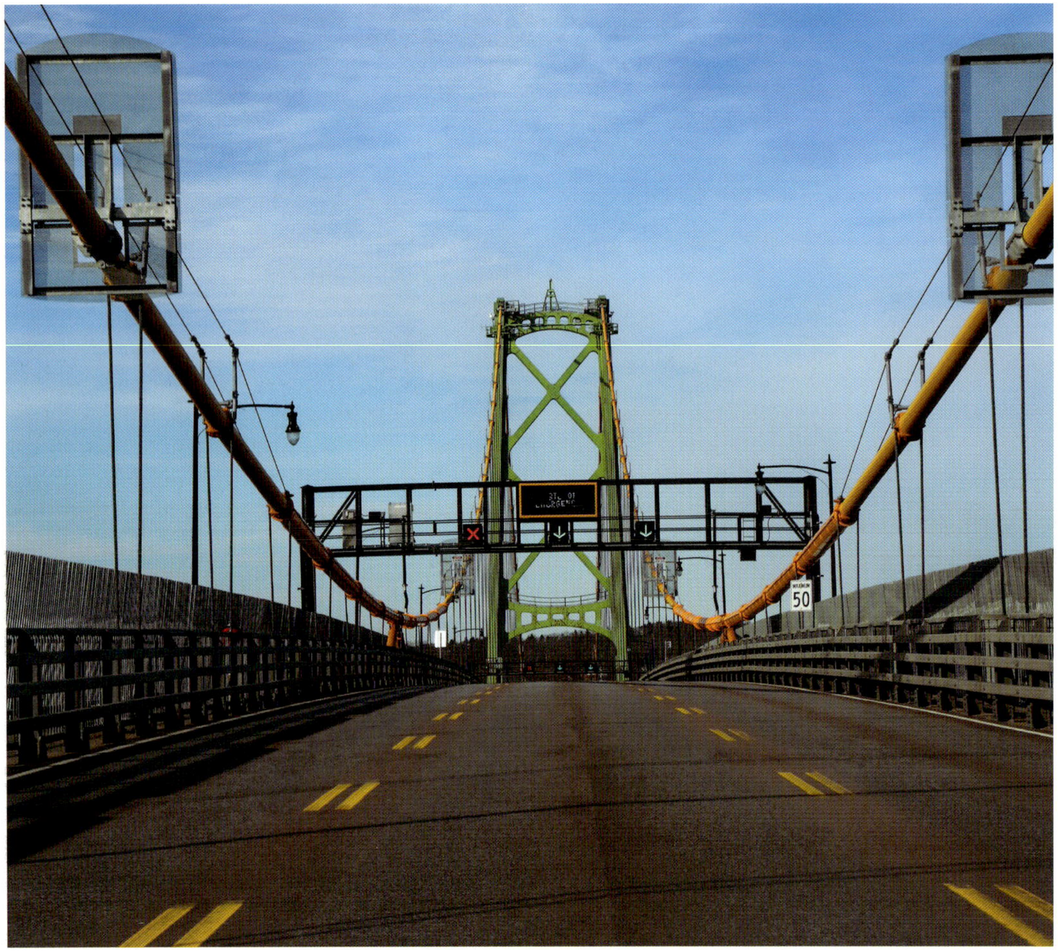

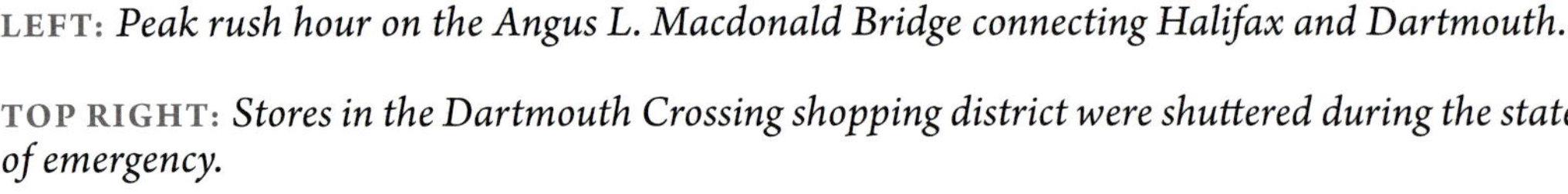

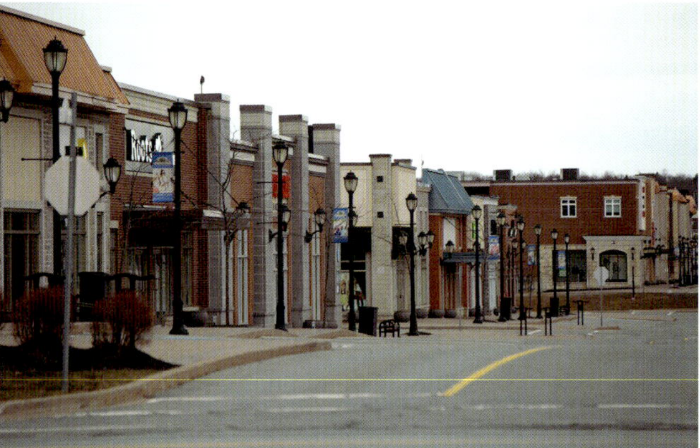

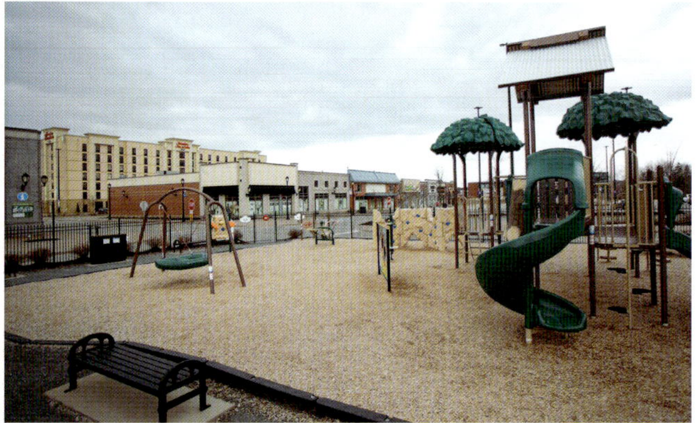

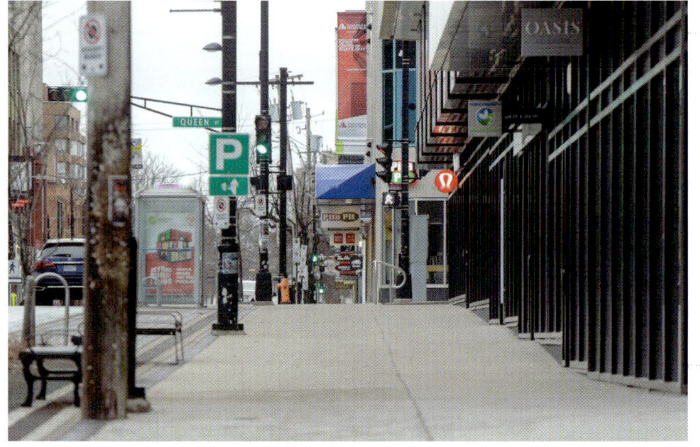

LEFT: *Peak rush hour on the Angus L. Macdonald Bridge connecting Halifax and Dartmouth.*

TOP RIGHT: *Stores in the Dartmouth Crossing shopping district were shuttered during the state of emergency.*

MIDDLE RIGHT: *A closed-off community playground at Dartmouth Crossing.*

BOTTOM RIGHT: *The nearly empty sidewalks on Halifax's Spring Garden Rd.*

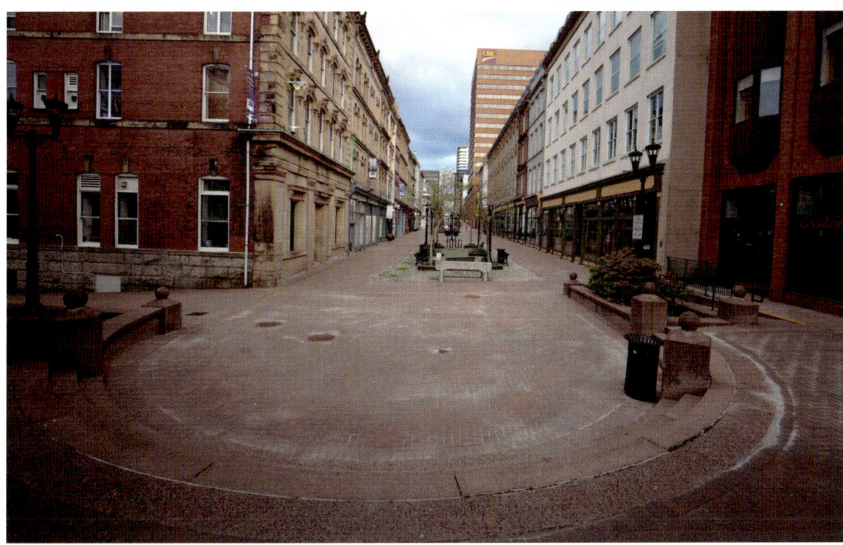

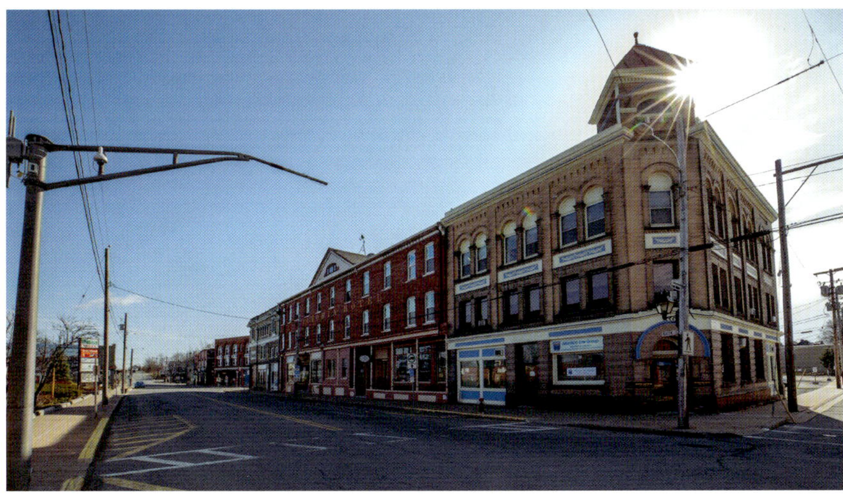

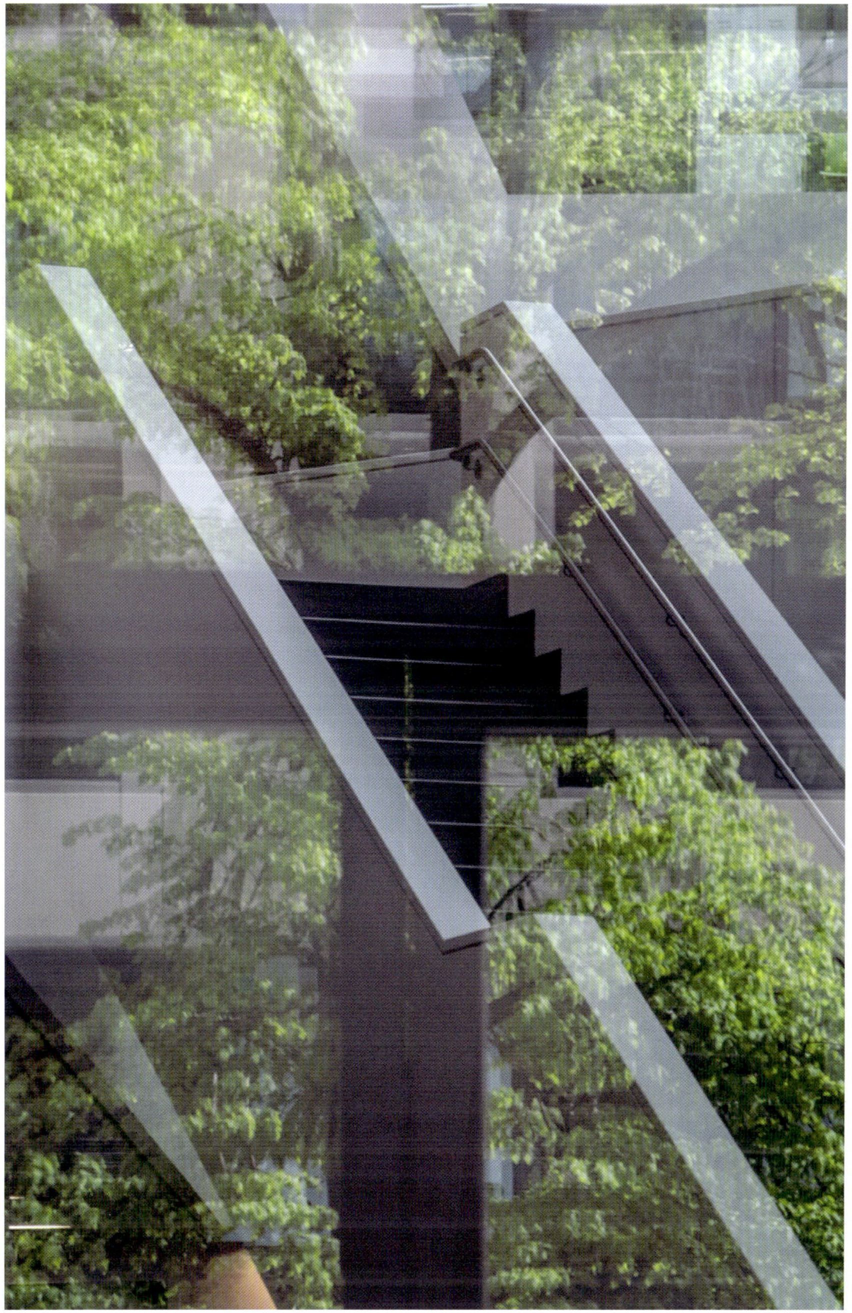

TOP LEFT: *The Granville Mall in downtown Halifax.*

RIGHT: *The empty main staircase at the Halifax Central Library. (Yoriko Miyata)*

BOTTOM LEFT: *The intersection of Water and Gerrish Streets in Windsor on a Saturday morning.*

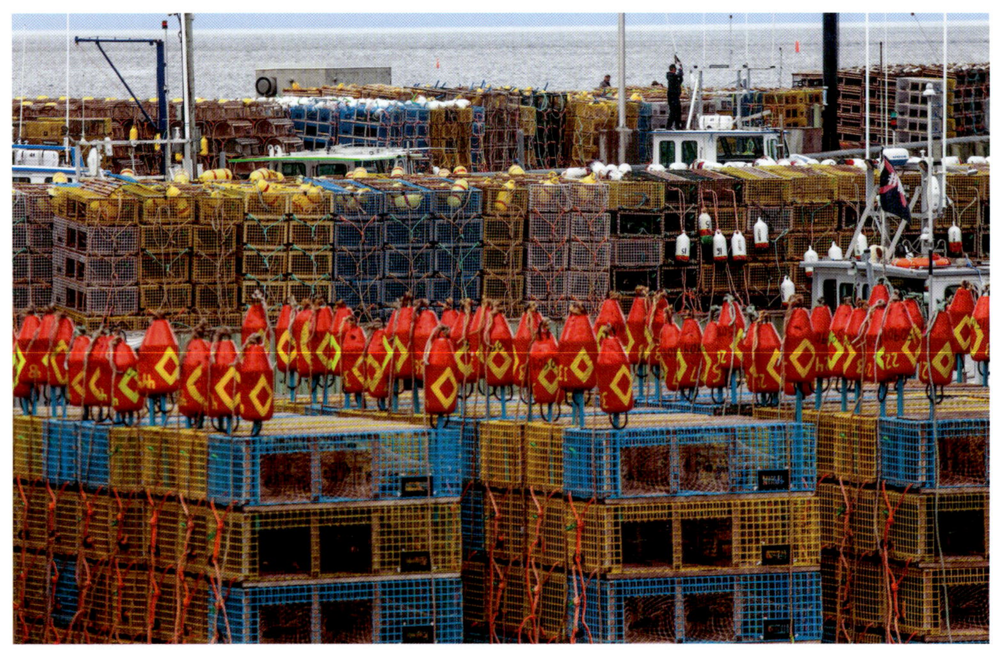

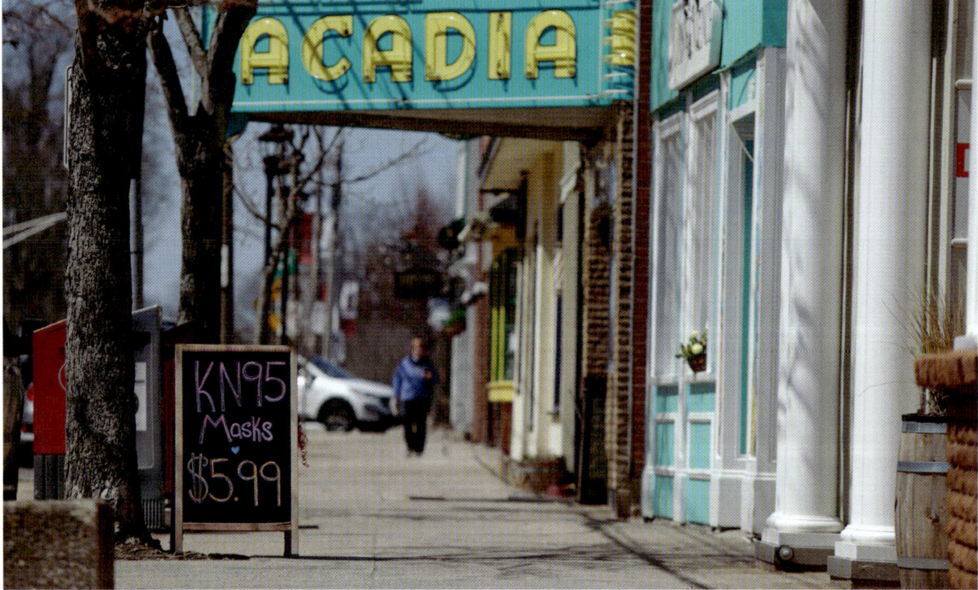

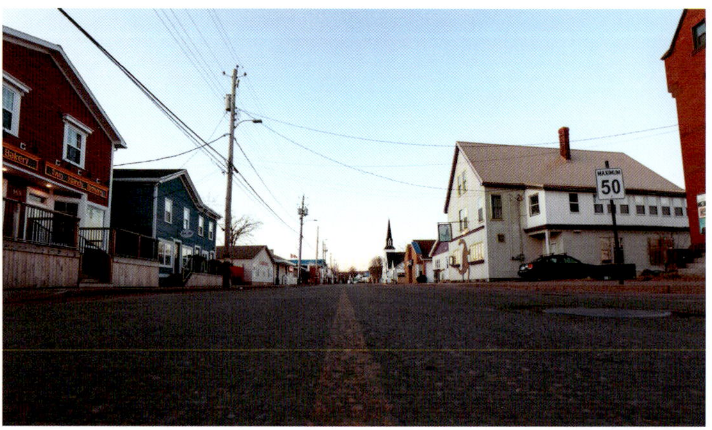

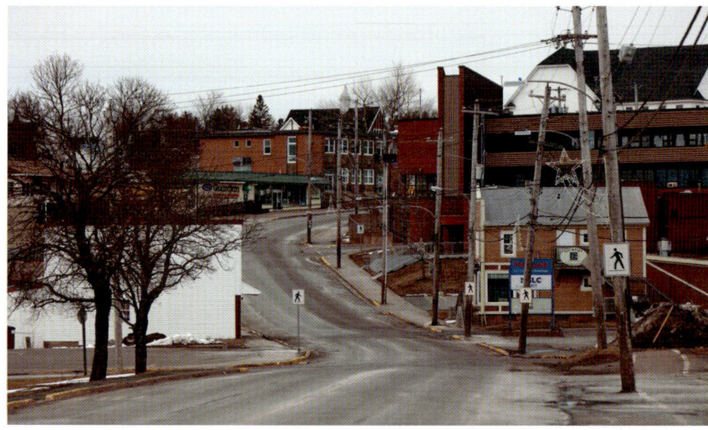

TOP LEFT: *Wharves were closed to anyone not directly involved in the fishing industry. Here, in Caribou, fishers were preparing for the upcoming lobster season.*

TOP RIGHT: *Empty streets in Springhill.*

BOTTOM RIGHT: *Closed shops on Main St. in Parrsboro.*

BOTTOM LEFT: *Signs advertising masks, usually reserved for the Halloween season, began appearing all over the world during the pandemic, as this one did in Wolfville. Beginning July 31, everyone in Nova Scotia was required to wear a non-medical mask in most indoor public places.*

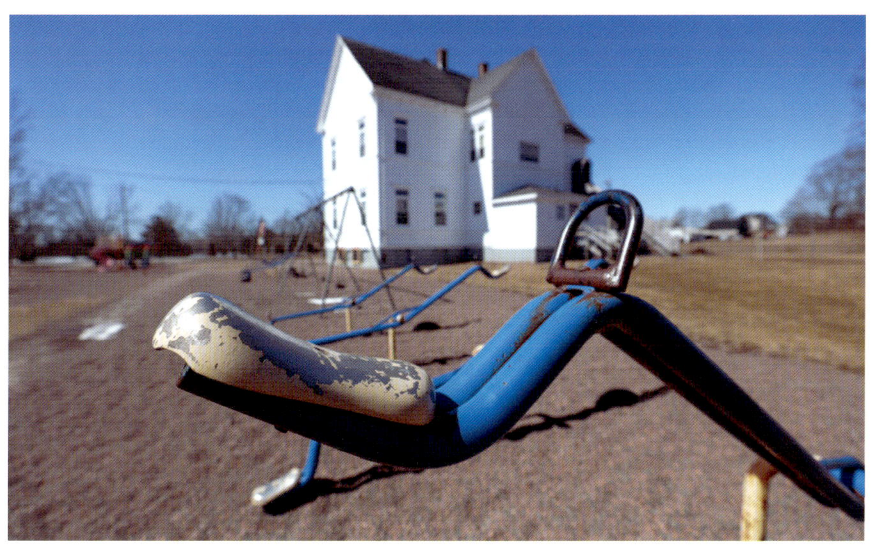

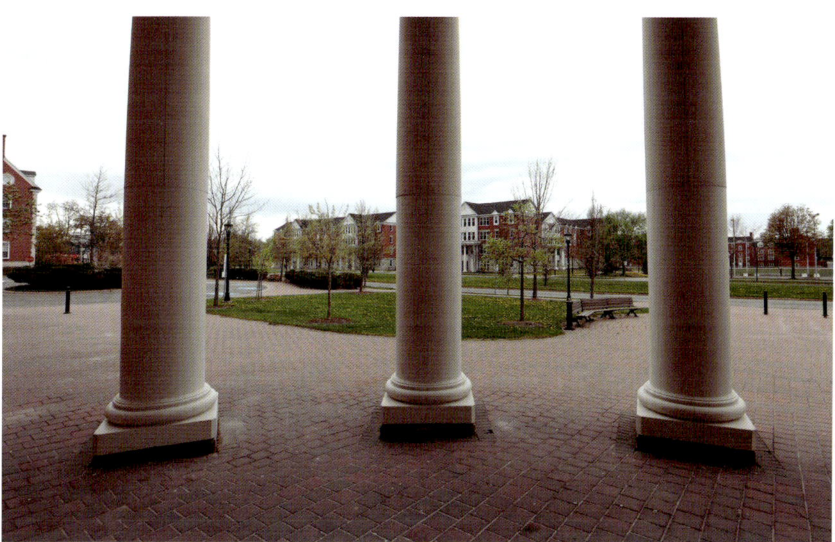

TOP LEFT: *When students and teachers headed home from this school in Great Village for the March Break they had no idea it would be the last time they would enter the school for the year.*

TOP RIGHT: *The St. Francis Xavier University campus in Antigonish.*

BOTTOM RIGHT: *Traffic was diverted into a check-point at the border of Nova Scotia and New Brunswick. Before the "Atlantic bubble" opened up in early July, anyone coming from out of province was required to self-isolate for fourteen days. The bubble exempted travellers from other Atlantic Canadian provinces from that requirement.*

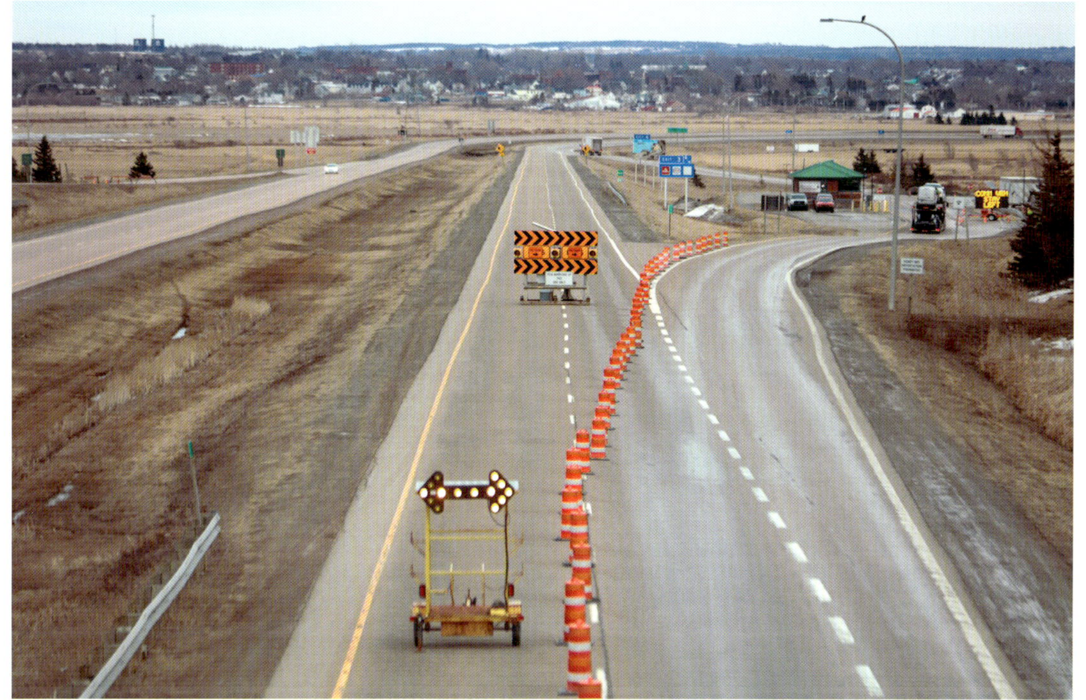

NO PLACE LIKE HOME:
Trapped in New Zealand

In early February 2020, Alf Baldwin, a retired RCMP officer, and his wife, Sue, a retired high school teacher, headed off to New Zealand on a two-month bucket-list trip. When they arrived, they rented a vehicle and set off on an 8,800-kilometre trek, driving through lush countryside, over mountains, and across glaciers; the plan was to stay in Airbnbs all along the way.

But about a month into their travels, they began to receive emails and messages from home telling them about a pandemic that was spreading across the planet.

"Our travel agent sent us an email and said, 'It's getting bad here; you should think about cutting your trip short and heading home.'" Alf and Sue didn't put much stock in the warning. "We were just kind of in this little wonderful travel bubble. It's New Zealand—not really noticeably affected by the virus."

So they carried on, driving until they received another email from their travel agent, who strongly suggested they reschedule their return date. "We were in the northernmost part of New Zealand. It's very remote," says Sue. "It's a beautiful country; the weather's beautiful; the people are beautiful, and we're saying, 'Well, it's only another ten days before we go home.' In New Zealand there was really not a lot of mention of COVID-19."

The next day another email told them they'd better book right away because there was a chance there would be no flights for them to get home on. The message finally hit home. "We thought, 'It must be getting serious,' so we decided to switch. Within twenty-four hours we were booked straight back to Vancouver." But their flight was not for another seven days.

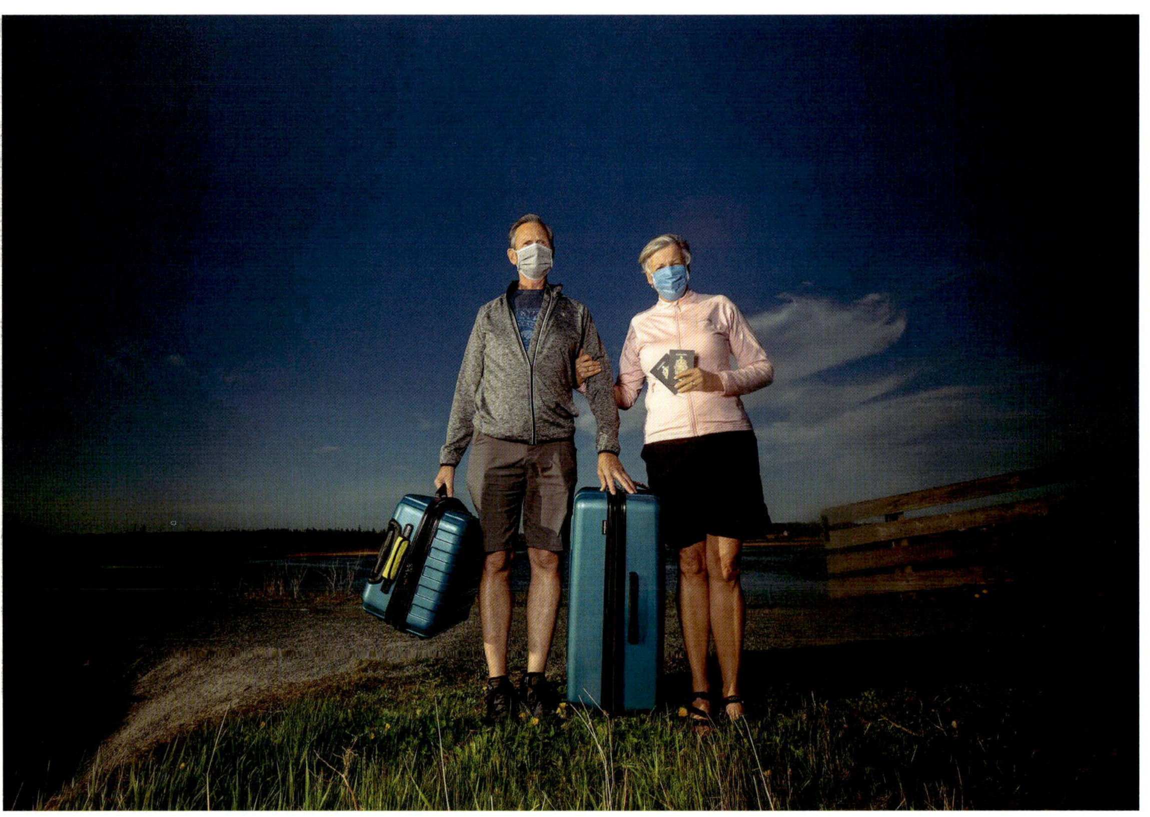

Alf and Sue Baldwin pose for a photo with their travel gear. The two were in New Zealand when international borders began closing and they had to cut their trip short.

"That's when I started to get really nervous."

As they waited, they began to realize the gravity of the situation. Hotels started to empty out and restaurants closed or began operating at reduced capacity. They still had several days before their flight was scheduled to leave.

"We knew what was happening at home to some degree. But when you're not home, even though you're hearing it's getting bad, it's hard to relate, especially when you're on vacation. It's not in your mindset," says Sue.

They were experienced travellers and had learned to roll with schedule changes, but things were happening fast. On the day of their flight, they didn't want to be "those people running to the departure gate," so they got up early and got on a bus that would take them to the airport. Having heard about social distancing and mask use, Alf and Sue cracked open a package of masks Alf had bought two months earlier when he was travelling in Vietnam and put them on.

As the bus picked up more and more people en route to the airport, says Sue, "the look of terror and fear in so many people's faces was everywhere. People were staring, wondering if we were carriers. By the time we got to the airport, the bus was jammed to the gills. There was no distancing."

Alf remembers looking over to a parking lot that had held a few dozen motorhomes available for rent to tourists when they'd arrived; the lot was now filled with hundreds of motorhomes, packed in tight. The tourists were gone.

The usual hustle and bustle of the international airport was gone, too. The doors to International Departures were sealed and security officers stood out front. All travellers were asked if they were feeling well, and whether they had a passport and a ticket. If they answered no to any of those three things, they were not allowed into the airport.

"The majority of the international flights had been cancelled, so if you didn't have a ticket for Air Canada you couldn't get in," says Sue.

Alf says he was concerned they could get bumped off the flight. "I'll always remember [thinking] 'This is not the time to be the nice Canadian. You [need to] get on that plane. This is not the time for kindness."

"We felt a tremendous sense of relief when we actually went and sat in our seats on the flight," says Sue.

When they got to Vancouver, they were surprised to discover that only they and a few others on the plane had been wearing masks. "When we arrived, [officials] didn't seem to be too concerned; we weren't asked any questions whatsoever. It was just like business as normal," says Alf. They flew from Vancouver to Montreal, but it wasn't until the two arrived at Halifax Stanfield Airport that they were asked about their travels and instructed to quarantine.

"We were greeted with professionalism. It was so different. Two different teams of people asked us how we were feeling and ensured we knew exactly what we were to do. We were to self-isolate," says Sue.

"They did a fantastic job," Alf agrees.

When they arrived at their apartment they discovered a bag hanging on the door. It held a gift from their upstairs neighbours: a roll of toilet paper and a loaf of bread.

"They welcomed us home in East Coast fashion," Alf laughs. "It was universal! What the hell was up with the toilet paper binge purchasing?" During their two weeks of self-isolation, Alf and Sue often found packages at their front door containing food and treats from neighbours.

"New Zealand—it's a beautiful country and so clean and very green. They're very conscious of the environment," says Sue. "But when you come down to a crisis like this, not knowing what's lying ahead, there's no place like home."

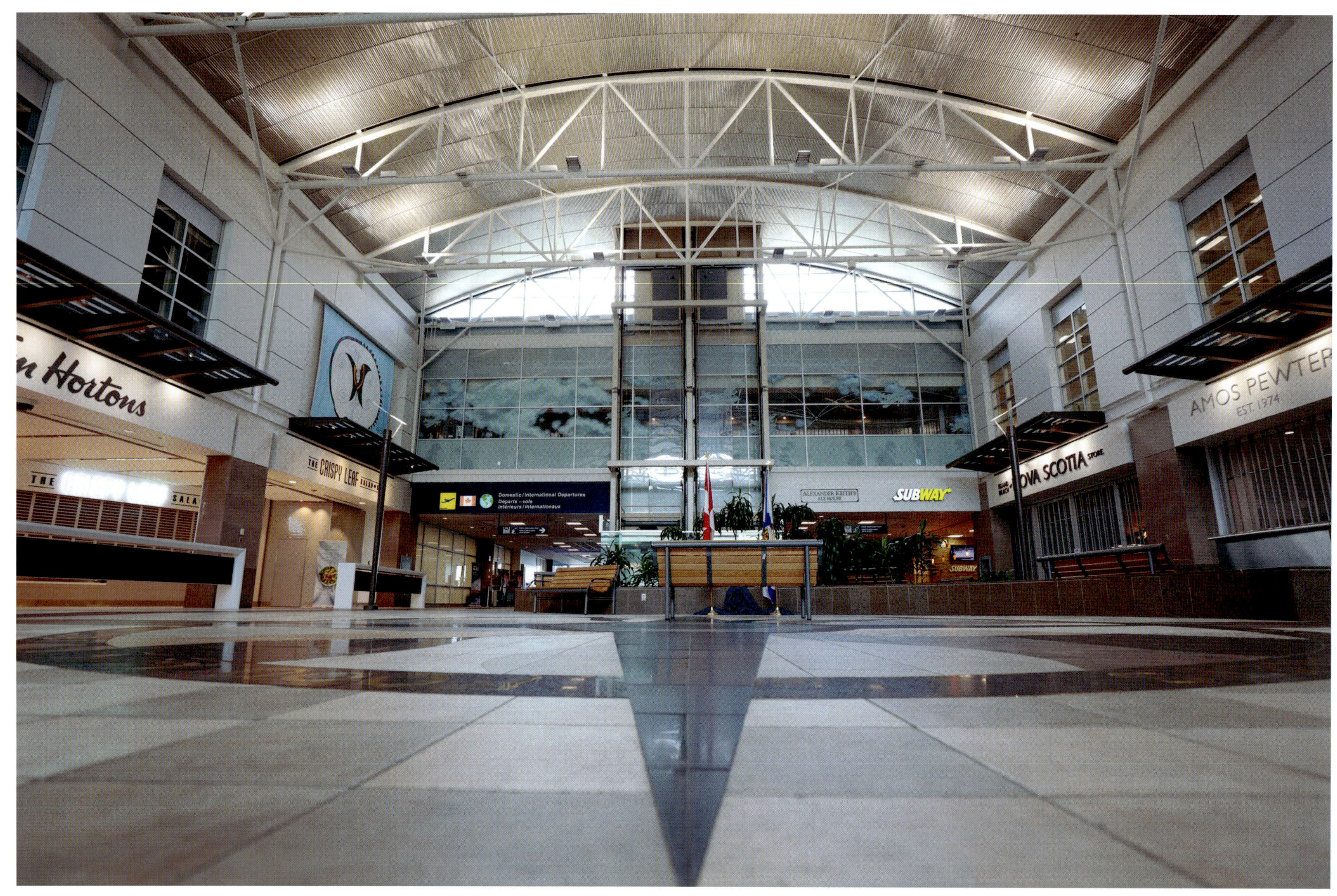

This lobby at Halifax's airport is normally filled with travellers saying goodbye to their loved ones before heading through security, but on this day it was like a scene from a post-apocalyptic movie.

PULLING TOGETHER TO GET IT RIGHT:

Halifax Stanfield International Airport

It is surreal.

There are no announcements in the departure area for flights boarding.

There is no final boarding call for the family who has checked in but has not yet arrived at the gate.

There are no excited children clutching their mini superhero carry-ons as their parents go through their boarding passes and passports.

In fact, there is no one here at all.

This is the departures lounge at the Halifax Stanfield International Airport. The shops, except for a single coffee shop for staff, are all closed; the lights are low; the escalators are still. A cleaner walks by and sanitizes the armrests between chairs.

It is surreal.

This airport has been the working home to Joyce Carter for twenty years. She joined the Halifax International Airport Authority in 1999 and was appointed President and CEO in 2014. But right now, she says, the place is in a state of "induced coma." The number of passengers that passes through the building—typically eleven thousand each day—is down 98 percent. In a normal year, the airport's economic impact on the province is valued at $3.8 billion.

Joyce knew sooner than most that the global pandemic was going to have a major impact on the province. She had travelled to China on a trade mission in the fall of 2019—to the very area where the virus originated. In January she saw that cargo numbers had dropped dramatically, and when Canada's first case of COVID-19 was reported on January 25, she realized the impact here would be significant.

"I had two thoughts. I had travelled to China in November and I immediately thought about that trip. We had been in the Wuhan area. My second thought was—the pandemic has moved to Canada," says Joyce.

"A big challenge for me professionally was just kind of admitting to myself: 'We've got to start to shut things down. We've got to get it right,'" she says,

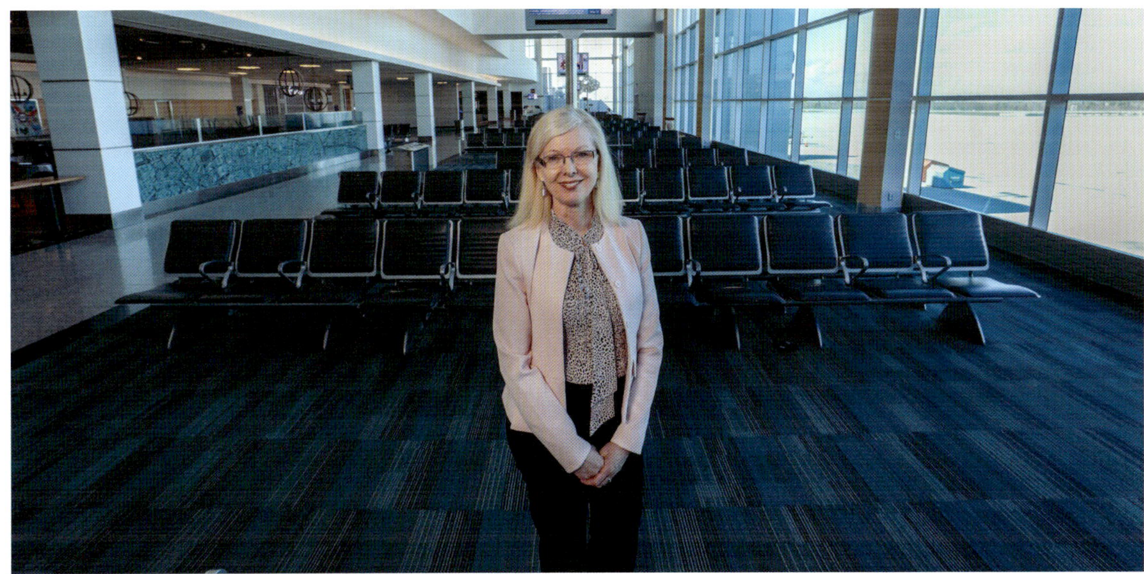

Joyce Carter, President and CEO of the Halifax International Airport Authority, stands in the empty departure lounge at the airport. Airline travel was affected all over the world. In April and May, the airport saw fewer passengers each month than they would have on a typical day in 2019.

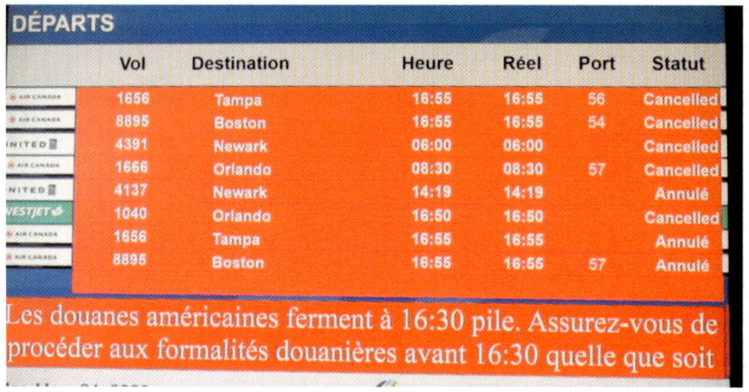

The departures board at Halifax Stanfield, filled with cancelled flights.

adding that it became evident very quickly that not only did the airport have a role to play in keeping travellers safe, it also had to look after its own employees' safety. "When we heard about the first case in Toronto... we got our pandemic plan out and we exercised it. We stepped up all of our cleaning protocols; we put up social distancing signage," she says. "We were really careful to be sure that our essential workers were protected."

When the Nova Scotia government recommended that workers stay home, Joyce's team quickly launched a work-from-home program. "By the time the state of emergency was declared, we'd already exercised that, so it was not an instant transition, but it was fairly seamless."

At that point the airport was still processing a lot of passengers. "We were welcoming back Canadians who wanted to get home to Nova Scotia," she explains. "The biggest thing I saw was that people felt relieved to be home, without a doubt."

Information was changing daily, and as the world began to learn more about the global pandemic, travellers were becoming more and more desperate to get home.

"Initially there were commercial flights; you could just call up Air Canada and get a flight to Halifax. But as the messaging got tighter and as the border started to close, people were told they should get home as soon as they could, and that created a tremendous amount of stress," she says. "People were calling me and saying, 'My son is in wherever; what options does he have?'"

Canada closed its borders to foreign nationals except Americans, and to Canadians why had symptoms of COVID-19, on March 18.

"Arrivals is a pretty emotional place for me to watch the business that we've built up. I've been here over twenty years, and in a matter of a week or two, it had kind of shut down," she says.

Joyce is proud of how her team stepped up. "Everybody together is doing what needs to be done, knowing that we will come out the other side. I think about our physical health and well-being, and then I think about the health of the businesses and the economy. That's never going to be right if we don't get this right," she says.

"We are good at crisis management; we do it all the time, and this is another crisis. It's a very big one, and we absolutely see that we play a big role and a very important one in helping curb the spread."

A LIFELINE ON THE ROAD:

Crystal Blair

Crystal Blair, owner of the Glenholme Loop Petro Pass Restaurant, is standing behind a barrier of tables that are entirely covered with muffins and fresh fruit. She looks up from a stack of letters and cards. "It just goes to show you, kindness travels faster than COVID-19," she says of the enormous outpouring of gratitude and support she's received in the last several weeks from truckers and their families across Canada and the United States.

When the state of emergency was declared and businesses and restaurants were forced to close down, Crystal told her staff that, for the first time in her thirty years there (first as an employee and since 2007 as the owner), the restaurant would have to close to the public. But then she saw a social media post from a trucker in the US wondering how he'd manage when truck stops were closed and even their washrooms were shut down.

"I just panicked. I looked at my husband and I said, 'I can't do this to my drivers. I have to do something,'" Crystal says.

"I just got right on Facebook and said, 'I'm trying to help the drivers with my washrooms. They're open. I'm going to be here. I'll be here for breakfast in the morning, but I'm a staff of one, so this is what we're going to do: I'm going to try doing a breakfast sandwich and home fries and it's only going to be four dollars. Free showers, free coffees." That post went viral overnight.

"I couldn't believe it; the response was amazing. The next day somebody called in and said, 'I see what you're doing and I'd like to buy ten drivers their breakfasts.'"

It took off from there. "Another call was from a lady in New Brunswick and then, the next thing I know, it's two months later and we're still feeding the drivers for free. Some of them would pay it forward—'I'll buy the next guy's breakfast'—and it just kept going from there."

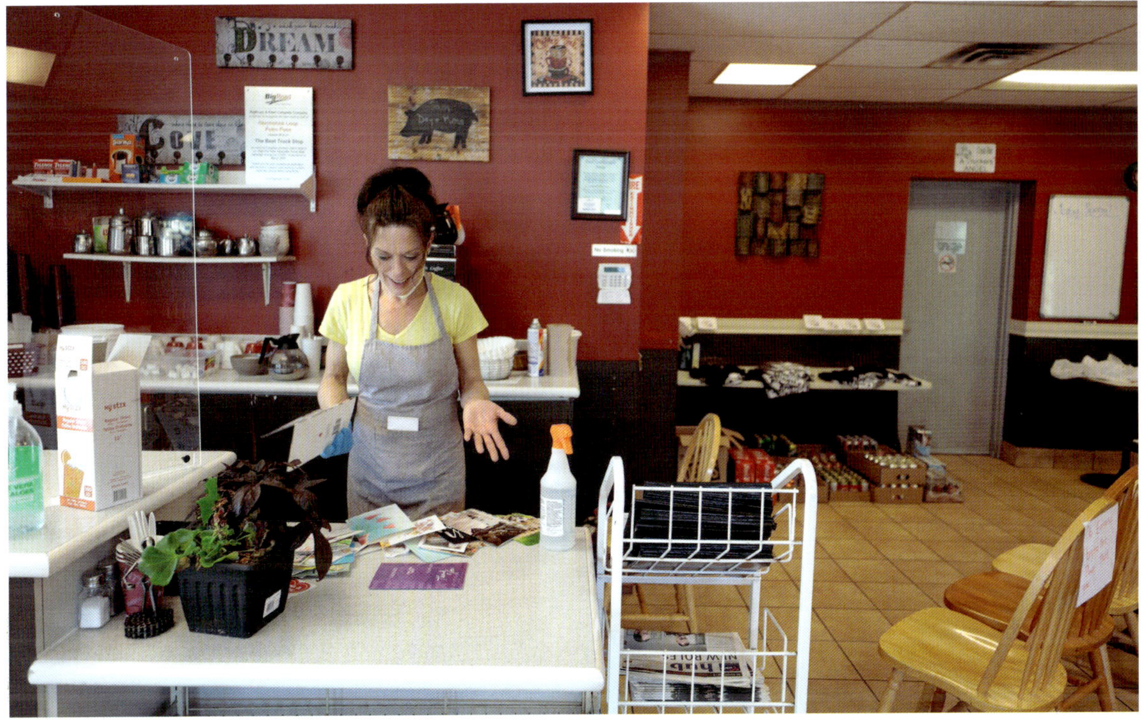

Crystal Blair, owner of the Glenholme Loop Petro Pass restaurant, looks over the cards and letters she has received from truckers and their families from all across North America. Crystal provided a vital lifeline by staying open during the pandemic.

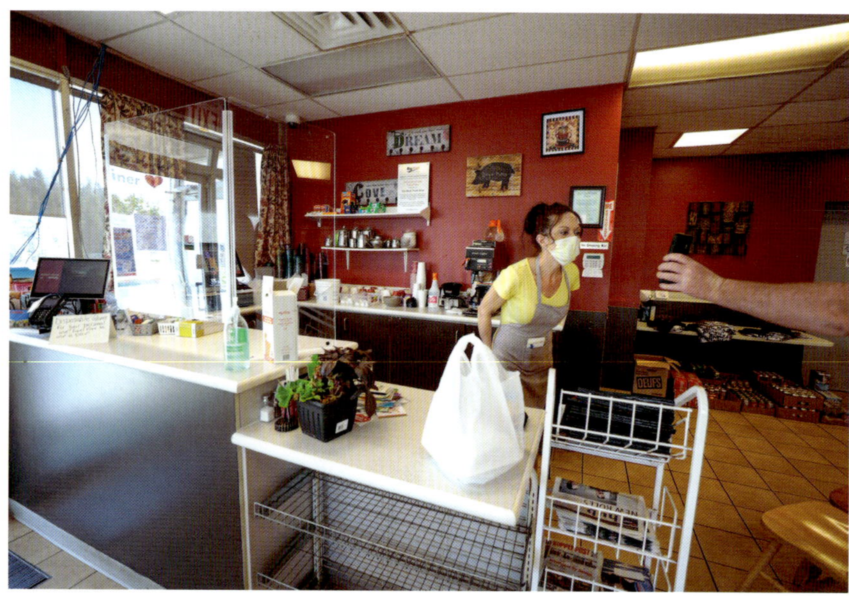

A truck driver shows Crystal a photo on his phone as he picks up a free meal.

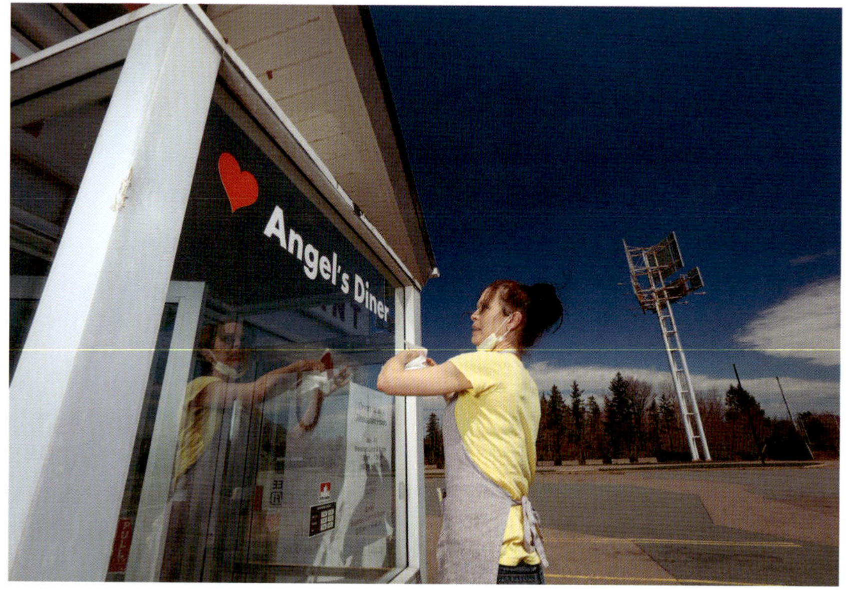

Crystal hangs the sign a grateful trucker gave her. Thanks to donations from across the country, she was able to provide free meals to truck drivers when they had a difficult time finding places to eat and shower.

Crystal was featured on newscasts and stories across the country and donations and accolades started rolling in. She received financial support from trucking companies across the continent and an outpouring of recognition in both Canada and the US for her work.

"I've gotten so many letters, it gives me goosebumps every time I think about it," she says. "So many people just tell me that I've restored their faith in humanity; they are blown away by what I'm doing here."

She says the truckers who walk through her door are some of the most experienced social distancers around, given that they're essentially confined to their trucks most of the time. But Crystal knows her face-to-face contact with them is important.

"It's close to one of the only places they still feel human," she says. "When they come in they get a little conversation, they get a hot meal, they're allowed to use the washroom, take a shower. Nobody's saying, 'No, no—you're not allowed to use the facilities here. You've crossed the border—you stay in the truck!'"

Her "new normal" is working eighty hours a week—and she loves it. "You should see how busy I get: the parking lot will be full for hours. When the maximum number is in here, there'll be a couple in the foyer, and they'll be lined up outside—and it's just me." Her husband comes in at night and helps her mop the floors and clean the showers, and her kids run errands for her.

Despite the hard work, she wouldn't have it any other way. "We're in it together," she says. "The drivers treat me like I'm a saint." She points to a package that was sent to her as a gift from a trucker who had recently stopped in. She takes it, grabs a ladder, and climbs up to affix the package's contents to the window.

As she peels the back the paper, the words on her new sign appear:

"Angel's Diner."

MOVING DAY

Contributed by Jennifer Hutton, Middle Sackville, NS

For at least fourteen years my husband and I had been planning to move—someday—from Ontario to Nova Scotia. We were just sort of waiting for the stars to align, and one February afternoon while we were sitting in our hot tub in Cambridge, Ontario, we looked at each other and said, "Now." A week later, our house was on the market. A week after that, it was sold. We rushed home from the realtor's office, booked our flights, and flew the next morning to YHZ.

Over the next three days we saw sixteen homes—some more than once. Finally, on Saturday, March 14, we sat in a Bedford hotel room waiting to hear whether an offer we'd made would be accepted. At 11:01 P.M. our realtor called to tell us we had just purchased a home! We were giddy with excitement.

Eight hours later we were back in the rental car headed to the airport. The flight back to Toronto was on a packed Boeing 777, with not a mask in sight. The only sign of COVID-19 was the absence of hot towels in the business-class cabin.

By the time we arrived back in Toronto, news about the pandemic was starting to ramp up. We learned after we landed that Nova Scotia had declared its first case of COVID-19, that the Ontario government was preparing to extend school closures, and that stores and restaurants would likely be closed in the coming days.

My husband had worked as a transit operator for thirty-one years, and we planned his retirement on May 15 to work with the closing dates on our homes. We'd assumed that somewhere in the mix there would be a farewell/retirement party. What actually happened was that my husband's retirement was moved abruptly up to April 6 because of an 80 percent drop in transit ridership in the Toronto area. My husband stepped off his bus that last day without a wave or a handshake, got into his truck like he had every day for thirty-one years, and drove home without fanfare.

Then we learned that, while moving companies are considered essential, cross-country moving was going to be a challenge. Our movers would be permitted into Nova Scotia without isolation orders, but with one important stipulation: they would not be allowed to enter our new home unless we had first completed a fourteen-day quarantine there. Fortunately, the sellers of our new home (also moving inter-provincially) asked if we could close early. Given the circumstances, we agreed to take possession a month early—on April 20. Our closing was done virtually with our lawyer in Dartmouth.

Next, we prepared for a trip that was more complicated than I could ever have imagined. In the days leading up to our departure we had been warned we wouldn't be able to use bathrooms anywhere outside of Ontario, and aside from picnic-area rest stops in Quebec, that was absolutely true. Our drive took us through four provinces and included three intense checkpoints where our VIN number, health, and travel history were recorded, and where we had to present identification and proof of property ownership. During an overnight stay at a New Brunswick motel, public safety officers were posted at the exit to ensure we didn't leave the motel grounds for food or otherwise, and to make sure we got right back on the Trans-Canada the next morning.

We arrived in Middle Sackville on Sunday, May 3, to the sound of Canada's Snowbirds flying over Halifax. Relatives had brought in folding chairs, air mattresses, and bed linens, and had left groceries in our fridge. We settled in for our two weeks of isolation. Within a few days, in true Nova Scotia form, a neighbour we didn't even know arrived on our doorstep with a lasagna, and my husband's cousins delivered prepared meals and desserts throughout our quarantine.

On Monday, May 18—Victoria Day, 2020—we were finally allowed to step through the door of our new home and into our new life here in Nova Scotia. We felt a huge sense of relief.

We walk around our new neighbourhood now as if we are in a dream. The air in Nova Scotia just feels different—I can't explain it. And I have never felt more at peace in my entire life.

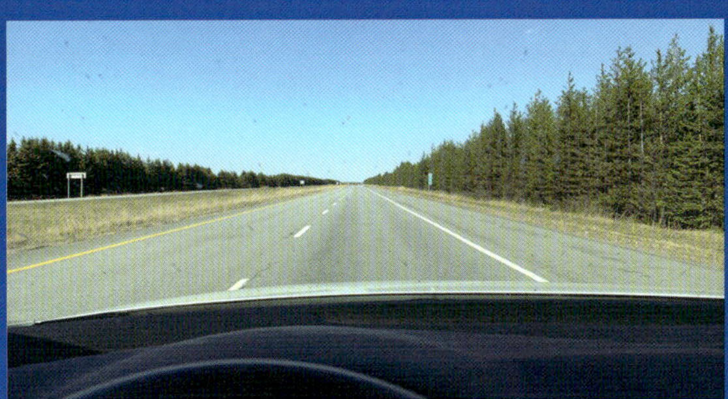

Jennifer Hutton says she and her family didn't pass a single car for ninety-six kilometres as they drove through northern New Brunswick on a Sunday morning in early May. (Jennifer Hutton)

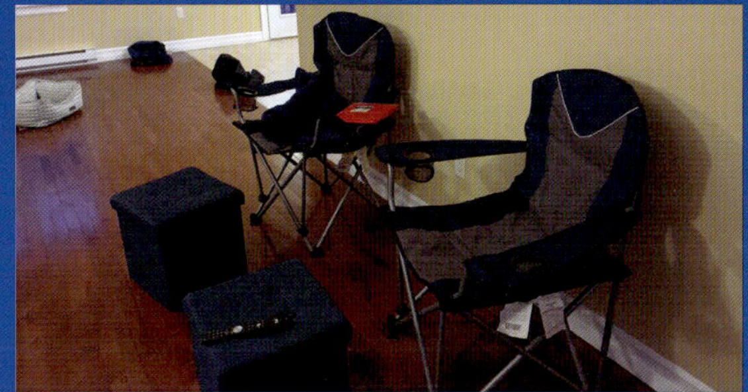

"Quarantine life" for the Hutton family after moving to Nova Scotia in the midst of the pandemic. This was their only living room furniture as they hunkered down for fourteen days. (Jennifer Hutton)

KEEPING OUR DISTANCE

In the first months of the lockdown, only essential businesses were open. When Nova Scotians dared venture out for necessities, we all had to get used to a new protocol: social distancing, or maintaining a distance in public places of at least two metres (or six feet) from other people.

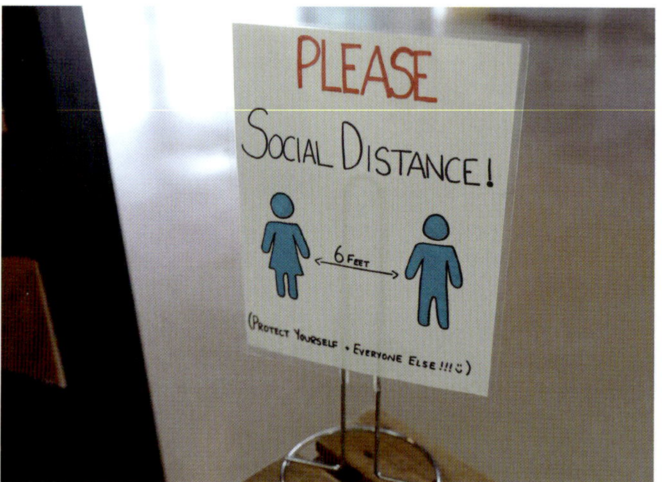

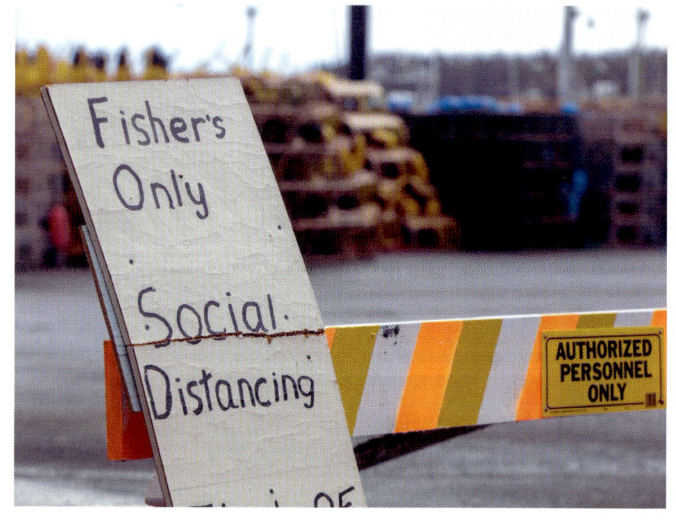

LEFT: *Early in the pandemic, parks and trails were closed, frustrating many who were growing bored with staying indoors.*

TOP RIGHT: *Signs telling people where and how to stand became a part of everyday life. (Paul Darrow)*

BOTTOM RIGHT: *Signs limit access to the Caribou wharf on the Northumberland Strait.*

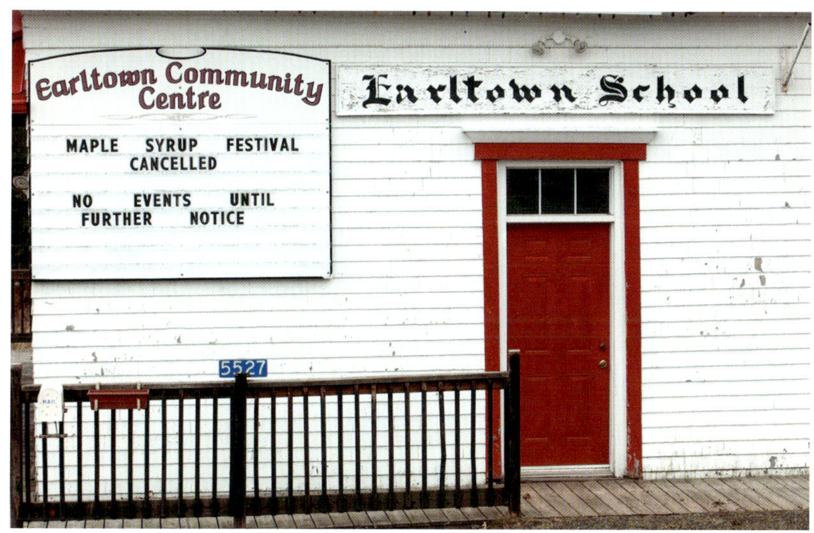

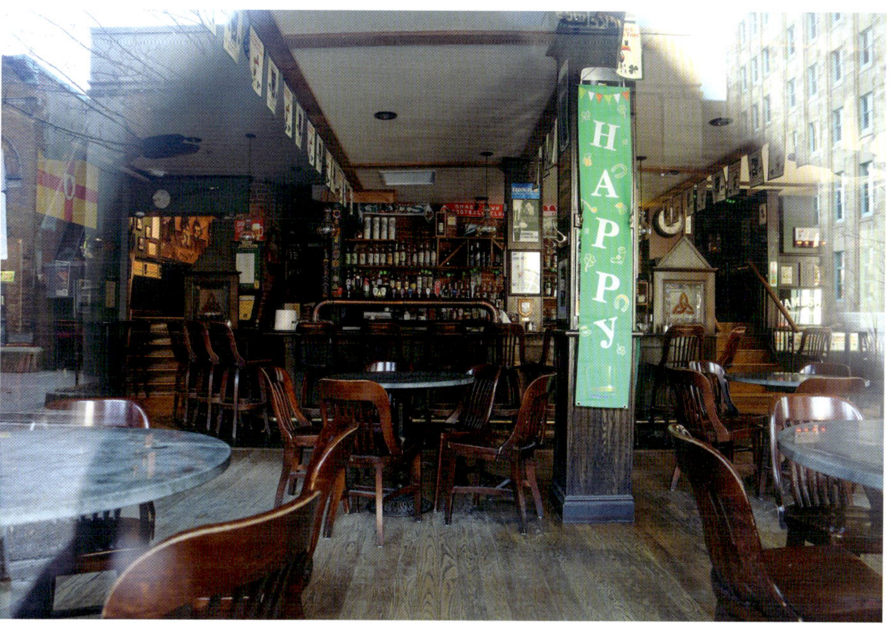

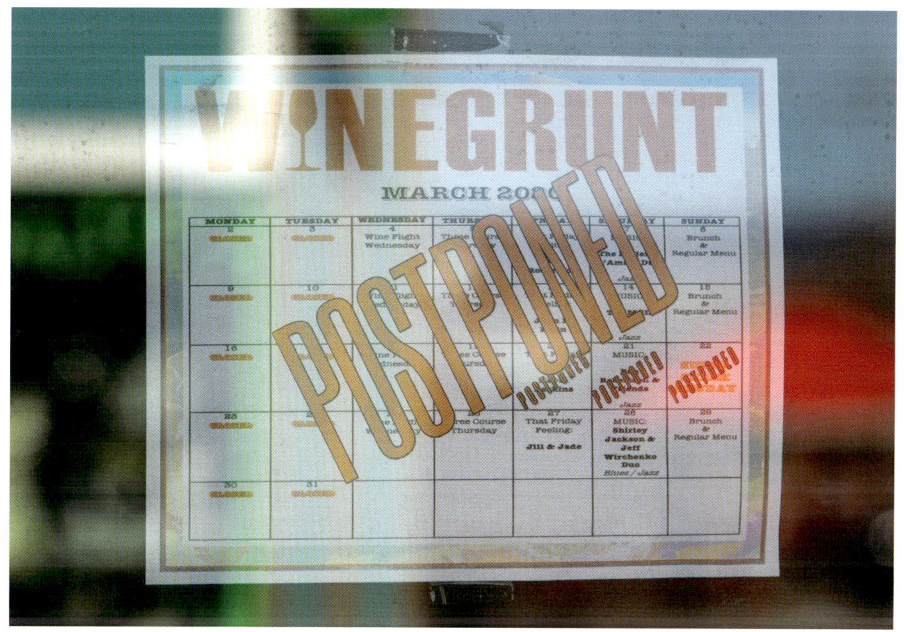

LEFT: *Not only was the Maple Syrup Festival in Earltown cancelled—practically every Nova Scotia festival and gathering scheduled during the spring and summer of 2020 was cancelled or held virtually. The economic impact on small communities and businesses was enormous.*

TOP RIGHT: *Awareness of the pandemic was growing just as bars were prepping for one of their biggest days of the year: St. Patrick's Day. Most events were cancelled, and bars soon shut down altogether. The Old Triangle Irish Alehouse in Halifax closed in mid-March with its decorations still up.*

BOTTOM RIGHT: *When things started to shut down, the Spitfire Arms Alehouse in Windsor decided to formalize it. Postpone March!*

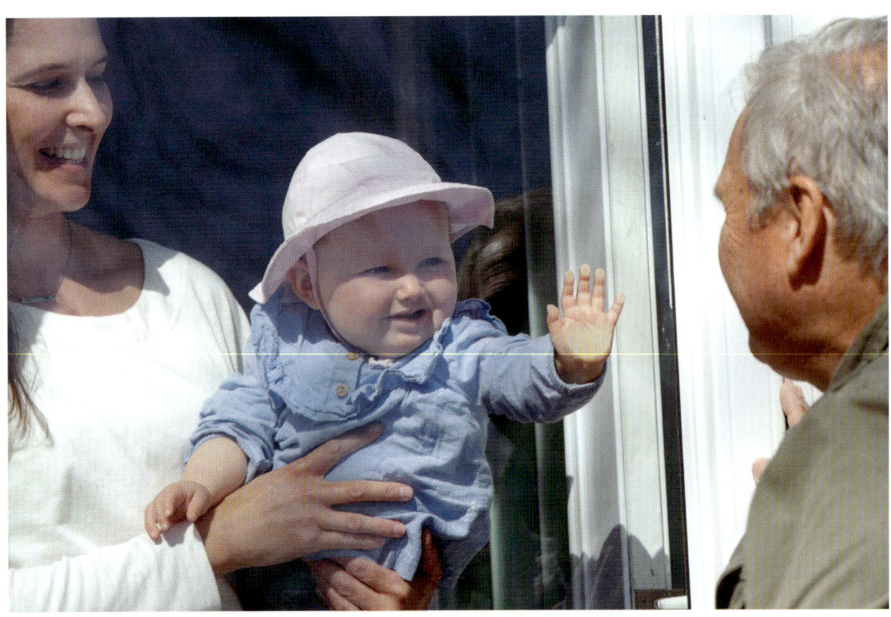

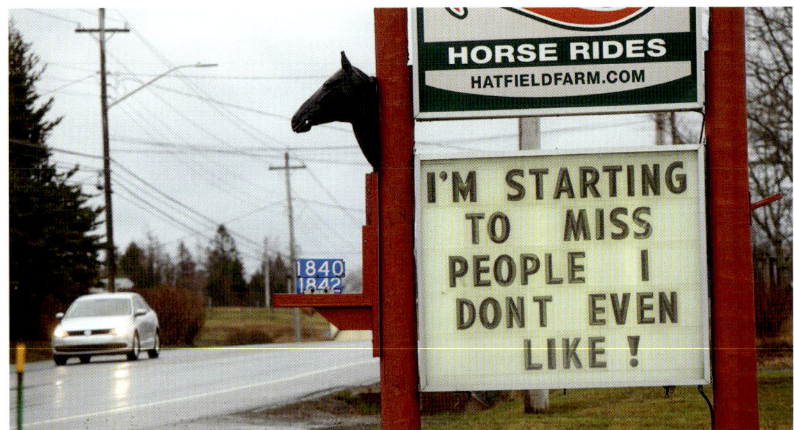

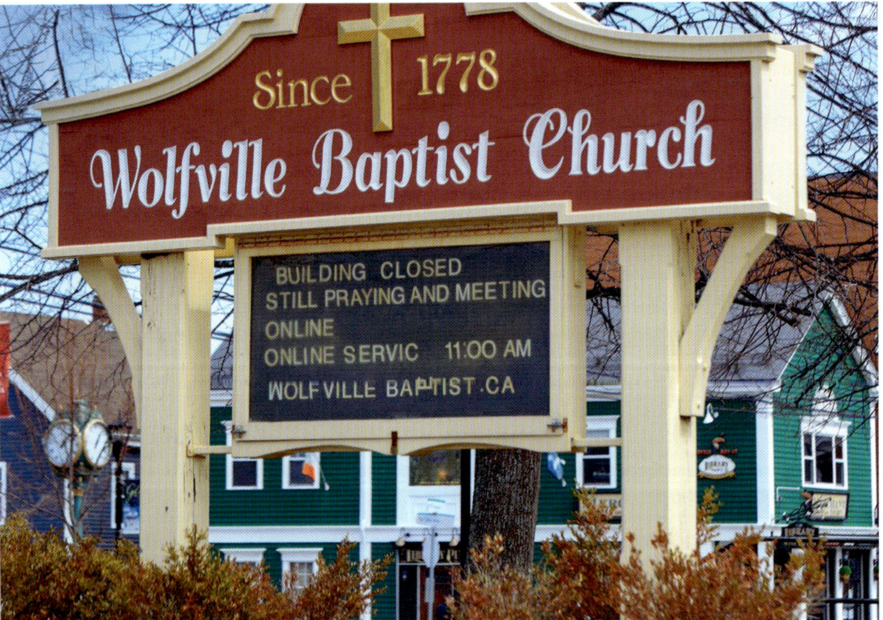

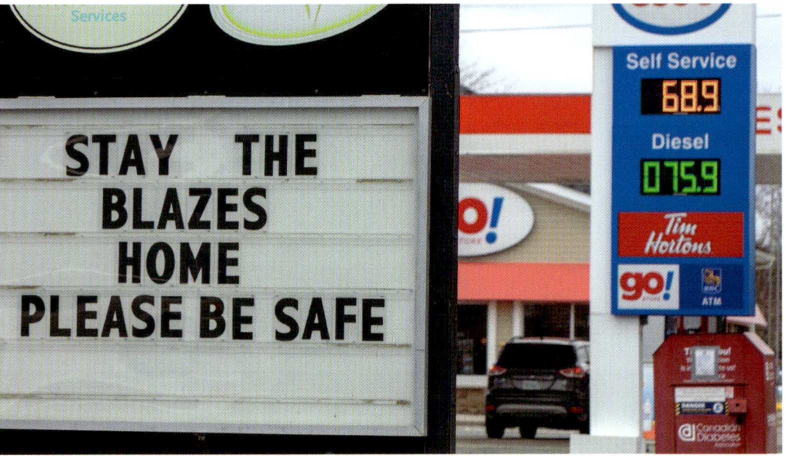

TOP LEFT: *Jac Whitmore of Dartmouth holds her daughter, Vienna, as she plays with her grandfather, Jerry Lawson, through the glass. During the lockdown, parents and grandparents were forced to come up with creative ways to maintain contact.*

TOP RIGHT: *Hatfield Farms in Hammonds Plains showed a sense of humour as the days dragged into weeks.*

BOTTOM RIGHT: *The worldwide decline in economic activity pushed gas prices down to the lowest levels in decades.*

BOTTOM LEFT: *Places of worship had to close to their congregations and many, like the Wolfville Baptist Church, went online.*

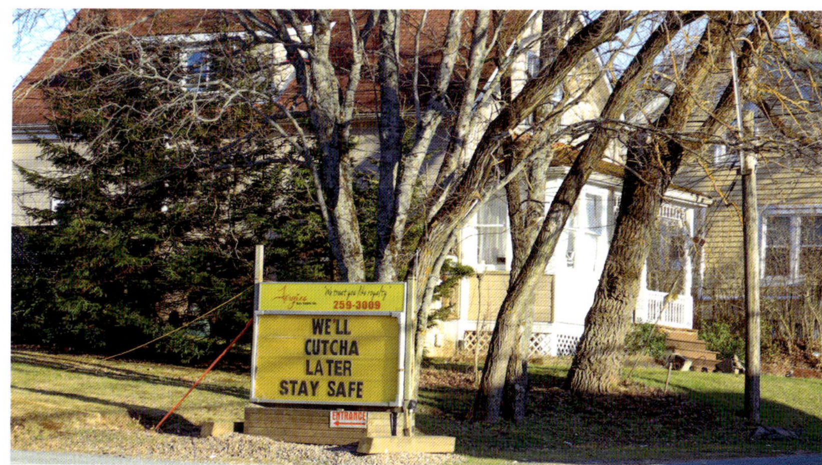

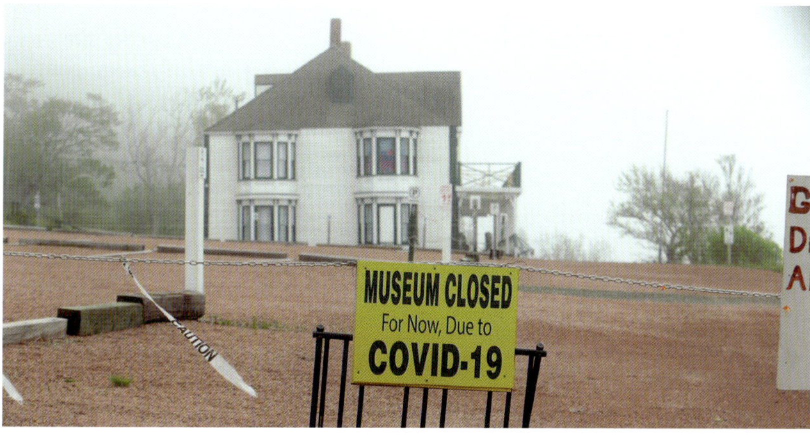

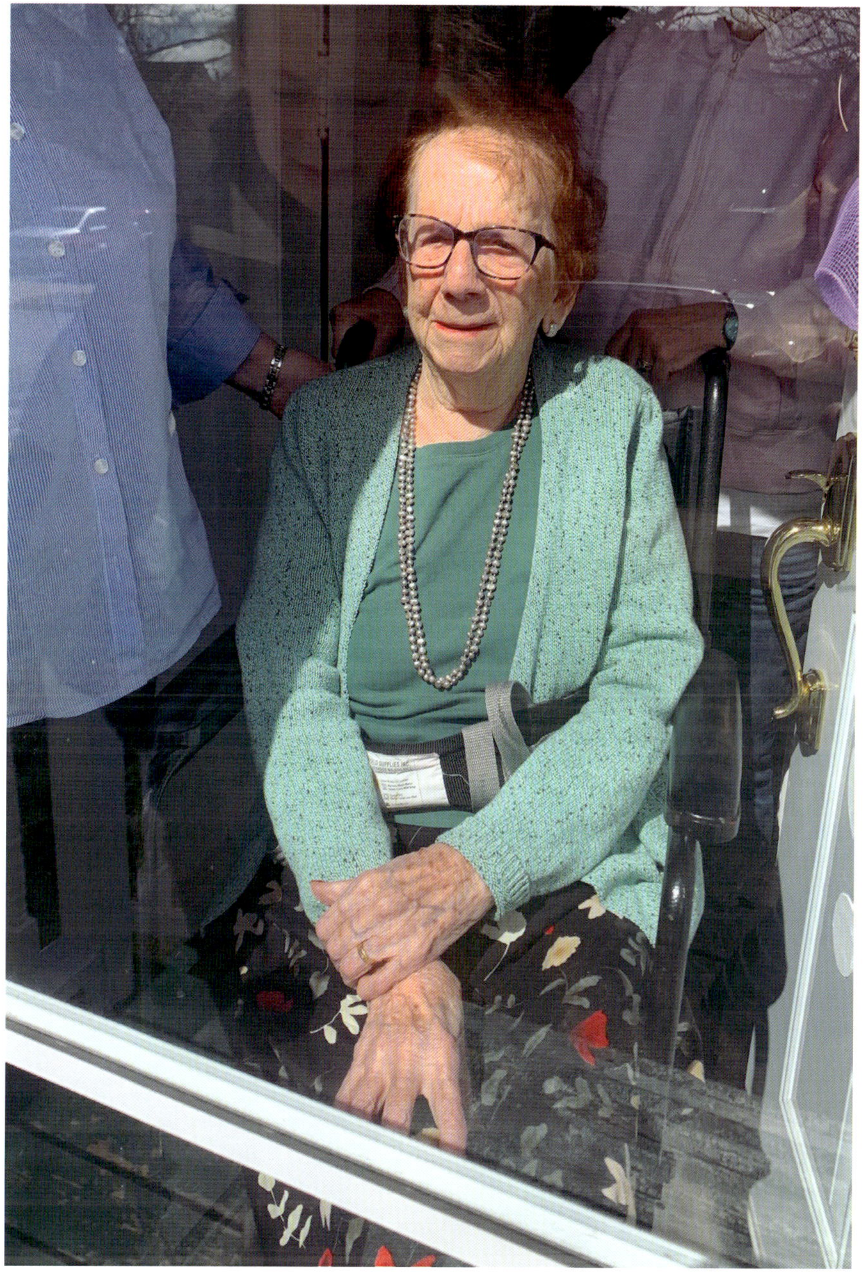

TOP LEFT: *As businesses closed, Fergie's Hair Studio in Enfield showed a bit of lighthearted humour.*

BOTTOM LEFT: *While some museums opened in midsummer, a number of community museums, such as the Ottawa House Museum near Parrsboro, remained closed for the season.*

RIGHT: *With distancing came many emotional challenges. This image of Catherine Williams's grandmother was taken during a window visit on Easter Sunday, April 12, 2020. Her grandmother passed away on May 4 at the age of 103. Her death was not related to COVID-19. (Catherine Williams)*

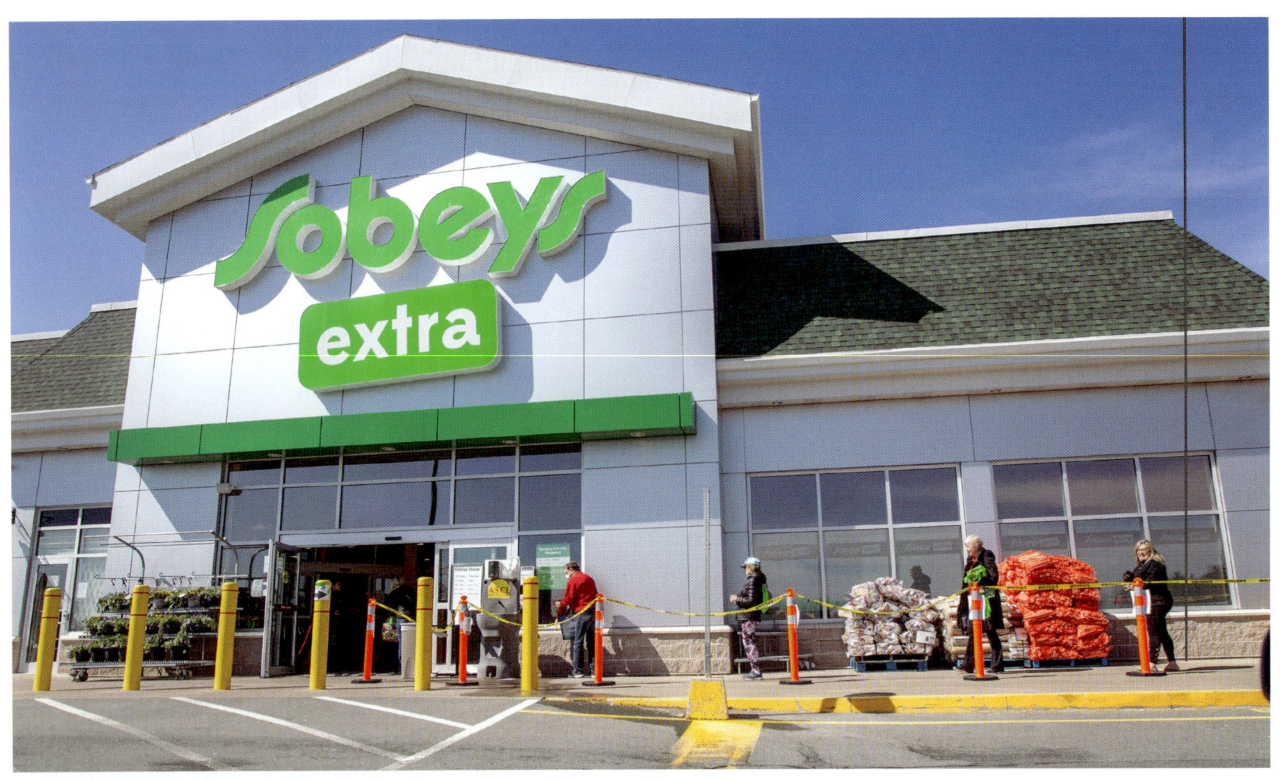

TOP: *Lineups and masks became the norm as stores limited the number of people allowed inside at one time.*

BOTTOM LEFT: *Some people discovered home cooking when their favourite restaurants closed. A renewed interest in baking led to shortages of things like flour and yeast all across the province.*

BOTTOM MIDDLE: *Grocery shopping meant learning to follow a map as aisles were designated one-way to help customers limit contact with others.*

BOTTOM RIGHT: *Stephanie Watson of Cole Harbour, NS, says she stood in line on many occasions during the pandemic, as she did on this trip to get toilet paper and paper towels. "I was not a hoarder...just trying to get regular supplies!" she says. (Stephanie Watson)*

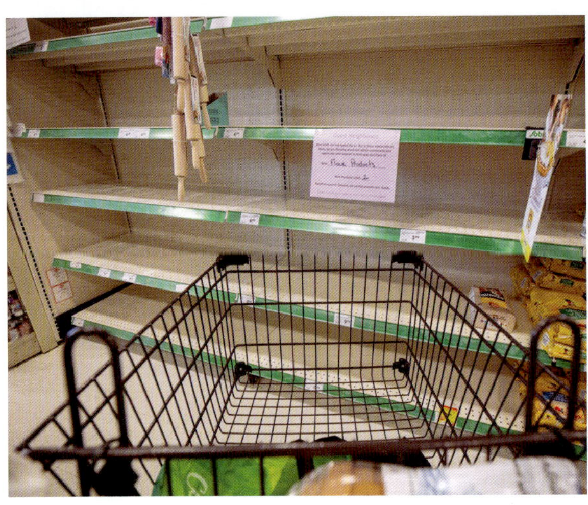

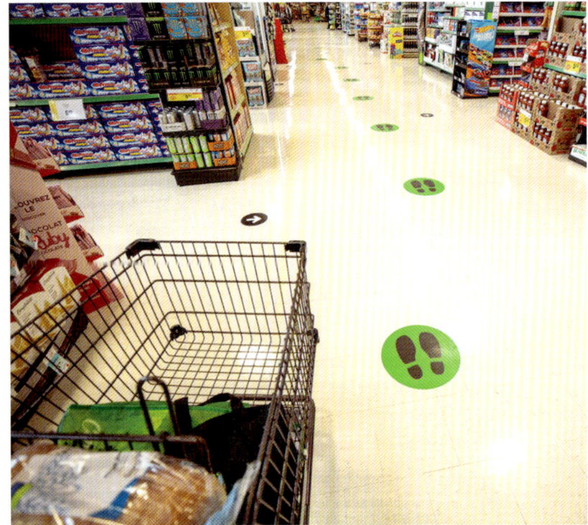

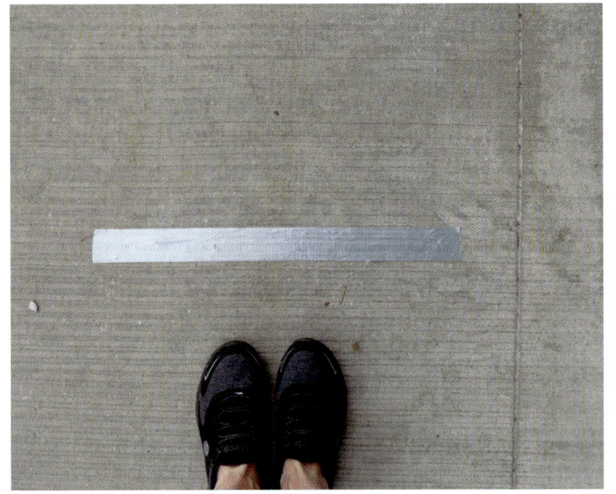

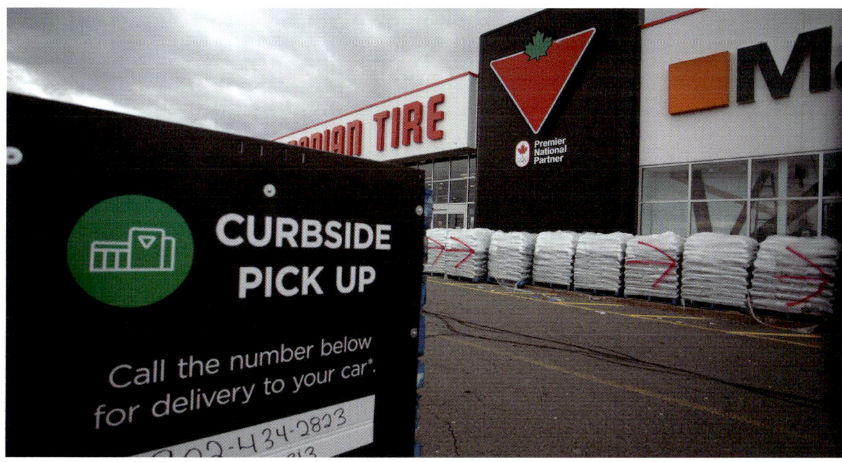

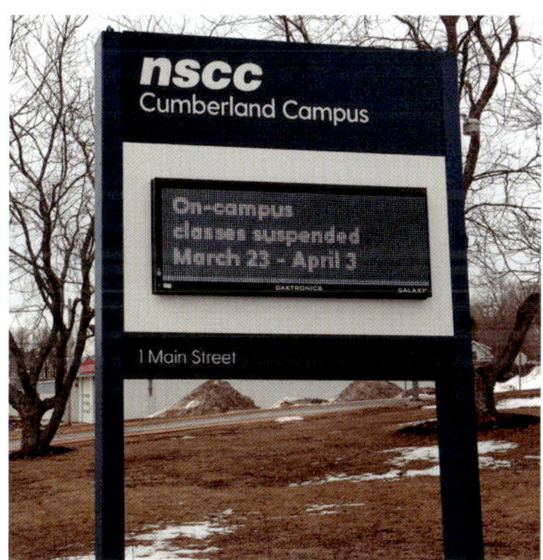

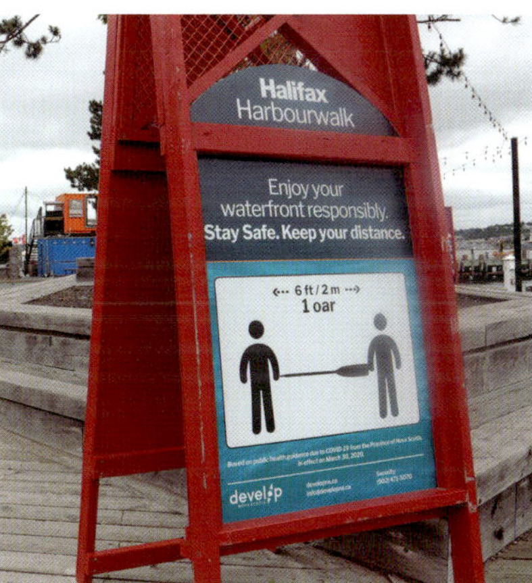

TOP LEFT: *Shopping for essentials became a challenge during the pandemic. This store in Dartmouth was one of many that offered curbside service so customers could avoid entering the store.*

RIGHT: *Stores were required to limit the number of customers in order to adhere to the rules around physical distancing. (Paul Darrow)*

BOTTOM LEFT: *Classes at the NSCC campus in Springhill, like those at post-secondary schools across the province, were shut down.*

LOWER RIGHT: *Humorous signs like these on the Halifax boardwalk encouraged people to stay "1 oar" or "12 large donairs" apart.*

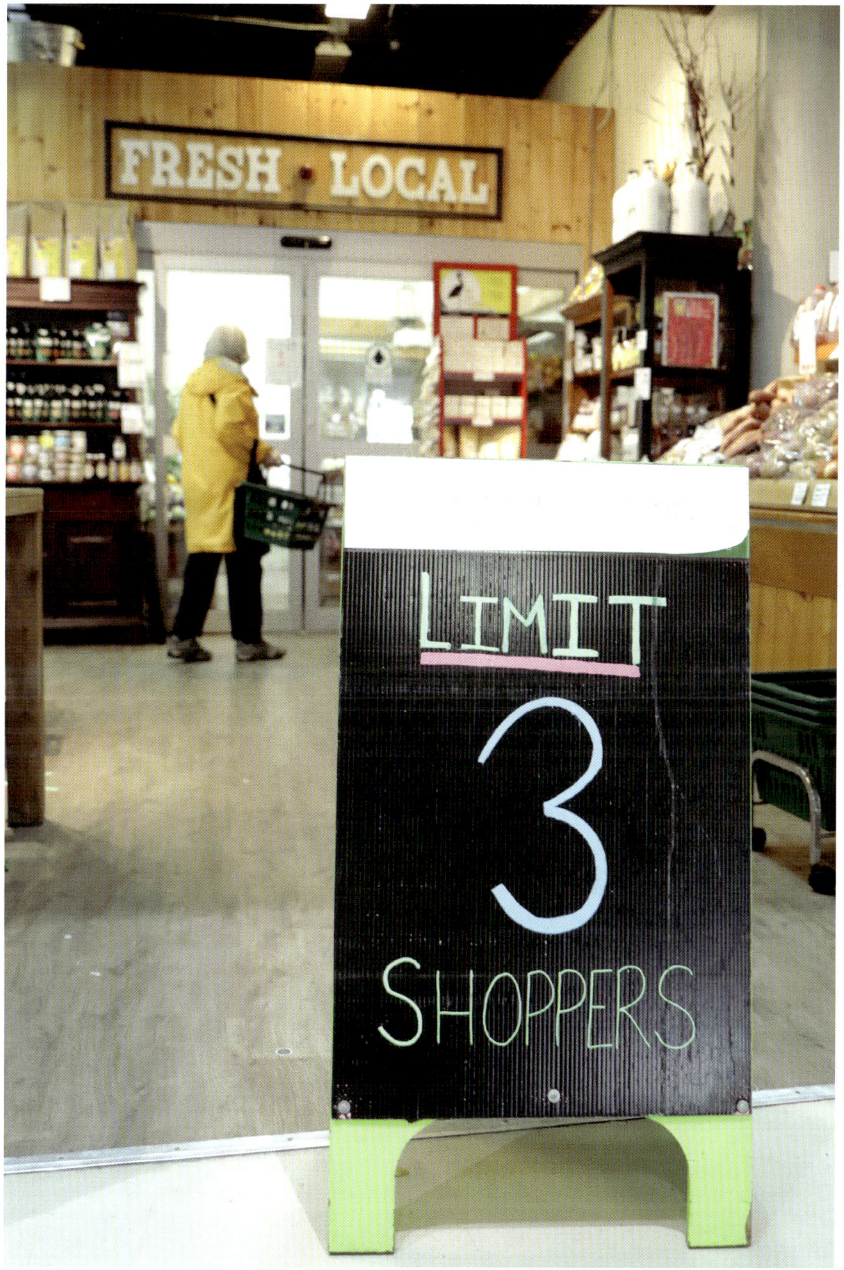

TOGETHER APART:
Video Calling

The lockdown and social isolation orders meant Nova Scotians were really *missing their family and friends. Zoom and FaceTime became the new buzzwords. Video calling became one of the best ways to connect—for both business and pleasure.*

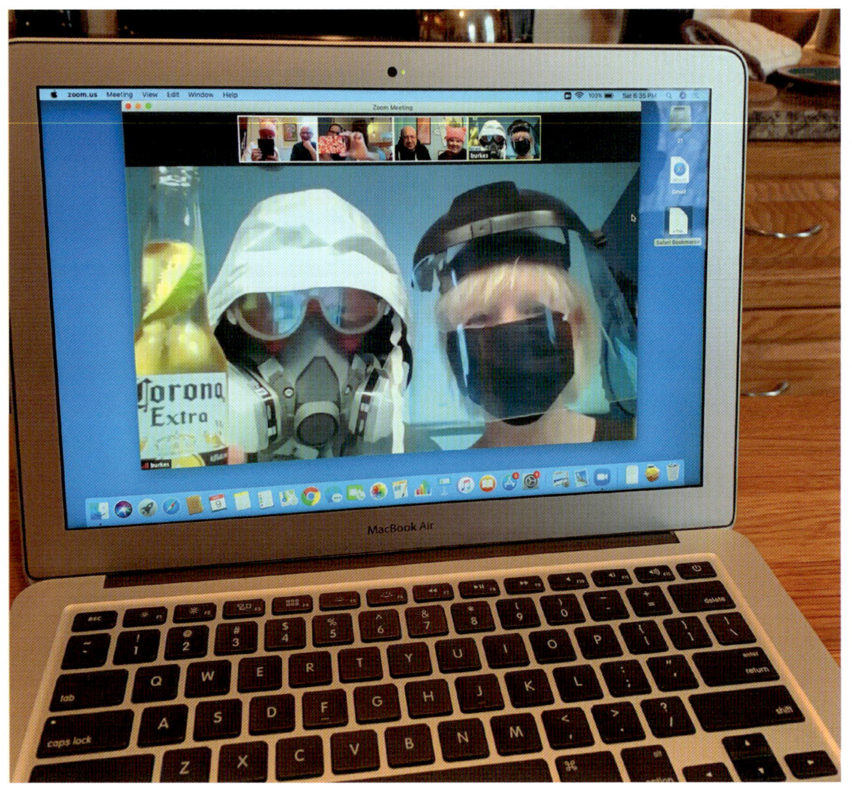

LEFT: *Kristine MacDonald of Port Hawkesbury, NS, says she had many video calls with her grandmother, who lives in a long-term care home. (Kristine MacDonald)*

RIGHT: *Shawna Burke and John Somers suit up to share a lighter moment during an "appetizer club" meeting with John and Mary Whidden of Halifax. The group normally gets together regularly for a bite and drinks, but met virtually during the state of emergency. (Mary Whidden)*

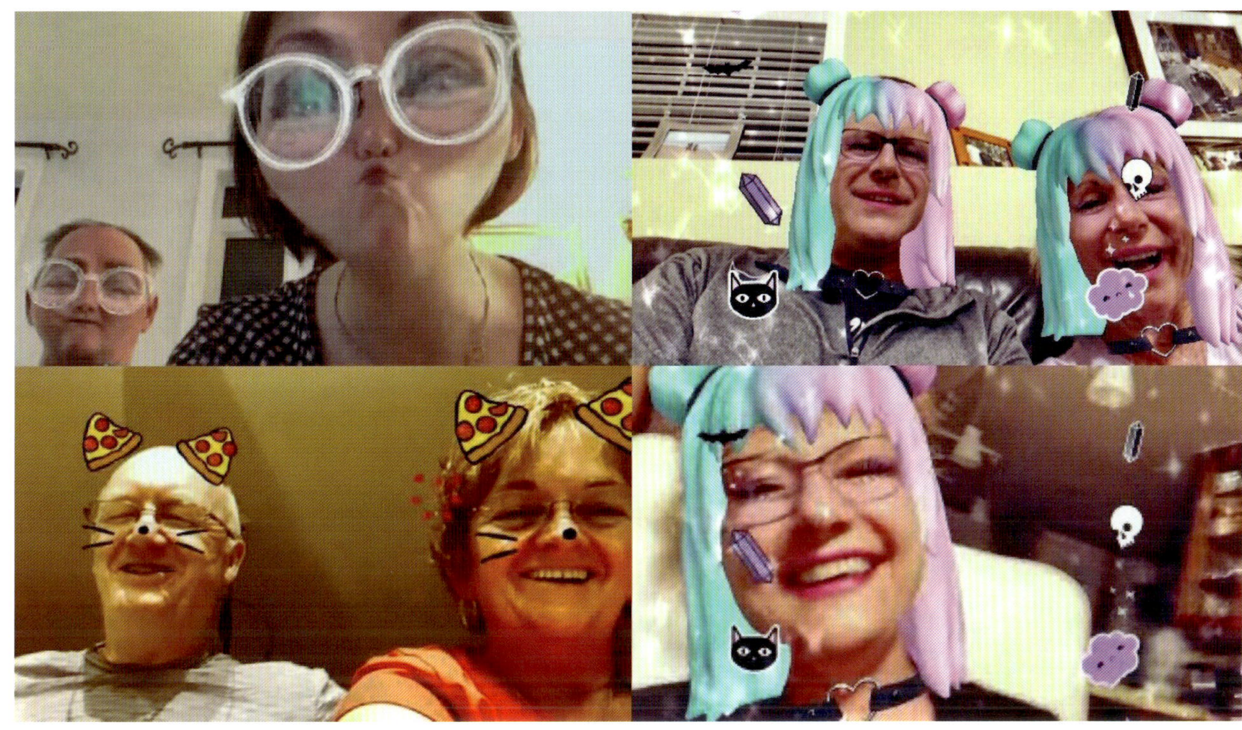

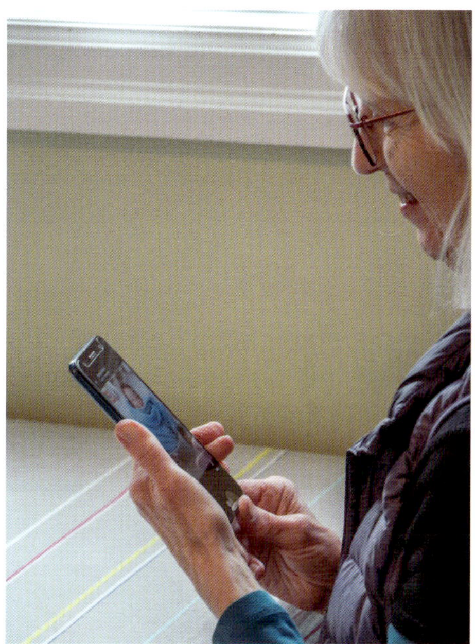

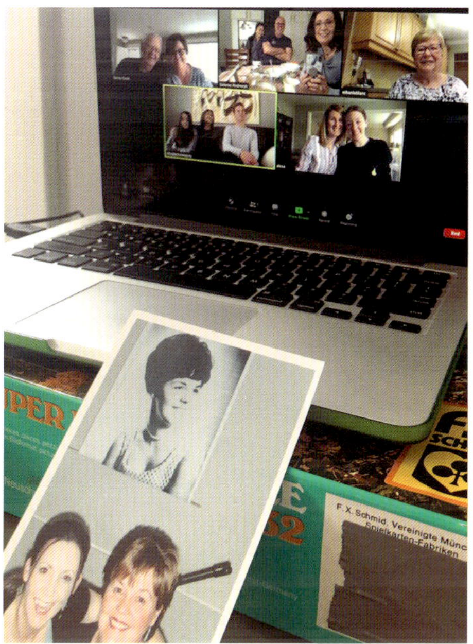

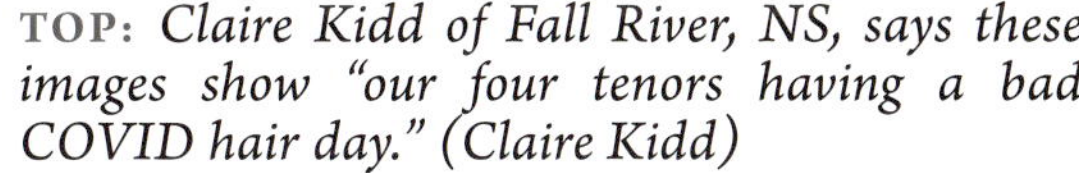

TOP: *Claire Kidd of Fall River, NS, says these images show "our four tenors having a bad COVID hair day." (Claire Kidd)*

TOP RIGHT: *Madeline Comeau of Halifax has only been able to interact with her new granddaughter, who lives in the US, via smartphone. (Yoriko Miyata)*

BOTTOM RIGHT: *Leanne Andrecyk of Halifax and her family celebrated Mother's Day with a Zoom family brunch. (Leanne Andrecyk)*

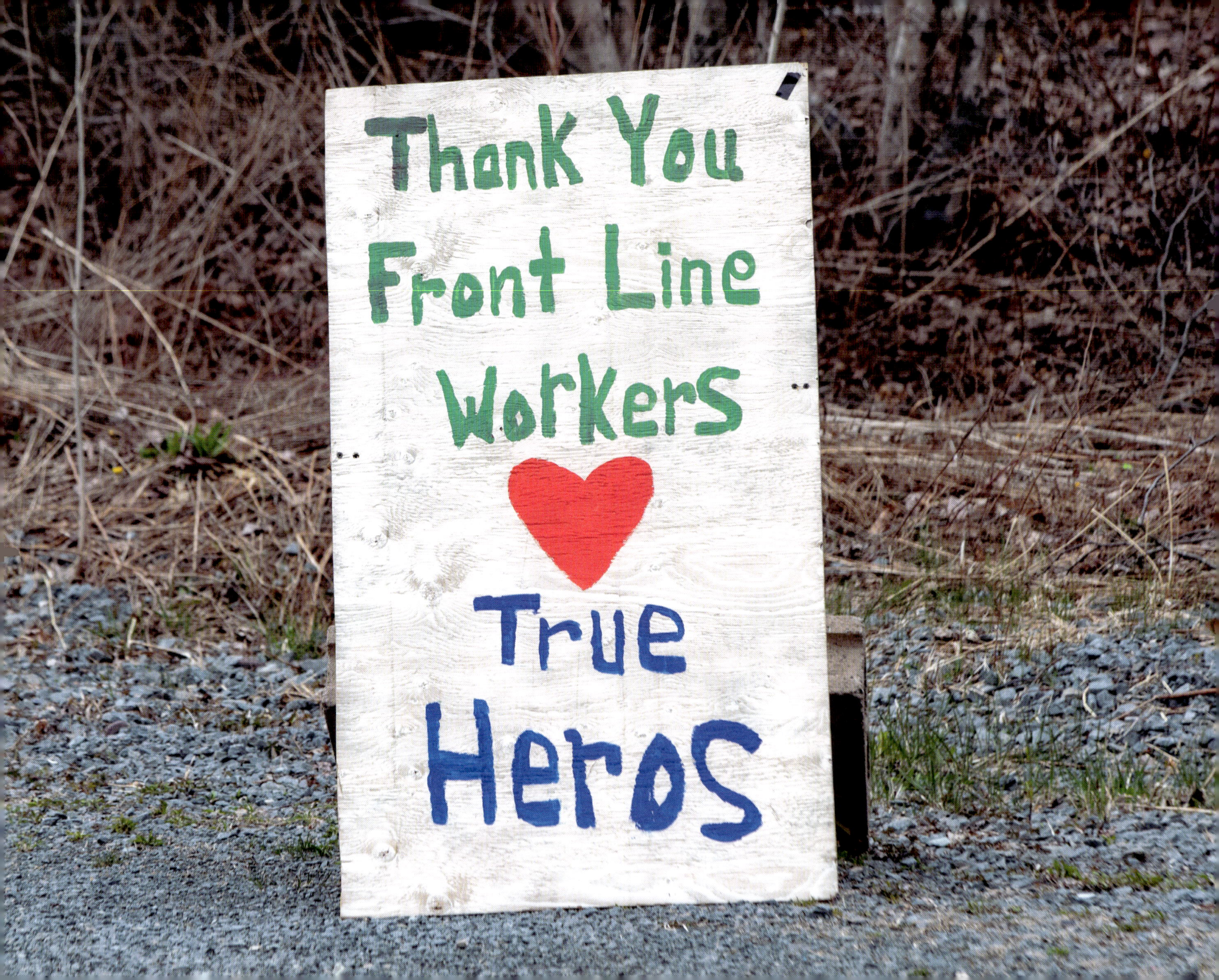
Thank You
Front Line
Workers
True
Heros

Part Two: LIFE ON THE FRONT LINES

| *A simple sign beside the road in Windsor Junction.*

SIGNS OF APPRECIATION

Many, many Nova Scotians work in jobs considered essential during the COVID-19 pandemic, and those who didn't have to put their lives on the line went to great lengths to find creative ways to let essential workers know how appreciated they are.

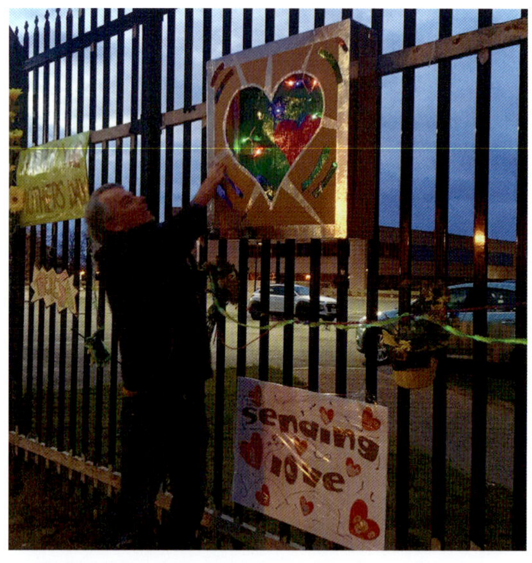

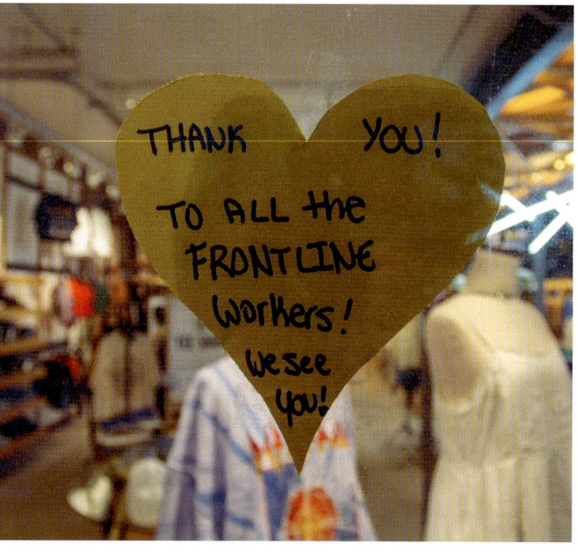

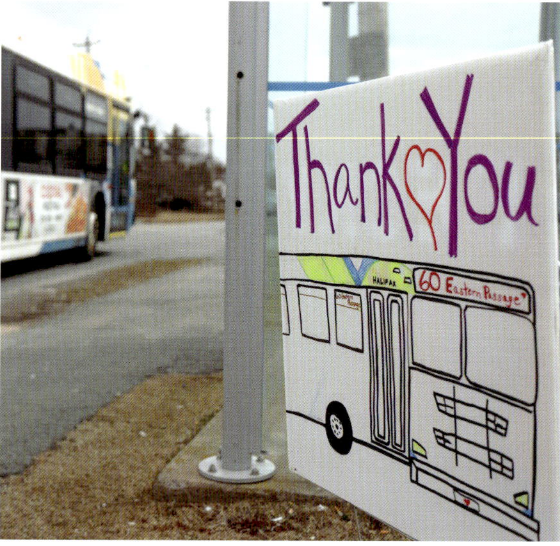

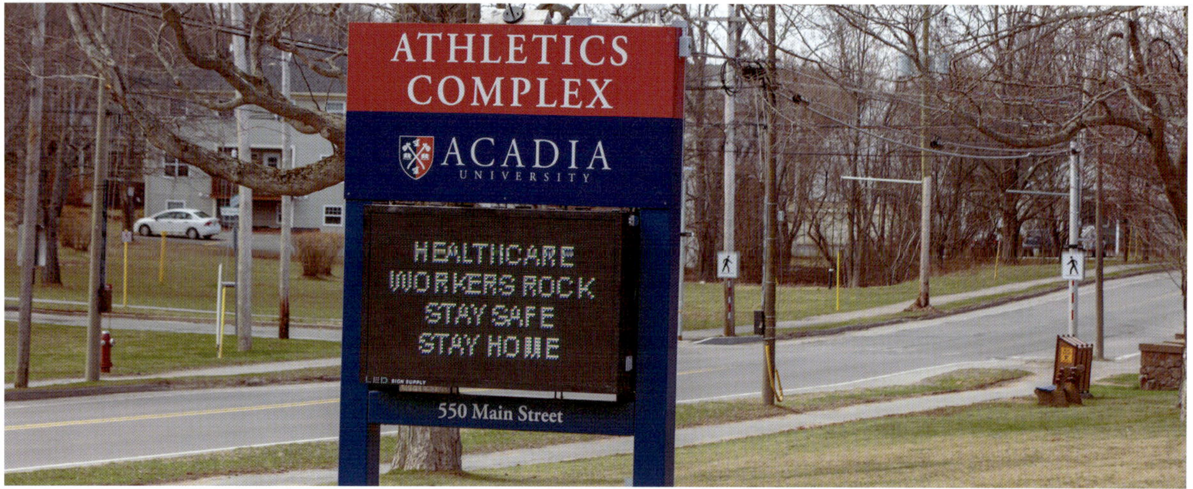

TOP LEFT: *Peter MacDougall of Halifax affixes a sign with words of support for the residents and workers at Northwood to a fence on Gottingen St. The sign was made by his wife, Ginette Cyr. (Ginette Cyr)*

TOP MIDDLE: *A Halifax store offers a message of thanks.*

TOP RIGHT: *A sign of thanks in Eastern Passage. (Paul Darrow)*

BOTTOM: *Words of support at Acadia University in Wolfville.*

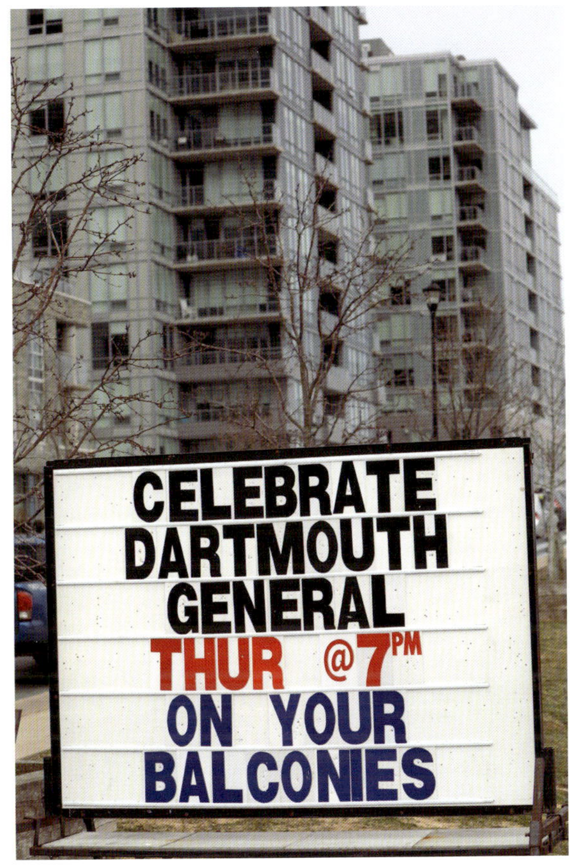

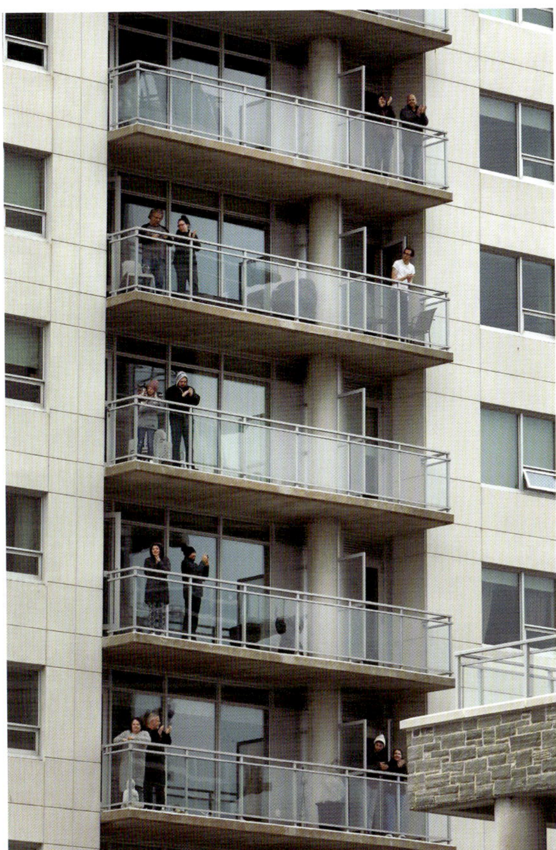

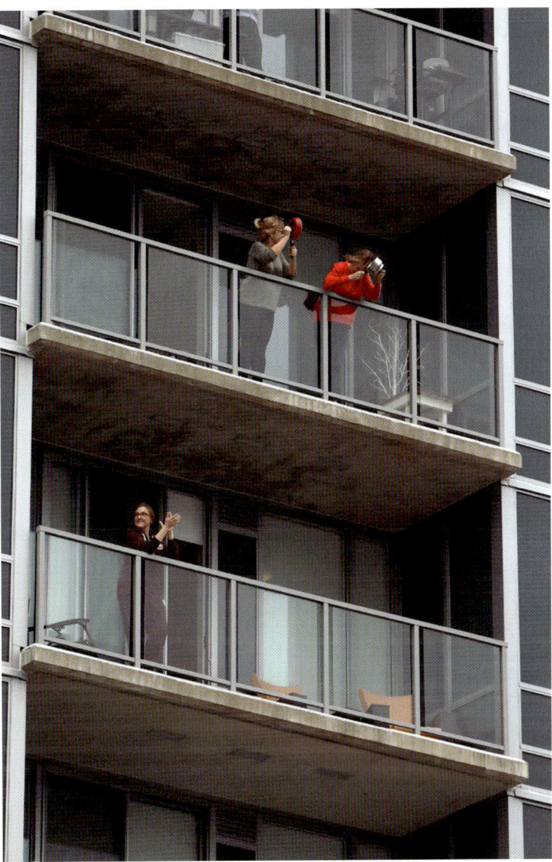

Residents of a Dartmouth apartment complex celebrated front-line health-care workers during shift change at the Dartmouth General Hospital by banging pots and pans from their balconies. (Paul Darrow)

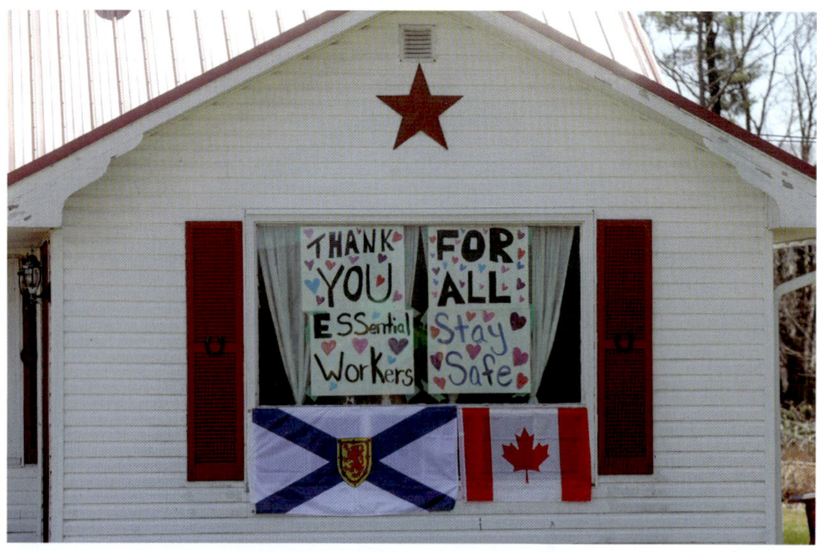

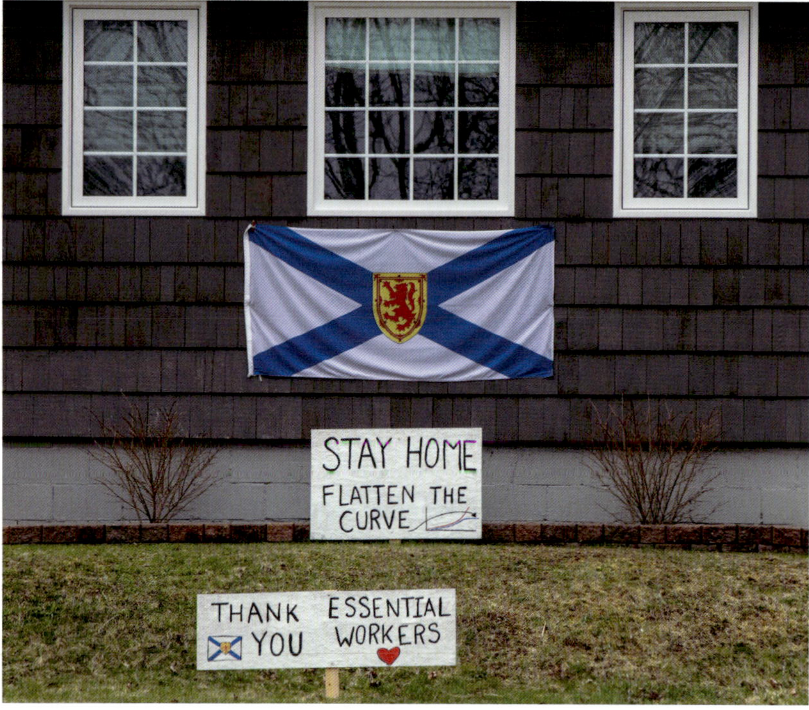

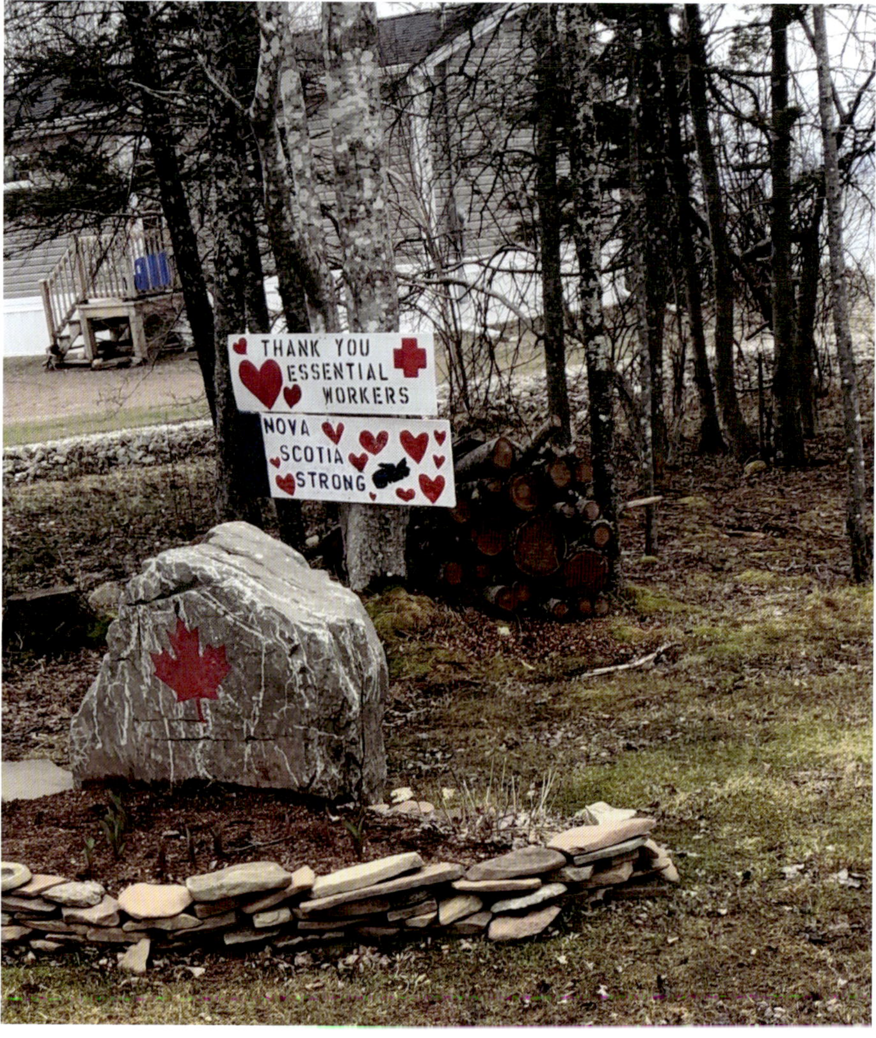

TOP LEFT: *People in in Cambridge show their appreciation to front-line workers in late April.*

BOTTOM LEFT: *Signs in Windsor Junction.*

RIGHT: *Carol and Morgan Dalrymple of Little Narrows, Cape Breton, offer a few words of thanks. (Morgan Dalrymple)*

ABOVE AND BEYOND:

Nurse Andrea Jenkins

Andrea Jenkins is standing in front of Northwood, a long-term care facility and seniors' residence in Halifax. The building has been the epicentre of Nova Scotia's COVID-19 outbreak; by late July, sixty-five Nova Scotians had died from COVID-19, fifty-three of them residents of Northwood.

Andrea, a twenty-year veteran nurse, is wearing scrubs; she has a mask in her hand and a stethoscope around her neck. Across the street, a passerby yells, "Thank you for everything you do!" and waves. Behind her, handmade signs of thanks and inspirational messages directed at the residents and staff have been affixed to anything that doesn't move.

Originally from Newfoundland, Andrea has worked for the last fifteen years at the Halifax Infirmary as an acute-care nurse. Like everyone, she watched as the virus spread around the world knowing that, at some point, it would reach the shores of Canada. What she didn't know was how that might affect her.

"I was just working a normal shift [at the infirmary] and I was seeing a patient, and my manager came in and said, 'We have a meeting in about five minutes.' That never happens. So we all went, and we were told then that the floor I was working on was being converted to a COVID unit," she says.

"Everything was changing. All the patients that were on that floor were being moved out and we were shutting down, preparing for COVID patients. I realized that it had arrived."

She says she and her colleagues were a little apprehensive. "Anytime something big and new [arrives and] you are going to be on that front line, of course it is a little concerning.

"We knew we would be receiving education specific to COVID-19," she says. "We knew we would be appropriately prepared. We knew we could do the work—we do the work every single day. All the things that we could control, we felt very confident in. The unknown was where the worry lay."

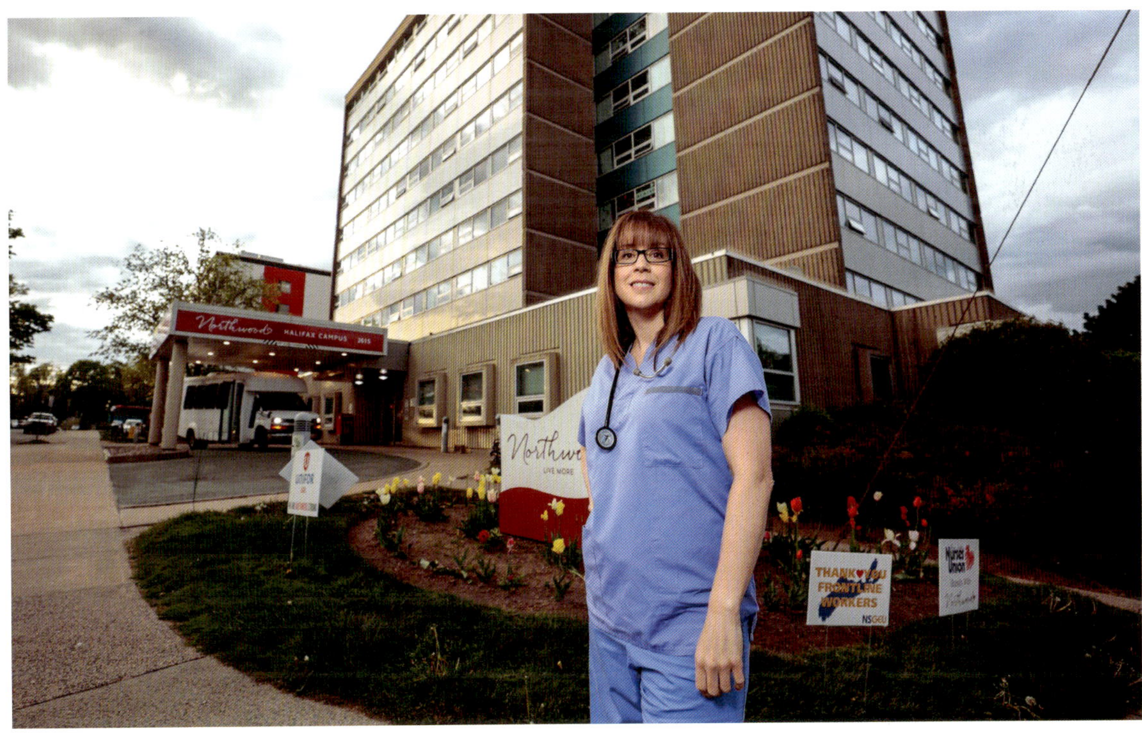

Acute-care nurse Andrea Jenkins stands outside the Northwood seniors' complex, the epicentre of the pandemic in Nova Scotia, where she and her colleagues battled COVID-19.

Given that COVID-19 was having such a large impact at Northwood, Andrea's unit was redeployed there. "They had a lot of staff sick. They had a lot of residents that were sick. Without extra help, how could they possibly, possibly manage?"

Like many, her team had heard the news reports about long-term care facilities in Quebec and Ontario where the residents hadn't been well cared-for. That wasn't the case at Northwood.

"Everybody was washed and clean and dressed and well-fed," she says, adding that the staff who worked there were like family members to the residents. "They were heartbroken at what was happening."

One of the nursing challenges was going to be to deliver acute care in what was essentially a residential environment. "If we showed up at your house tonight at seven P.M. and tried to convert it into a hospital, it would be impossible, because it's your home. You roam about in your home; you touch everything. You might get dressed in your bedroom, you might get dressed in your bathroom, but at the hospital, we have very strict designations."

Andrea was also concerned about making sure family members, who were barred from visiting due to the state of emergency, could chat with their loved ones who were under her care. She arranged phone calls so they could stay in touch. If a resident wasn't able to operate the phone, she would act as a go-between.

"I would take my cellphone and put it in a plastic bag and let them have a chat or FaceTime—whatever worked," she says. "They loved it! Everyone was always excited.... I think letting people have a quick glimpse into what the day would look like or how their family was doing made a big difference."

She says things can get very emotional when people are connecting like that in difficult circumstances. "It's very emotional, but it's a good emotion.... At the end of their conversations, when their kids are like, 'I love you, Mom,' there were very heartfelt 'I love you's. You knew everyone was scared." But she also noticed one other thing: many people would end their calls with "stay well" or "be careful." In this context, Andrea says, those words carried so much more meaning—meaning that was brought home to her whenever she returned to her own home after her shifts.

"For so many of the nurses that I work with, the concern was that we would bring it home. We have chosen to do this work and to put ourselves out there, but our families haven't necessarily signed up for the same."

Her concerns were tempered by the gratitude people showered on her and her fellow health-care workers. Community members regularly dropped off meals and gifts at her house. And in the same way people all over the world were honouring health-care workers during shift changes, people stood outside Northwood ringing bells, banging on pots and pans, and hollering words of thanks each time she came and went.

"It was very humbling, but that's the job. You are there to be a help," she says. "We are all called to do and be what the world needs us to do and be.... Our responses to that call may vary, but none is too insignificant to not make a difference. None is so remarkable to warrant being called a hero."

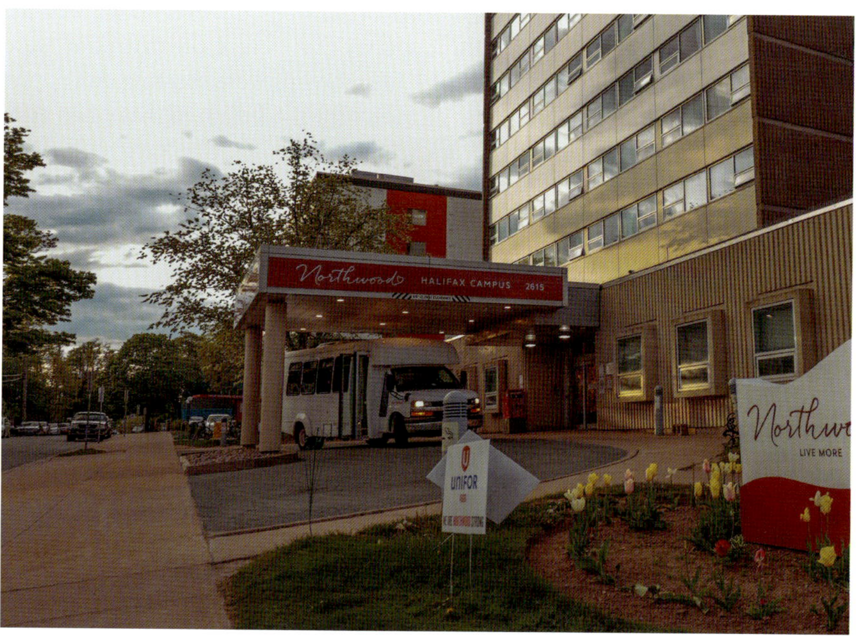

"The first time I showed up to see the early morning shift-change outside Northwood in late April, it was grey, windy, cold, and raining. Dozens and dozens of staff were lined up in the rain, waiting to be screened to enter and be given their assignments. They looked like soldiers. I was so moved by their silent resolve. As the night staff left the building, many of them burst into tears when I made eye contact and said 'thank you' to them.

"I knew then I would keep coming back for the early shift-change."

– Jan Marriott, retired nurse and daughter of Northwood resident

EMERGENCY ROOM: *Dr. Krista Watson*

Krista Watson has been an emergency room physician at Fishermen's Memorial Hospital in Lunenburg for the past eleven years. In mid-February she had just returned from a trip to Miami with her family and she had seen on the news what was happening with COVID-19 in European cities and hospitals, so she started to prepare for its imminent arrival here. That meant that, in addition to brushing up professionally and taking courses on managing ventilated patients and infectious diseases, she also redid her will and made sure her own personal care directive was up to date.

"Risk, I think, is always part of what we do, especially in terms of infectious disease," she says. "I think health-care workers accept some degree of risk as just being part of their work." She's glad her town was spared an outbreak of COVID-19, and says the numbers show that people have heeded the calls to distance and to limit social interactions.

In an attempt to limit physical contact with patients, Krista says she's focused on having people explain verbally what they are experiencing. "It's like, 'Tell me your story; tell me about your symptoms.' And only then do I kind of zone in for the very targeted physical close-contact exam, to try to limit my own exposure."

She is, however, seeing fewer patients in the ER. "I would say we went down to seeing maybe a quarter of our normal patient flow initially, because people really only wanted to come out only for emergencies," she says. "I think really the citizens kind of took up that call, and I feel very grateful."

She doesn't have to look far, though, to see what her fellow health-care workers are going through. "I'm grateful, but also a little guilty. I know that the workers at Northwood and the workers at the Halifax Infirmary have been very, very busy," she says.

"If anything, I really owe a huge thanks to the people who stayed home, who took the precautions really seriously. [They] protected me from exposure."

And like health-care professionals all over the world, she's seen the outpouring of appreciation and support on lawns, in windows, and on signs near the hospital.

"I did receive a number of really lovely emails saying, 'Thanks for what you do and thanks for being on the front lines,'" she says. "It's very humbling."

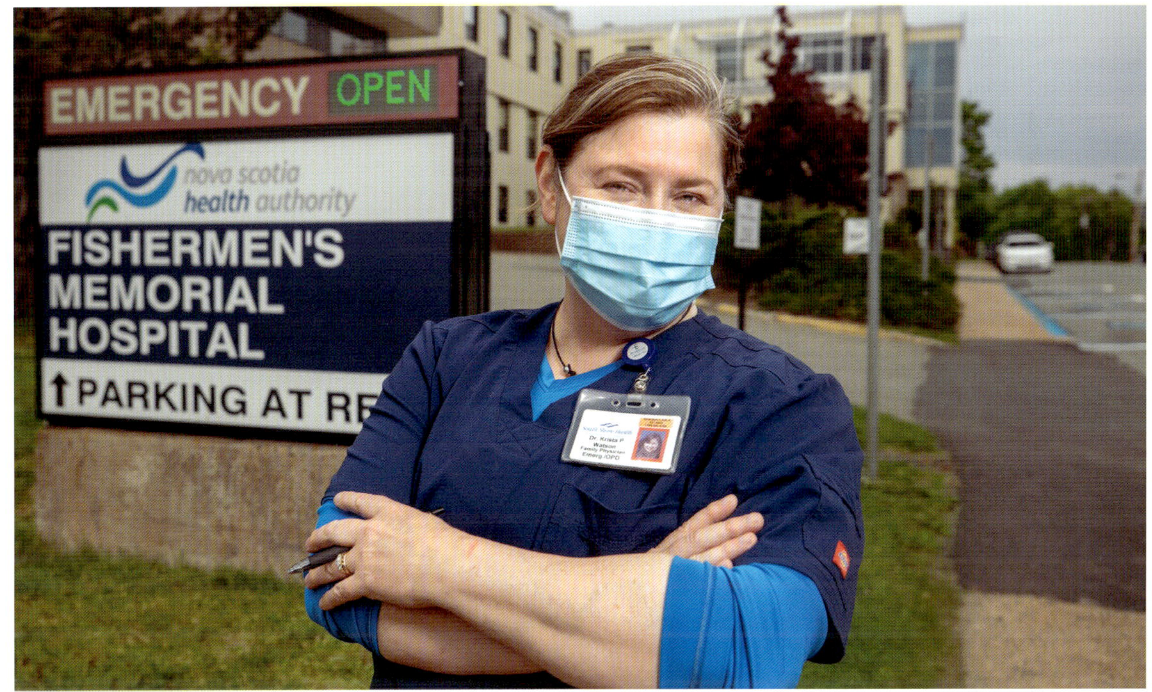

Dr. Krista Watson, an ER physician at Fishermen's Memorial Hospital in Lunenburg, says she's grateful Nova Scotians stayed home, minimizing the spread of COVID-19.

FRONT-LINE PHARMACISTS:
David LeBlanc and Maggie Arenburg

David LeBlanc steps outside the Harbour South Pharmasave in Yarmouth, NS, and takes off his mask with a sigh of relief. The pharmacist has spent the morning inside wearing his mask as he works behind the new Plexiglas panels that have been put in place to protect him and his colleagues in light of the COVID-19 pandemic. Other new safety protocols include extra cleaning, limiting the number of people in the store, and enforcing physical distancing requirements.

Both David and his wife, Maggie Arenburg, are pharmacists in Yarmouth—he at this pharmacy, Spears and MacLeod Pharmasave, she at Yarmouth Regional Hospital. Theirs was one of the professions that foresaw the upcoming disruptions when worldwide demand for pharmaceuticals increased as people stockpiled prescription drugs out of fear that they may not be able to get the medications they needed.

"Every pharmacy has a pandemic preparedness plan in place, whether it be [for] influenza or any seasonal sickness," says David, "but even this winter, when we heard of COVID going on in other parts of the world, we sort of anticipated that it may make its way here and [that we should] prepare for it."

He admits, though, that they weren't fully prepared for how things went down. At first, pharmacies throughout Nova Scotia were only refilling prescriptions for thirty days, rather than ninety, to prevent shortages caused by issues with the supply chain. This led to a backlash because it meant people had to pay dispensing fees more often, which created a financial strain on an already anxious population. Eventually the provincial government stepped in to pay the extra dispensing fees.

"We were looking at the big picture, certainly," says David, "but I certainly understand [why] people with [things like] asthma or respiratory conditions...thought of stockpiling medications just in case.... But from a pharmacy perspective, we tried to be fair so that everybody could get the medication they needed."

He says working through the pandemic has meant working longer hours, which has taken a toll on his family. On the other hand, Maggie, who has spent the last year at home on maternity leave with their two children—Cate, three, and Ben, one—almost regrets having missed out on the chance to contribute her skills during the pandemic. "It's the

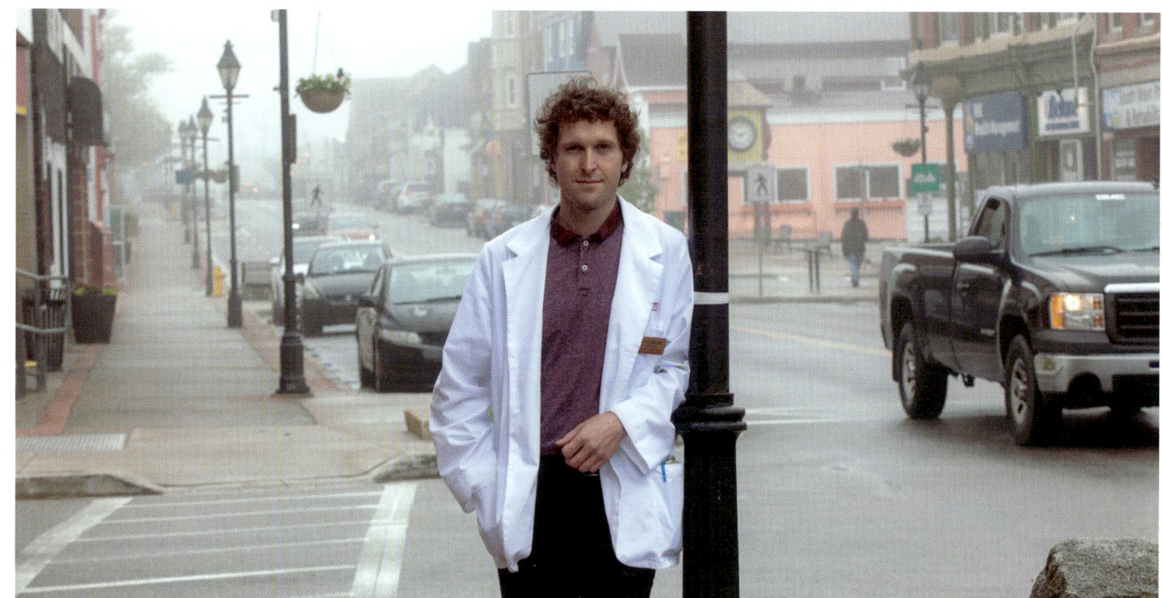

Pharmacist David LeBlanc outside the drugstore where he works in Yarmouth.

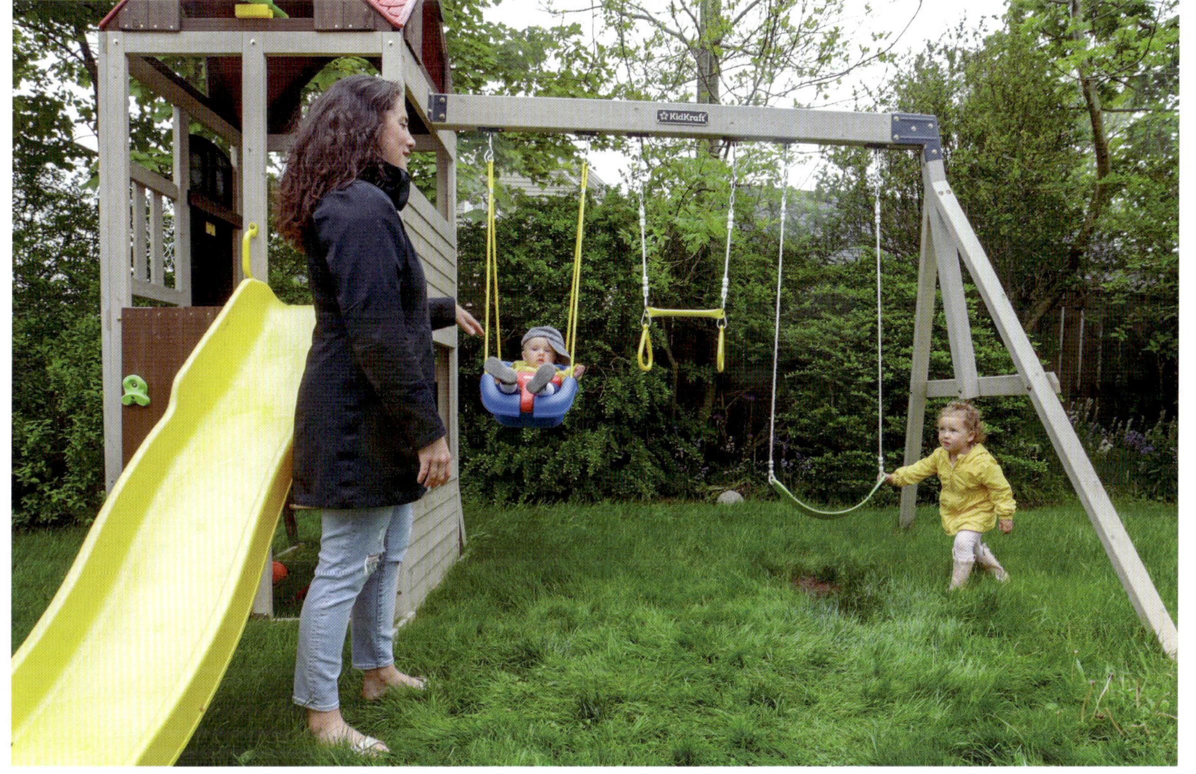

Pharmacist Maggie Arenburg has been on maternity leave from her job at the Yarmouth Regional Hospital during the pandemic; here she spends time with her kids: one-year old Ben, centre, and three-year-old Cate.

biggest health-care crisis our generation will see," she says, "and in some ways, I find it hard to not be contributing to that via my profession."

But that hasn't prevented her from keeping her credentials up to date. "I've been trying to keep up with the scientific literature on vaccines and transmission and whatnot…and I feel like my knowledge base is certainly better off for it," Maggie says.

"I'm a really big believer in a team approach and team-building, and I feel like this is probably one of the biggest team-building exercises a department or a staff could do together."

When she goes back to work in August, it will mean implementing protocols at home that didn't exist before. Now, when David gets home from work, he showers downstairs and puts his clothes into the washing machine before he joins the family. "We just took it for granted before. I never would've considered having to shower before interacting with the kids, or having to change my clothes before picking them up from daycare," says Maggie.

"I would say [the pandemic] certainly has made us realize what's important."

HAULING THE ESSENTIALS:
A Trucker's Experience

Jumping down from his rig, Mark Goudge walks over with a big smile—a smile hidden under his mask, but visible in the corners of his eyes. "This place has great coffee. Do you want one?" he asks, his huge red Freightliner Cascadia with the nameplate "Baron 2" behind him.

As the COVID-19 pandemic has overtaken the country, as borders have closed down and stores have shuttered, Mark and thousands of other truckers have continued to work, driving day and night to deliver essential goods to where they're needed.

Being away from home for six weeks as Nova Scotians came to grips with the state of emergency was a challenge. "My whole thing has been the not knowing and the inability to be near my family and loved ones as the gravity of this unfolded," he says.

As restaurants and truck stops shut down, the simple task of getting a meal on the road became more and more difficult. His employer had volunteers create food packages and put together personal items to help the truckers on the road. Other folks stepped up in other ways—like Crystal Blair, owner of the Petro Pass Restaurant in Glenholme, NS, who reopened her restaurant to prepare meals that were provided free to truckers (see "A Lifeline on the Road," page 29). "Not all heroes wear capes, and Crystal is a superhero," says Mark.

Mark has had some touching moments on the road—kids waving signs that read, "Thank You, Truckers!" and people waving at him from cars along the way. He woke up on Easter morning in Lancaster, Ont., to the sound of knocking on the side of the truck. A woman pointed to a table she'd set up with coffee and muffins. "I looked at the breakfast meal and said, 'This is fantastic! What organization are you with?' She told me there was no organization—it was just her. She had done it because a long time ago she had broken down on the side of [Highway] 401 and the only person to stop and help her was a truck driver. She never forgot that.... It was her way of saying thank you."

The lack of traffic has made his job easier, but he says it feels surreal to drive through major cities like New York, Toronto, and Montreal and with no traffic. Crossing the border has also changed. "We now have to wear masks when we come to the border on the Canadian side; the agents don't touch any paperwork, and even our passports are just scanned. I have to say it feels good to know [Canadians] are taking it seriously and ensuring the safety of our CBSA agents and us as drivers."

He says living through the pandemic has changed him. "[I] truly appreciate the little things, for sure: sharing a beer with a friend; coming home from two weeks out and going out for a nice meal."

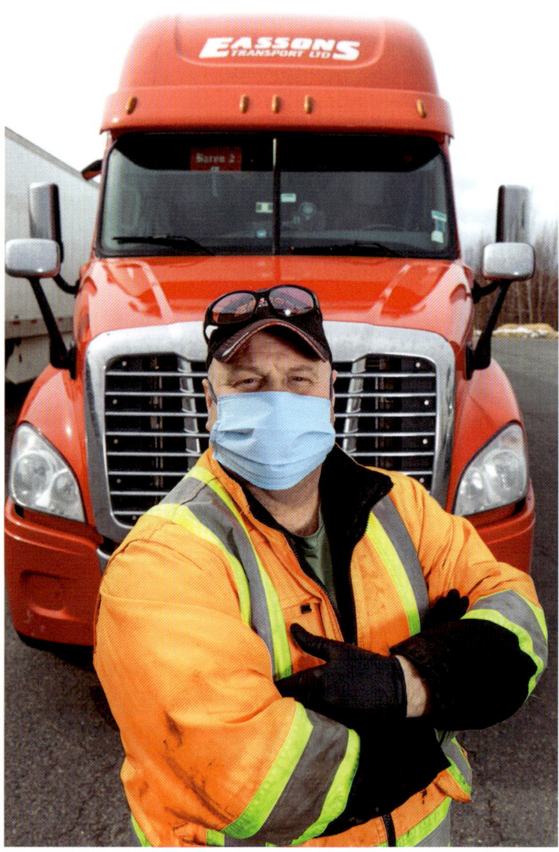

Mark Goudge of Westville, a long-haul driver for Eassons Transport, has travelled all over North America during the pandemic.

For now, though, that meal will have to wait. Mark steps up to the rig with his coffee. "The clock is ticking!" he says and climbs aboard.

"When I started this career I never even my wildest dreams thought I would be considered essential," he says. "The whole thing has been very overwhelming."

HYDROSTONE GROCER:
A Truly Essential Service

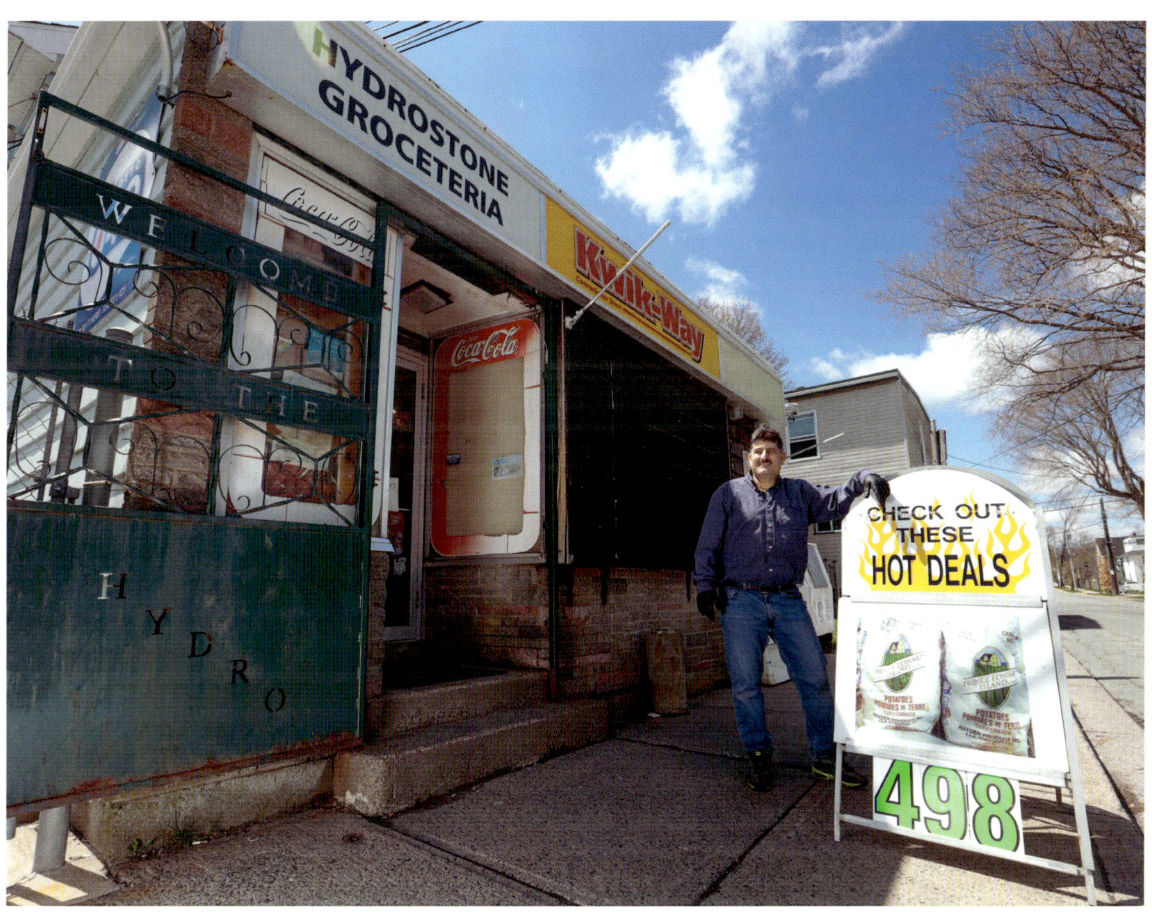

Eli Elrabahi, owner of the Hydrostone Groceteria, in front of his store on Isleville St. in Halifax.

Standing in the Hydrostone Groceteria on Isleville St. in Halifax as customers drop in is a bit like being in the middle of a family reunion. Owner Eli Elrabahi—who also goes by Lee—greets almost everyone by their first name and with a hearty hello as he stands behind the Plexiglas divider he has installed to limit the spread of COVID-19.

In some cases, he already knows what the customer wants and has it waiting at the counter for them. When Ron Alley, who is blind, comes in, the two go over his grocery list like old friends. Eli gathers up Ron's items for him and packs everything into a bag, ducking under the dozens of banners from winning lottery tickets he's sold.

"I've been coming here to see Eli since he's been here," says Ron. "I've watched his kids grow up." As Ron turns to leave, his dog, Frankie, looks over at Eli, who asks Frankie how many he wants today—as he reaches into the dog treat container behind the cash.

Eli emigrated from Lebanon to Canada thirty years ago—"the second-best thing I ever did" (the first, he says, was marrying his wife)—and has been operating the store for eighteen years. But recently he and his customers have come to realize what an essential role he and his grocery store play in the community.

"People were worried about us—if we were going to reduce our hours or shut down. We didn't do that. We increased our hours and we got more variety. We brought in items we never had before because people need them. We have medical supplies, cleaning supplies—everything we need for them," he says.

That also includes baking essentials, because so many people have taken up baking at home. As we speak, a man walks in and asks for yeast. Eli pulls some off a nearby shelf and explains that when the

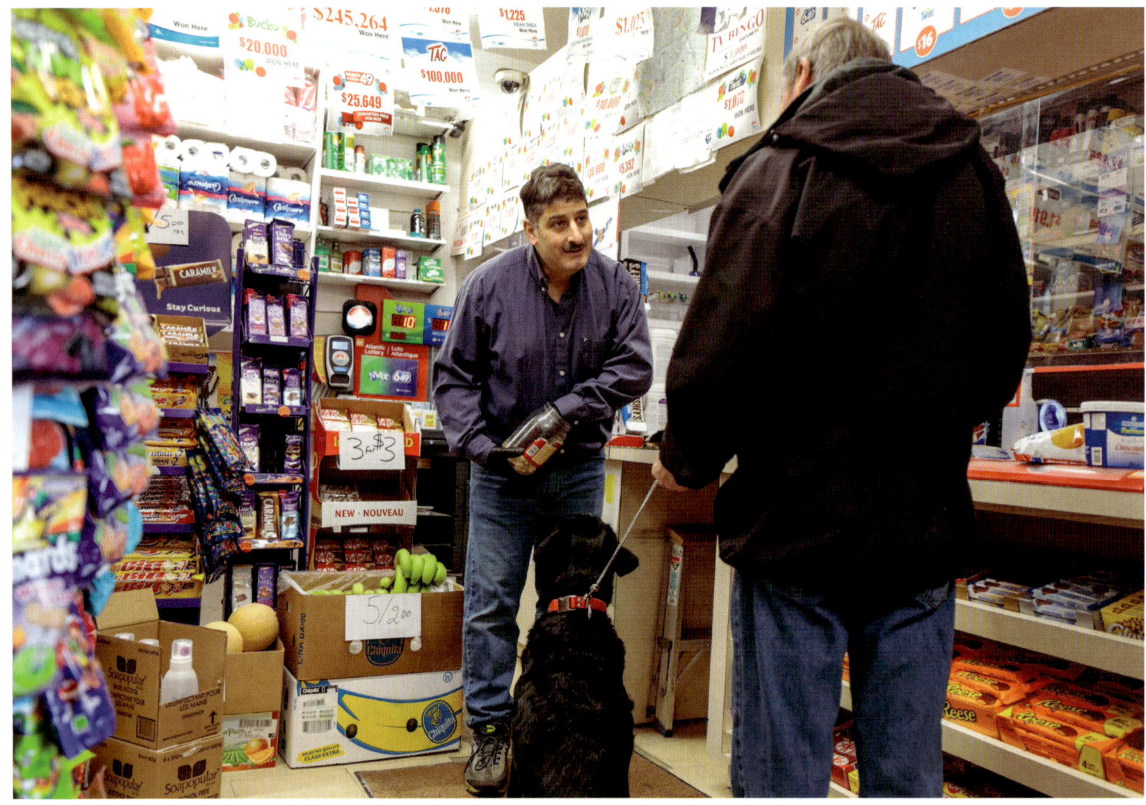

Eli asks customer Ron Alley if he can give Ron's dog, Freddie, a treat.

big grocery stores were closed, he was able to bring in a truckload of flour.

"I'm very, very proud of what we're doing here," he says. "I know my family was concerned. I'm exposed to the customers.... But it is very, very important to the community." Eli says between three hundred and five hundred people come through his doors every day, so he made sure he and his customers were safe early on by using gloves, plenty of sanitizer, and a Plexiglas shield.

But he admits he worries a bit. "Oh yes. I have four kids and a wife and they are concerned. You are exposed so much; you deal with so much. But... I'm very happy to be here and helping my community. It's like a part of me. If I don't come here every day, I think something is missing. This is my life. These are my people. I'm here in the sunshine; I'm here in the rain and the snow; I'm here in the bad times."

And he means it. The week before, a woman had come in to get flour and yeast and had forgotten her debit card. Eli told her to take her groceries and come back later to pay, even though he didn't know her.

It's easy to understand why the community loves him. "They bring me coffee or a cake that they made," he says. He keeps a little "bundle money," as he calls it, to help customers who can't afford the essentials. "You can tell when people walk in.... [They don't] have money for a loaf of bread or a jug of milk. We'll take care of it," he says with a smile. "Don't worry about it! Let's get through this pandemic together."

A NEW WAY TO GATHER NEWS:
Jean Laroche and Jayson Baxter

Veteran reporter Jean Laroche has told his share of stories over his thirty-two-year career at the CBC: the Montreal massacre, the Oka standoff, and the crash of Swissair Flight 111. He's covered enough legislative sittings to see six Nova Scotia premiers through their time in the house. And through all that, most of his reporting has been done via face-to face-interviews.

Now he's covering a global pandemic while working from home.

"The biggest kind of mind shift in this whole thing is the inability to go to where the story is," he says. "I really like being face-to-face with people when I interview them. You've got body language, you've got the raised eyebrow. You can go, 'Okay, well…[maybe] they didn't understand the question, or maybe there's something deeper there.' So I've had to shift my skills, listen a little harder, try and elicit what the body language doesn't tell you or what you can't get over the phone."

While working at home has it advantages—"two rolls to the right" and he is out of bed and at the desk in his home office—it also has its drawbacks. The line between work and home, thin at the best of times time for journalists, is now completely blurred.

"Because we're working at home, we're unable to disconnect from it," Jean says. "I think we're all in that same kind of boat, because normally I would only get emails during business hours from contacts or from the public, and now I'm getting them kind of all hours."

Jayson Baxter, co-host and producer of *CTV News at 5* is in a similar situation at work. When the state of emergency was declared, "anyone that could work at home…was told to go and get set up from their computer at home. Reporters left the building and started working remotely. Same with camera operators." The newsroom that would normally have had twenty people in it immediately went down to five.

The methodology for reporting also changed.

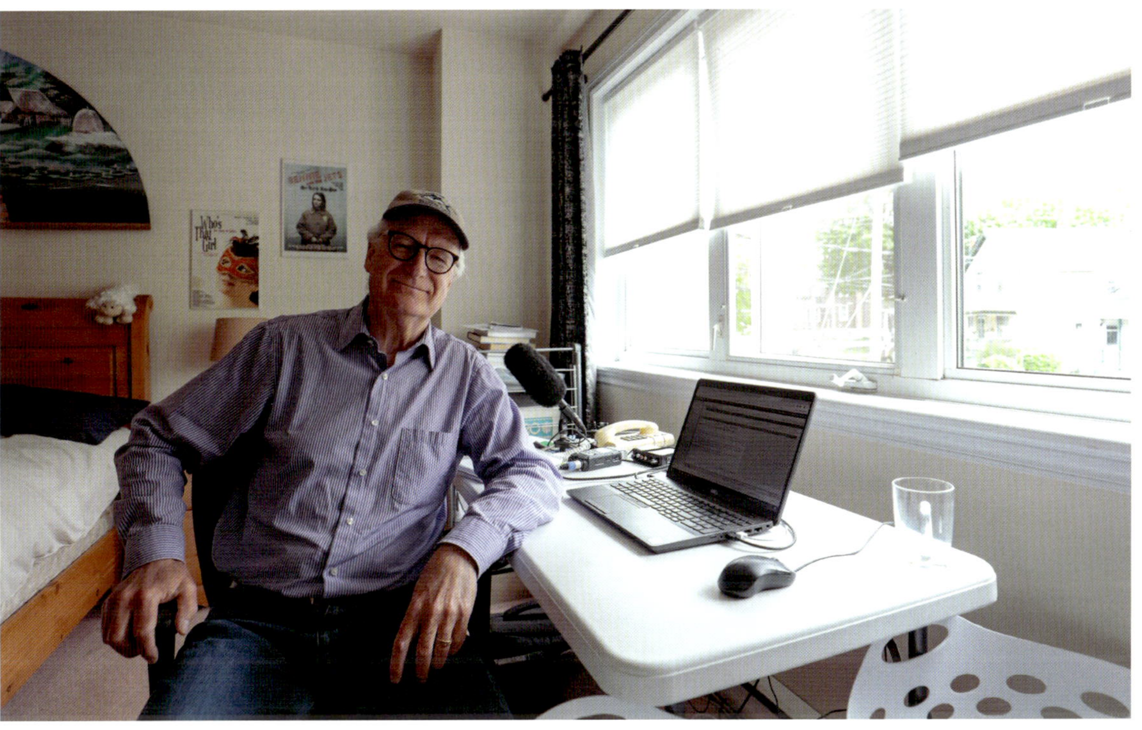

"Two rolls to the right" and veteran CBC reporter Jean Laroche is out of bed and at work in his home office—which is both an advantage and a disadvantage, he says.

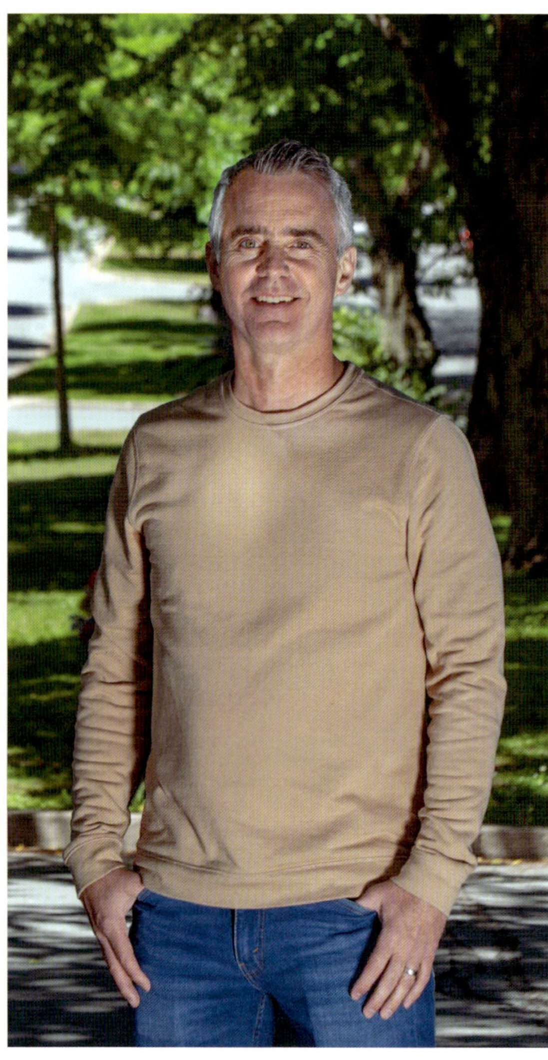

After twenty-five years in the news business, Jayson Baxter, co-host and producer of CTV News at 5*, says the three biggest three stories of his career happened at the same time: the worldwide pandemic, the Portapique shooting, and the Black Lives Matter movement.*

Where in-person interviews had previously been preferred over video conference–style interviews, that preference was now reversed.

And spring 2020 wasn't exactly a slow news cycle in Nova Scotia. In mid-April, Canada's worst modern-day mass murder happened in Portapique, NS, when a gunman went on a rampage and killed twenty-two people. In late April, six Nova Scotia-based Canadian Armed Forces members were killed in a helicopter crash off Greece. In early May, three-year-old Dylan Ehler went missing in Truro; his body was never found. In June, rallies and marches were held throughout the province in support of the Black Lives Matter movement. And that's all in addition to the pandemic.

"I've been doing this for twenty-five years and the ... biggest stories of my life, my career, happened back to back to back," says Jayson. "So there was a lot of fatigue, I think, mental fatigue in the newsroom."

Jean Laroche sees that fatigue, too. "I'm trying to be much kinder to colleagues and understand that people have a lot going on," he says. "I think I'm also that way with the people I talk to. Today I called somebody, and I said, 'How are you?' And there's not that automatic 'Fine'—there's a pause."

"It's made me a more careful listener," continues Jean. "When you're also living the experience, it affects you in a different way. You carry that around more than if it was a story about something else farther away."

Jayson and his crew realized their own fatigue was a sign people needed a break from the news, so they started a segment in which they solicited videos that would make people smile. It was instantly popular.

"People wanted to be informed, but we could see early on that there was a real need for moments of levity as well," says Jayson. "We've seen the worst of people, but we've also seen the best of people since this all happened."

He smiles. "People still want to laugh, you know?"

A SNOWBIRD LOST

In late April 2020 the Canadian Forces Snowbirds announced they would cross the country to lift the spirits of Canadians and to salute them for doing their part to fight the spread of COVID-19. The mission was dubbed "Operation Inspiration." The tour kicked off with flights over Nova Scotia and New Brunswick on May 3.

As the Snowbirds flew over Royal Canadian Air Force Base Shearwater outside Halifax, the team flew in the symbolic "missing man" formation in honour of the six military members who had been killed in late April in the crash of a Cyclone helicopter off the coast of Greece.

Tragically, on May 17, near the end of the Operation Inspiration tour, a Snowbirds aircraft crashed en route to Comox, BC. Capt. Jenn Casey of Halifax, the public affairs officer for the aerobatics team, died. The pilot, Capt. Richard MacDougall, was badly injured. The remainder of the tour was cancelled.

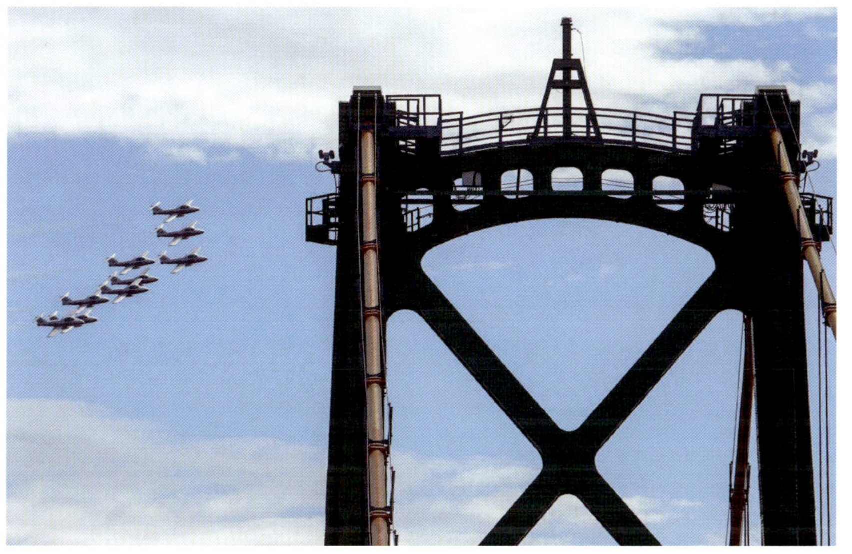

TOP: *The Snowbirds over Halifax.*

BOTTOM LEFT: *A hearse carrying the body of Capt. Jennifer Casey passes a mourner holding a Nova Scotia flag. People lined the roads to say goodbye and thank you as the procession made its way from Halifax Stanfield International Airport through the streets of the city.*

BOTTOM RIGHT: *A cadet and military member watch as the Snowbirds fly over Dartmouth in the "missing man" formation. (Paul Darrow)*

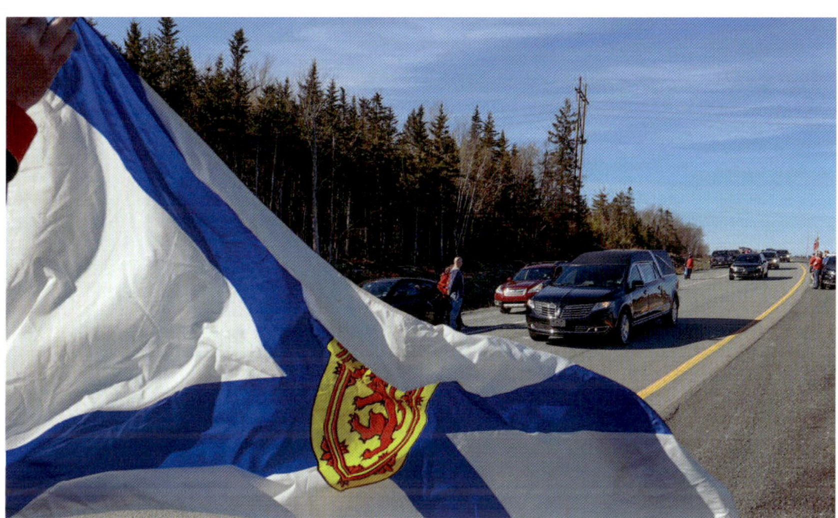

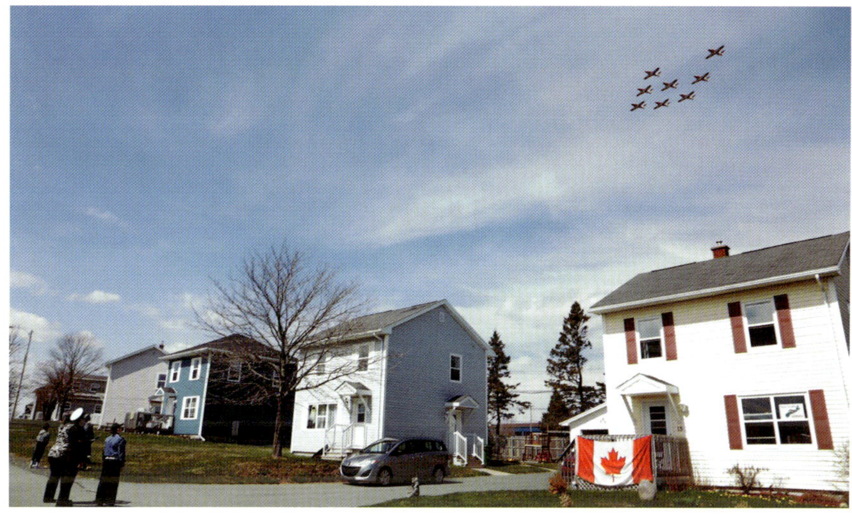

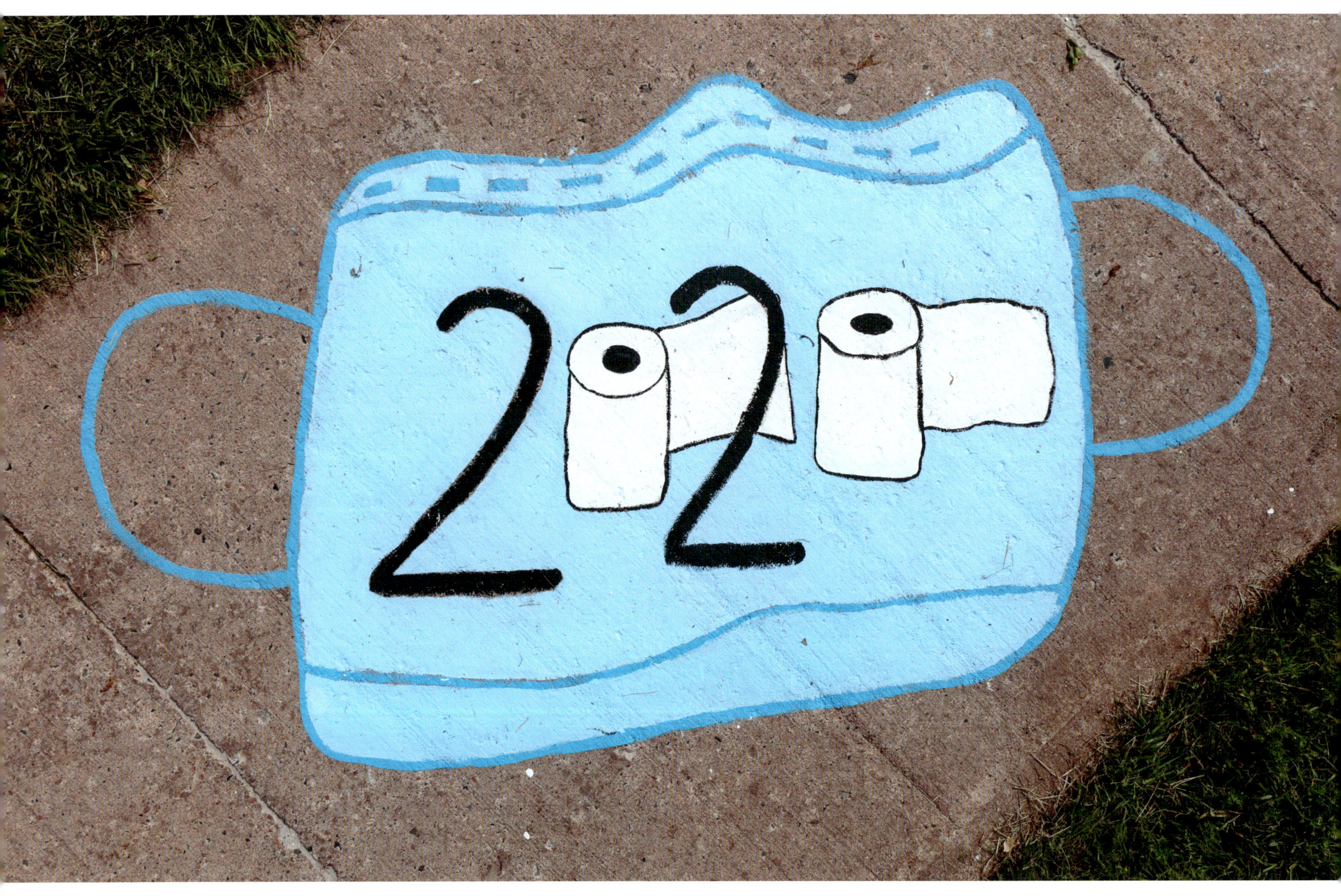

Part Three: MARKING MILESTONES

TOP RIGHT: *A chalk drawing in Amherst pretty much sums up 2020.*

WE'RE IN THIS TOGETHER: *Signs of Hope*

As we stayed the blazes home, Nova Scotians found ways to reach out and brighten the days for themselves and their neighbours.

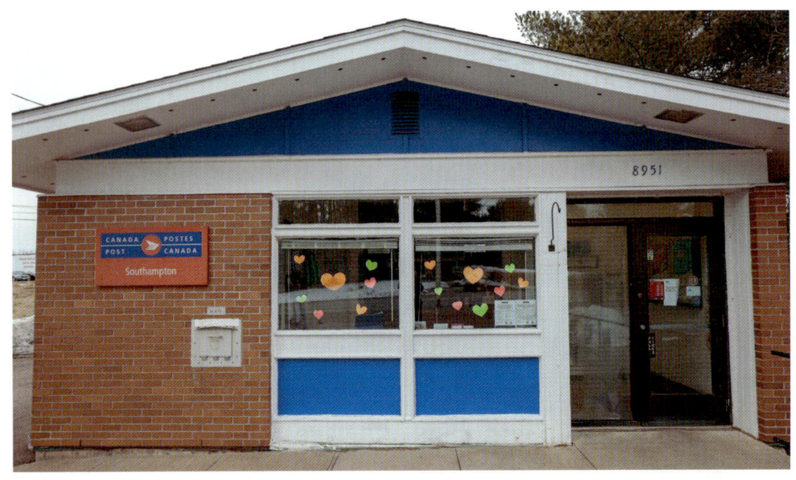

TOP: *The post office in Southampton shares a little love.*

BOTTOM LEFT: *Words of hope on a Portapique garage.*

BOTTOM RIGHT: *A homemade sign in Kentville.*

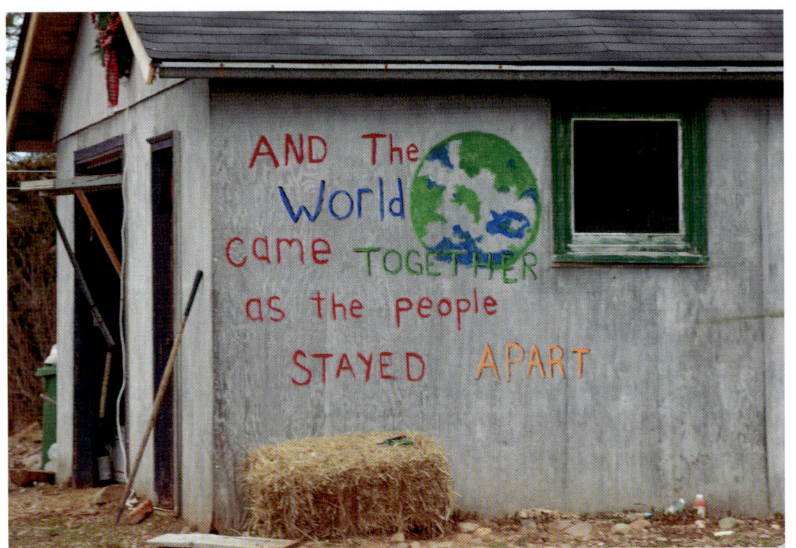

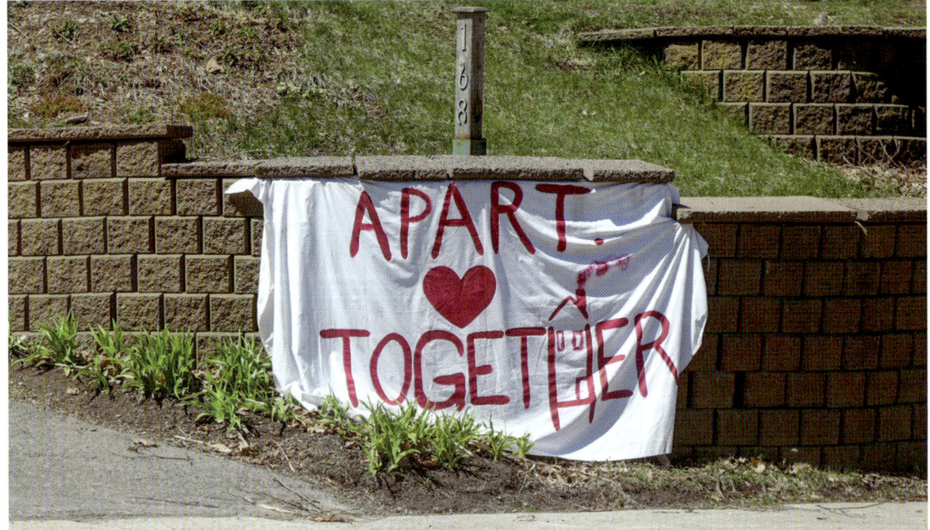

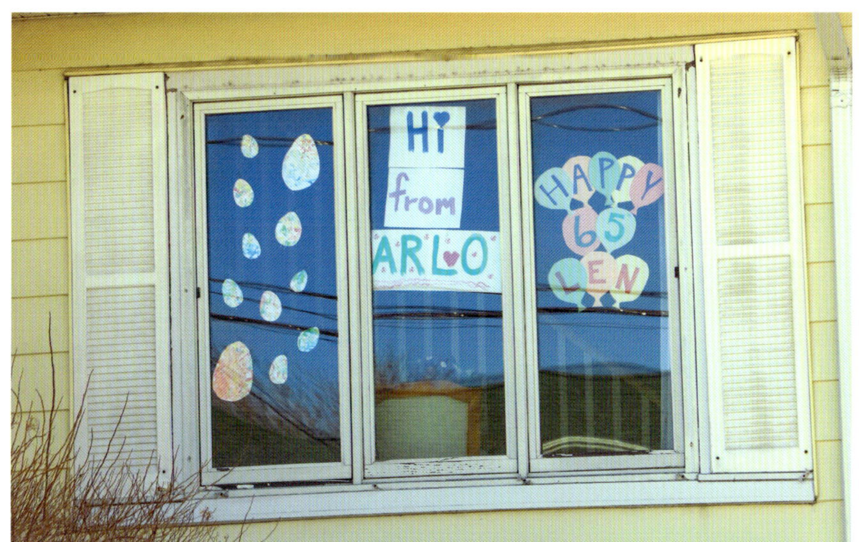

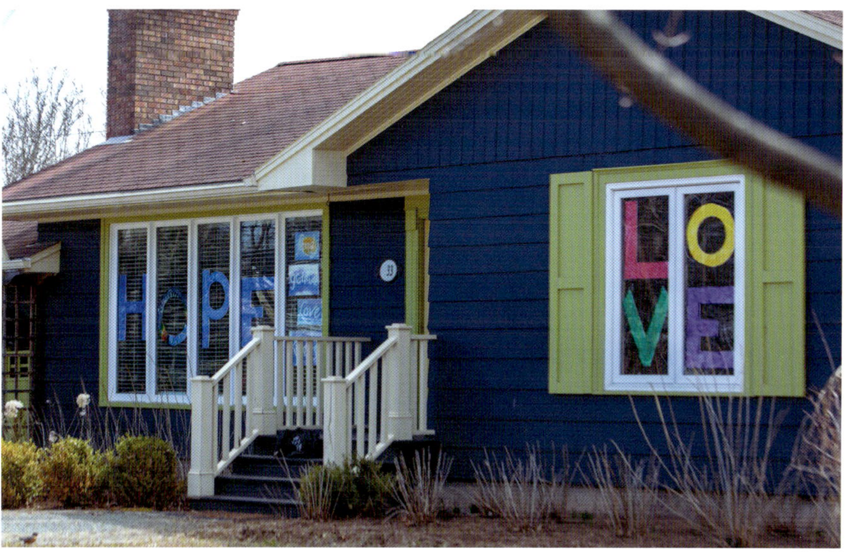

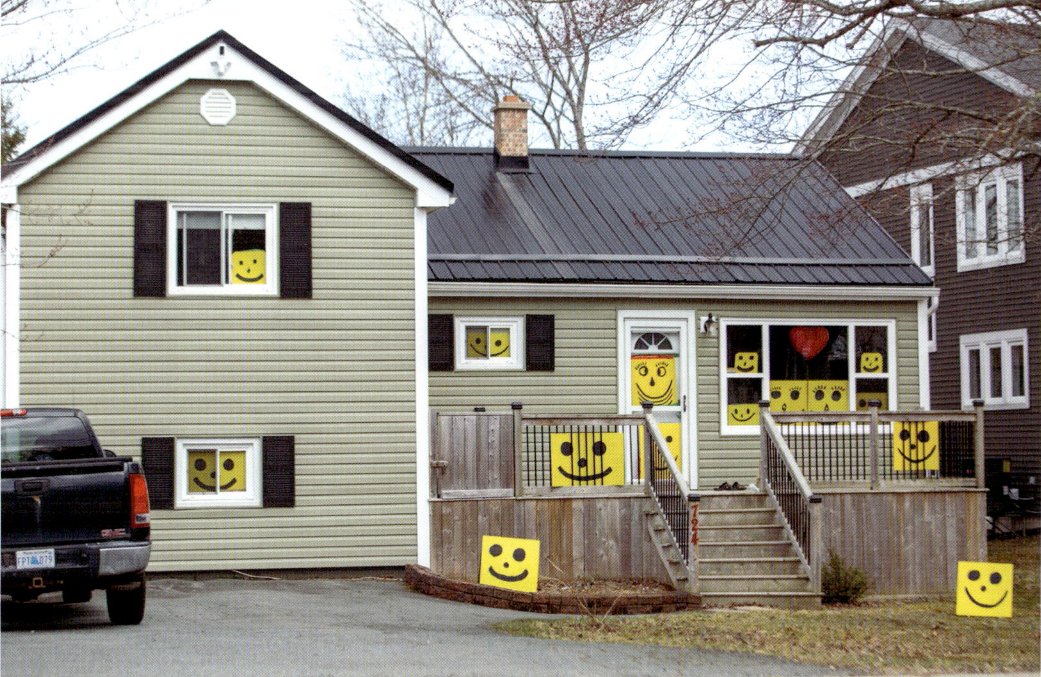

TOP LEFT: *Greetings from a distance in a Halifax neighbourhood.*

TOP RIGHT: *Hope and love in Wolfville.*

BOTTOM: *A home on Portobello Rd. in Waverley shares smiles with neighbours.*

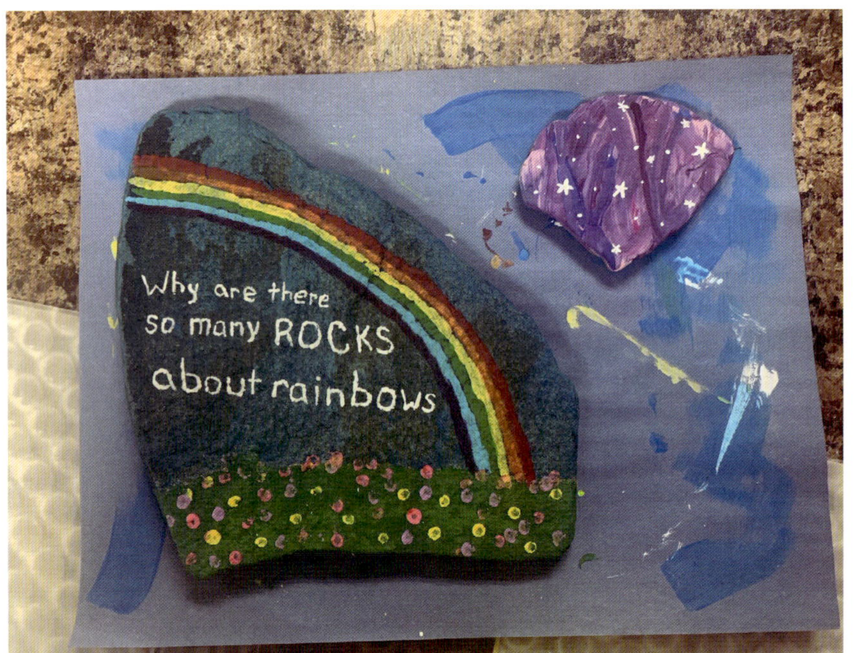

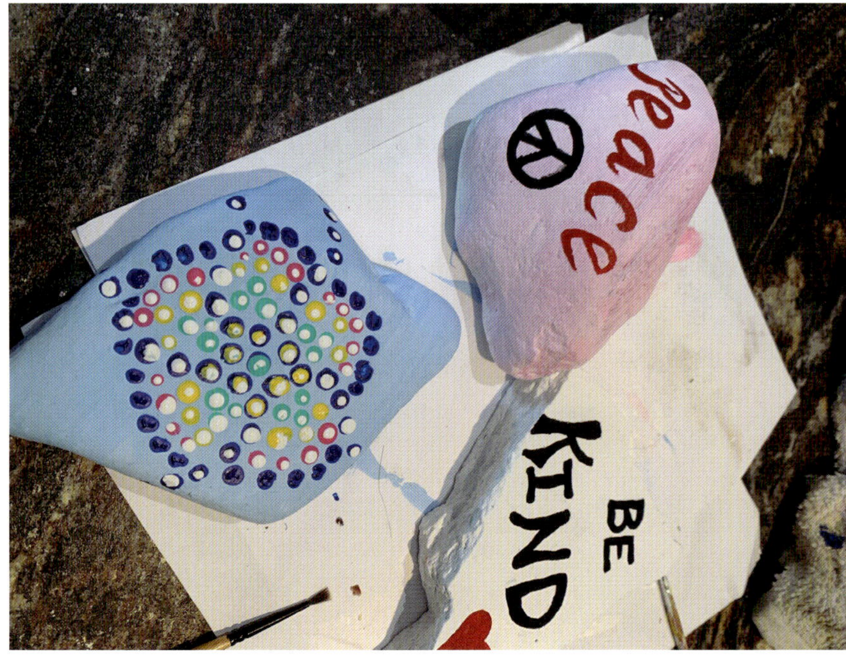

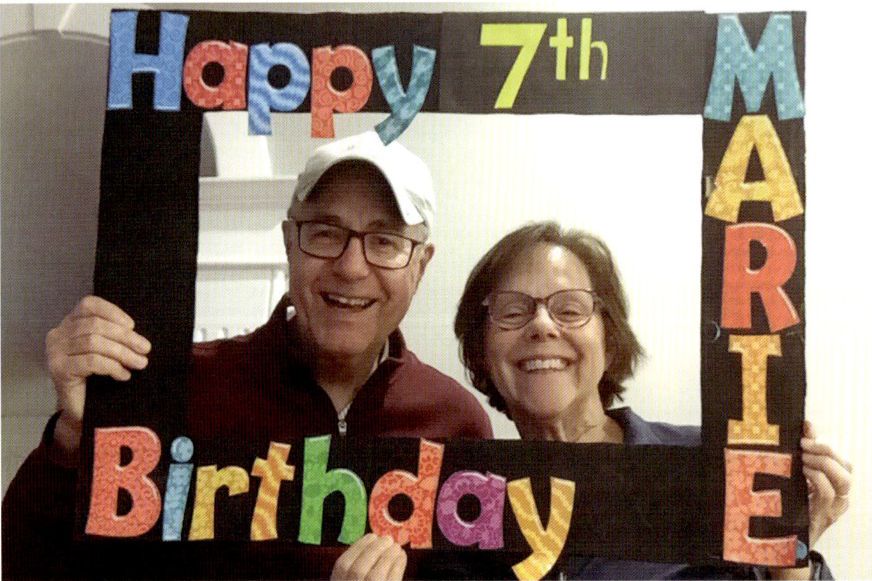

TOP LEFT: *Kristine MacDonald of Port Hawkesbury, NS, and her mother painted rocks and their windows to spread some cheer during the lockdown. (Kristine MacDonald)*

TOP RIGHT *Karen Brooking-Tinney of Fall River, NS, painted these rocks to brighten everyone's day. (Karen Brooking-Tinney)*

BOTTOM: *Jim Abraham and his wife, Andra, wished their granddaughter a virtual Happy Birthday since no physical contact was allowed. (Andra Abraham)*

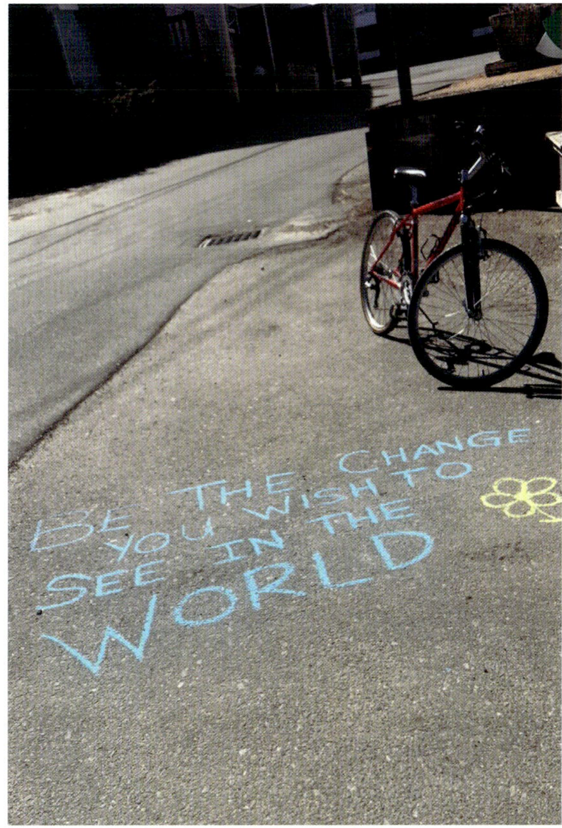

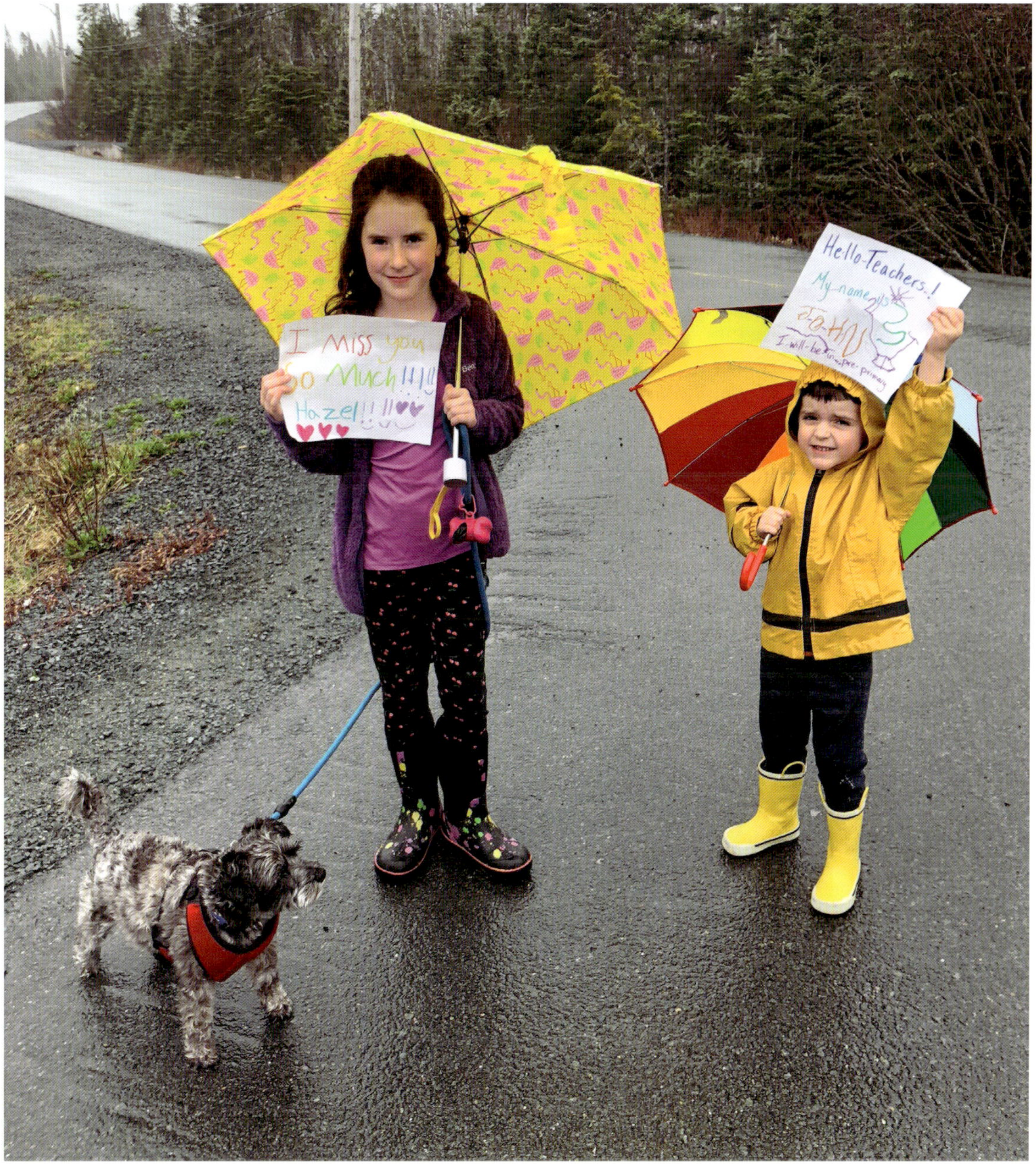

LEFT: *Catharine Fahie of Wolfville, NS, says this image is from a day she had fun biking around Wolfville, "playing with chalk and spreading love!" (Catharine Fahie)*

RIGHT: *Angela Roach Fraser of Whites Lake, NS, sent these photos of her kids waiting a "teacher drive-by parade." (Angela Roach Fraser)*

BIRTH UNDER LOCKDOWN:

Christian and Joanne

Joanne Firth had clearly envisioned how the birth of her first child would go. But sitting alone, in labour, waiting to be admitted to the hospital while her husband, Christian Laforce, waited out in the entry area wasn't matching her vision.

Joanne recalled the moment in March when it all started. "My water broke Monday morning at around one-thirty."

"It broke spectacularly," says Christian. Joanne, laughing, agrees. "They tell you it's not going to be like it is in the movies, but … it was."

That meant getting to the IWK Health Centre and getting registered right away. Unfortunately, a provincial state of emergency had been declared and visitor restrictions were already in place at the hospital to reduce the spread of COVID-19.

In advance of her due date, Joanne had already had her final ultrasound alone while Christian waited outside—a harbinger of things to come. "I never imagined that it would impact our birth the way it did," she says.

Christian recalls how it felt to wait outside while she registered. "I was standing out there in front of the security desk watching you in labour, waiting to get your room, and then just wandering around for an hour or something, waiting to get a call. I felt very apprehensive," he says.

"Obviously, we've never been through that before. I was just really just kind of trying to remember the moment. It was just me in front of the IWK, just breathing through my nose and saying, 'Okay, this is one step. I don't know what the next step is, but here we are right now, and everything seems to be okay—at least from my perspective.'"

Joanne laughs. "I was thinking, 'This sucks.'"

Eventually Christian was allowed into the birthing unit. Eliana Mary Gwendolyn Laforce made her appearance at 5:35 P.M. on March 24, 2020.

"Hic … hic … hic." Eight-week-old Eliana, swaddled in a warm blanket, tells her own version of events as she lays on her mom's lap, the two never losing eye contact for more than a few seconds as Christian looks on across the table.

"It was sad in the hospital not to have anybody come and visit; we had to do FaceTime so people could see her and take pictures," Joanne recalls. "It was sad for our family that they couldn't meet her … but in a way it was a nice bubble for us to get to know her."

"They say it takes a village to raise a baby, but when you have a baby in a pandemic, who's doing it? It was hard on you, not having the support of your mother, and I really grieved not having my family around. I wanted to cry," says Christian.

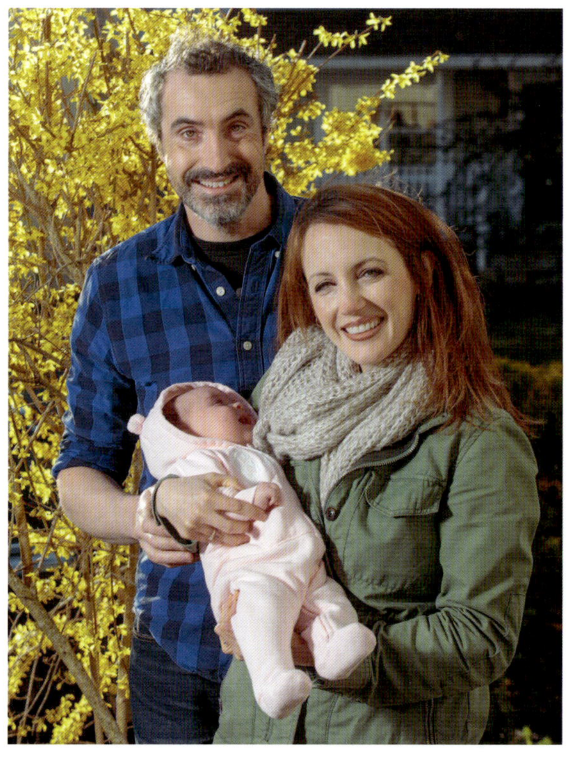

Christian Laforce, Joanne Firth, and Eliana.

Joanne particularly missed her twin sister, Karen. "There is a very close connection. It was really hard."

The first month after Eliana was born was filled with front-step drop-offs and FaceTime as the two navigated the challenges of being first-time parents without the family safety net.

"It's just not the same as having your mom come into your house and help you with your laundry or cook for you. When you have a baby, you want to share that joy, and it just felt like we couldn't do that," says Joanne.

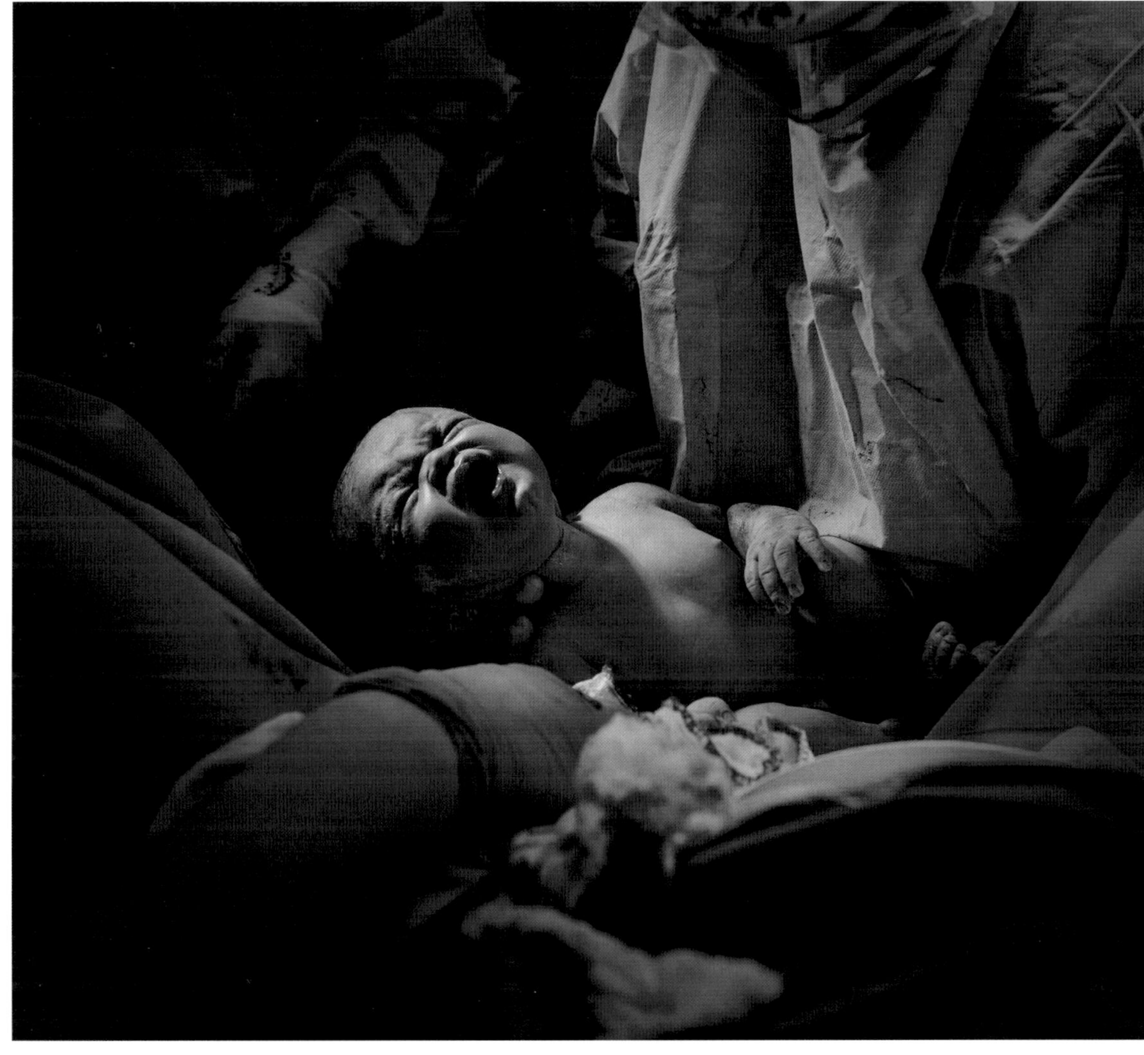

Eliana Mary Gwendolyn Laforce says hello to the world at 5:35 P.M. on March 24, 2020, in the midst of the global pandemic. (Christian Laforce)

Christian jumps in and tries to put his new life in perspective. "I feel like my world is actually kind of shrunk a bit. I think this would have happened with or without COVID-19. Being a new father… there are things that are just not as important when you have something like a new baby to focus on. Then they go away and you don't miss them."

Christian became very cautious about anything that came into the house, and when he did go out he made sure he wore protective equipment and changed before going near Eliana. "You so afraid of bringing something home to this little girl."

As the weeks went by Joanne realized she was experiencing postpartum depression. "The baby blues, anyway. To not be able to, you know, see your parents or see your family—it was really hard. You realize how much you value them."

They both remember the daily coronavirus updates with Dr. Robert Strang, and that he noted the restrictions could go on for months. "I remember that day thinking, 'Months! I won't be able to make it,'" says Joanne. "I did cry that day."

Joanne found some support on social media through a parent-support group. She read one story that put their situation into perspective—the story of a one hundred-year-old woman who had been born during the influenza pandemic of 1918. "Her mother told her, 'It was just me and you for a long, long, long time. But you know, we got through it. Things got better,'" says Joanne. "It was just a really nice kind of inspirational message…. If she can do it, we can do it! Her mother kept her safe. So yeah, that'll be the story we'll tell her: 'We kept you safe. It was just me, you, and your dad for eight weeks. But we did it.'"

She smiles. "I'm proud that we did it. We're stronger than we think we are."

HIGH SCHOOL GRAD WITH A TWIST: *Brooke Clarke*

Few other moments in life define the transition into adulthood like high school graduation. The celebration, the prom, and the coming together of friends and family make it one of life's great moments.

But like so many other moments during the pandemic and lockdown of 2020, this one appeared to be about to slip away from Brooke Clarke, a student at Lockview High School in Fall River, NS.

When Brooke left school for March Break, she had no idea she might not ever enter the school again—not even for graduation.

"I always expected…I would cross the stage with all of my friends, but I guess times have changed," she says. "You always picture your prom, getting all dressed up, going to prom with all your friends. Maybe getting a nice car to go in—all that, it's just taken away."

But while the traditional graduation celebrations did go by the wayside, communities and schools all over Nova Scotia found special ways to honour their grads. Communities posted signs, posters, and banners with graduates' pictures and names on them. Some schools organized drive-in graduations during which students and families waited in their cars until their names were called.

Brooke's school ultimately decided to allow grads and their "bubble families" to enter the building so graduates could experience the walk across the stage. Once the decision was made, school administration and staff jumped into action, decorating the auditorium, while community members fundraised to collect the nine thousand dollars needed to get the grad gowns, which had been cancelled earlier in the spring.

The students were given a ten-minute window. Dressed in her gown, her mortarboard cap with "2020" hanging from it, Brooke Clarke entered the auditorium, had some pictures taken with her "bubble family," and waited for her name to be called. The principal laid her diploma on a table. She picked it up, chatted for a moment, and then left her school for the final time.

It was, she said, "the most unique graduation ever."

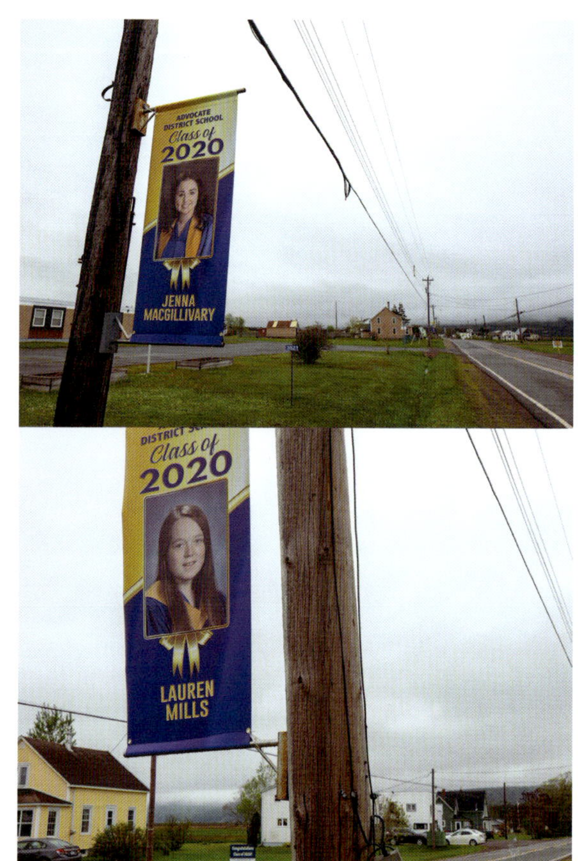

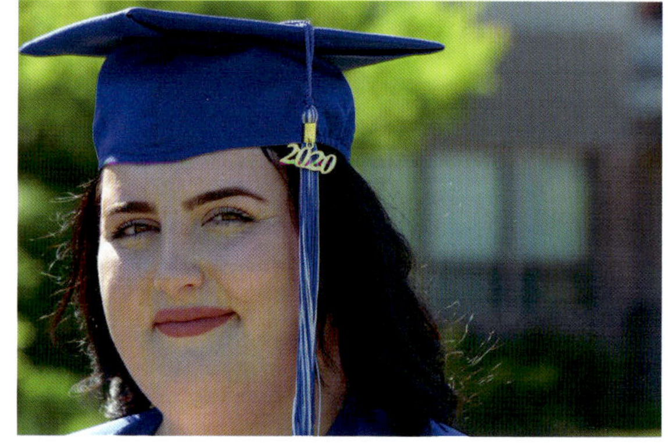

TOP AND MIDDLE: *High schools around the province found unique ways to honour their grads. Advocate District School made banners like these two for Jenna MacGillivary and Lauren Mills and posted them along the main highway.*

BOTTOM: *Brooke Clarke of Wellington ready for her graduation ceremony, which took place in a nearly empty auditorium at Lockview High School in Fall River.*

CONVOCATION CANCELLED:

A Creative Solution

University convocations are usually full of pomp and circumstance (thus the song) and many post-secondary graduation ceremonies have not changed for decades.

Until this year.

This year, with the continued closure of university and college campuses, convocation ceremonies had become virtually non-existent.

But Mikayla Halliday of East Clifford, NS, was having none of that. After working five years to earn a Bachelor of Fine Arts with a major in photography from the Nova Scotia College of Art and Design University (NSCAD), she had been eager to attend her graduation so she could see the students and professors she had spent five years of her life with one last time.

"I looked at my transcript, I went through pictures, I looked at the classes I took and the professors I had and I thought…'This is the day that finishes it all and I'm not going to get that.'"

So she decided that on May 11—the day her graduation ceremony would have been held—she would get dressed up as if she was going and take some photos. Using the skills she'd learned at school, she created her own diploma. "COVID-19 stole my convocation day, but not my degree," she says, laughing.

"I went out by the water, I took a couple of photos, I got dressed up and my mom bought me a little cake," she says. Then she posted her photos online.

The response was immediate. Grads and parents from all over liked, shared, and commented. "It reached a lot of people, and I was really happy to see that. I got a lot of people I didn't know saying how their son or their daughter was graduating this year, and [that] this was a really good, positive note to share with them," she says. "It definitely made me feel better about graduation. I wanted to create a reminder to other grads—like, this is a big deal. This is a big day. We worked years for this, and nobody should forget that."

The good news: she may get another chance. Mikayla found out a few days after the state of emergency was imposed that she had been accepted into a master's program in photography preservation and collections management at Ryerson University in Toronto.

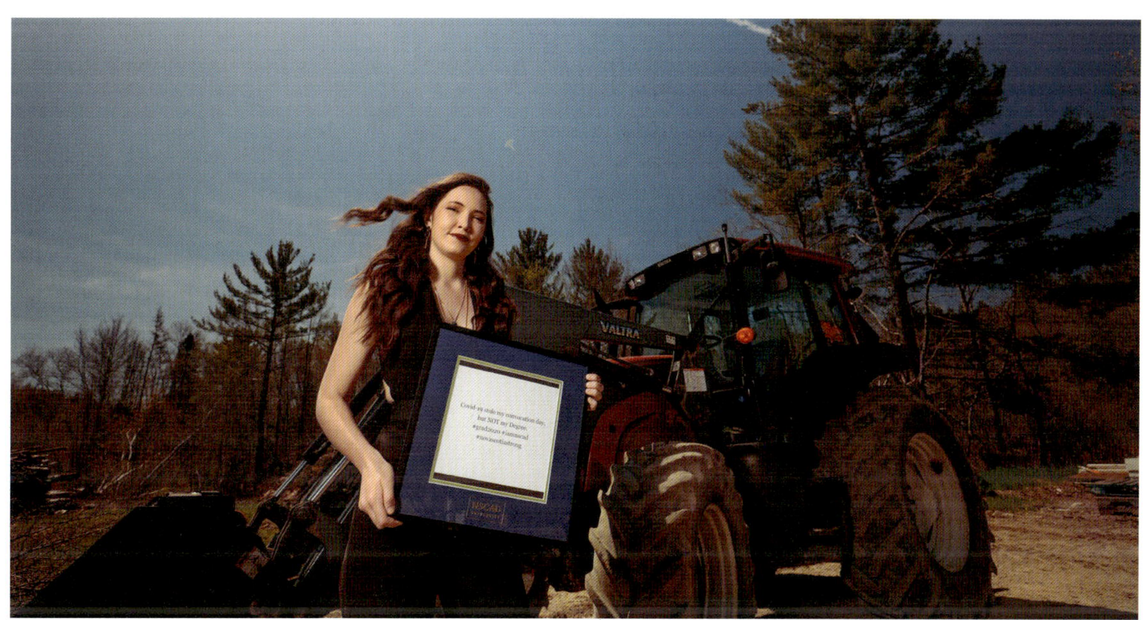

NSCAD graduate Mikayla Halliday stands with the certificate she created for herself after her convocation was cancelled.

DRIVE-BY CELEBRATIONS

Birthday gatherings and other in-person group celebrations were forbidden under the state of emergency, so Nova Scotians found creative ways to celebrate milestones with family and friends from a distance.

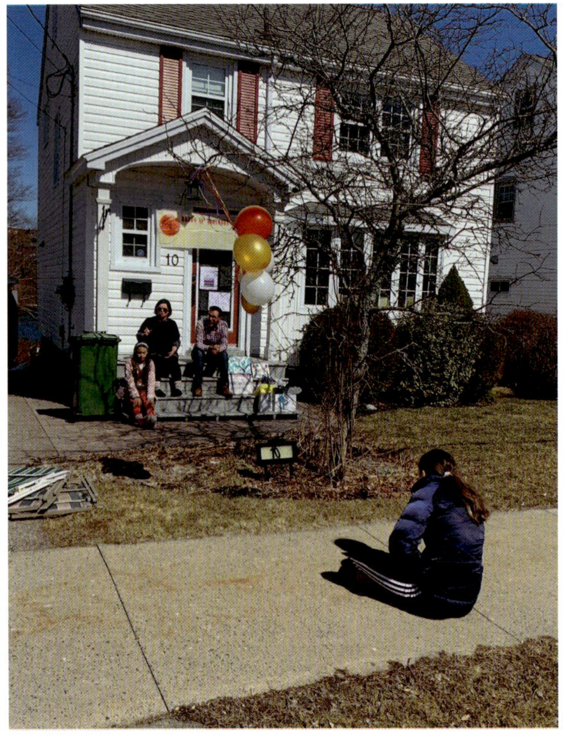

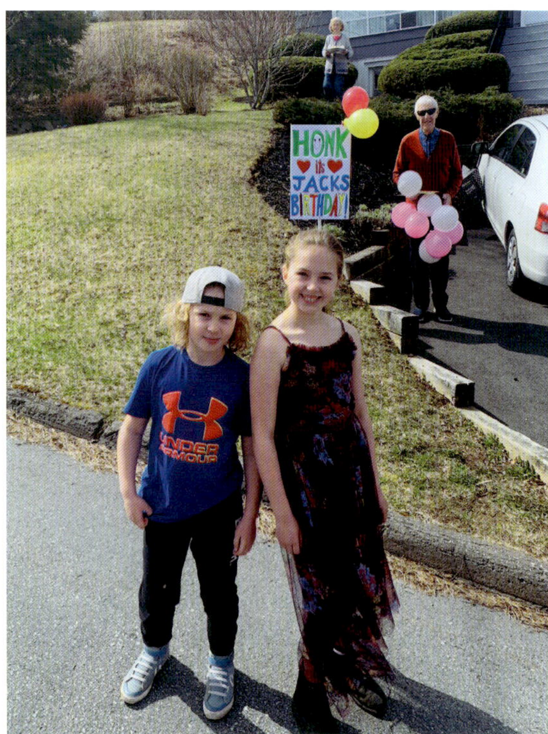

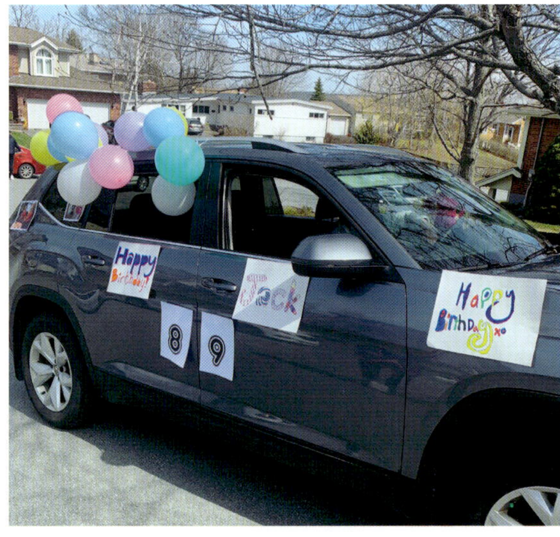

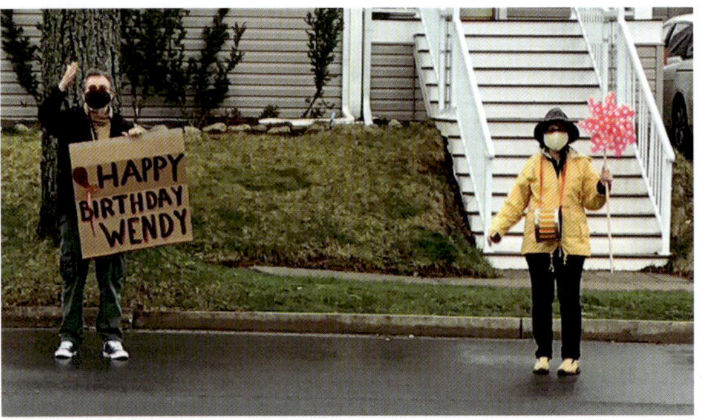

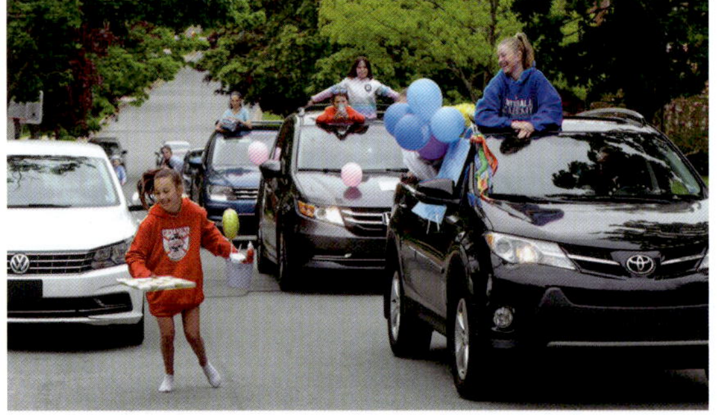

TOP LEFT: *A twelfth birthday visit from a safe distance. (Catherine Williams)*

TOP MIDDLE AND TOP RIGHT: *Lindsay Watters and her kids Charlie and Oliver Boyle of Halifax did a drive-by birthday party for their neighbour Jack's eighty-ninth birthday. (Lindsay Watters)*

BOTTOM LEFT: *When Wendy Purves of Halifax celebrated a birthday in late April, her friends Cheryl Pereira and Brian McConnell provided a cheery birthday parade from a safe distance. (Wendy Purves)*

BOTTOM MIDDLE: *Thirteen-year-old Julia Wilkie collects a gift from a friend as a drive-by birthday party, organized by her mom, passes her house in Halifax.*

LOVE IN THE TIME OF COVID:
A Pandemic Wedding

Shannon and Randy Krupp of North Sydney, NS, had been looking forward to their April wedding until the COVID-19 pandemic hit. Travel restrictions and restrictions against gatherings of five people or more meant they would have to postpone their big day until the state of emergency was over.

That meant no wedding guests, no reception party, no honeymoon—at least for now.

"A global pandemic in my lifetime? That never even crossed my mind," says Shannon. But as the news about COVID-19 only worsened, the pair began to worry there might never be a good time to have a wedding.

"We woke up one day and said, 'You know what? Let's just do it,'" says Randy. "We don't know when the quarantine's going to be over. I mean, it could last a year or two."

That's when Shannon, a musician who is used to performing online, came up with an idea: they would get married and live-stream the ceremony so their friends and family could experience it.

They settled on May 17 as the date, and the whirlwind of planning began. Stores were closed, so Randy ordered a suit from Amazon. A week before the wedding, they got a message that the parcel "may have been lost," so Randy opted to wear his grandpa's suit. Shannon, worried about similar shipping delays, found a wedding dress on Kijiji. The couple arranged to pick up rings from a local jeweller.

The two told their families about their plans. "They were kind of disappointed, in the sense that they wouldn't be there in person," says Shannon, "but they understood that under the circumstances

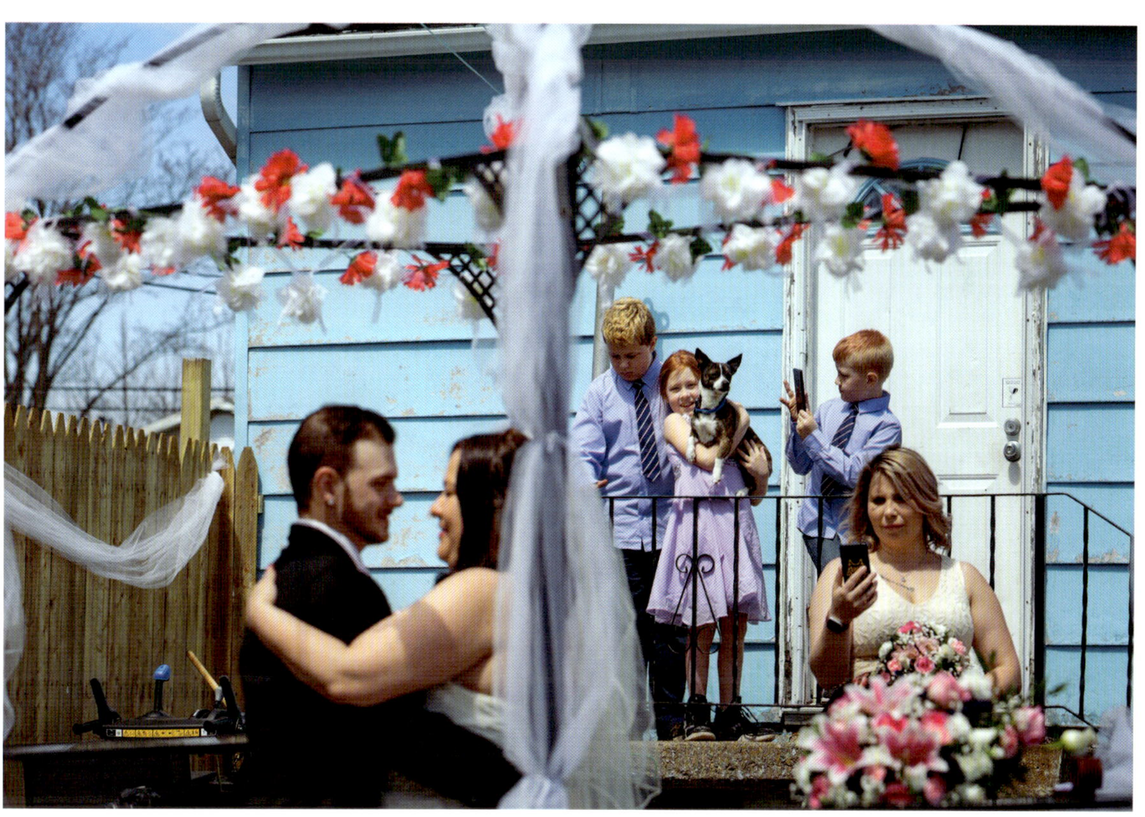

Shannon and Randy Krupp embrace as Shannon's children, Michael (at left on step), Rhiannon, and Xander, watch from the front step. Maid of Honour, Jessica Spooney, streams the event on Facebook as the couple's family and friends watch the live feed. (Steve Wadden)

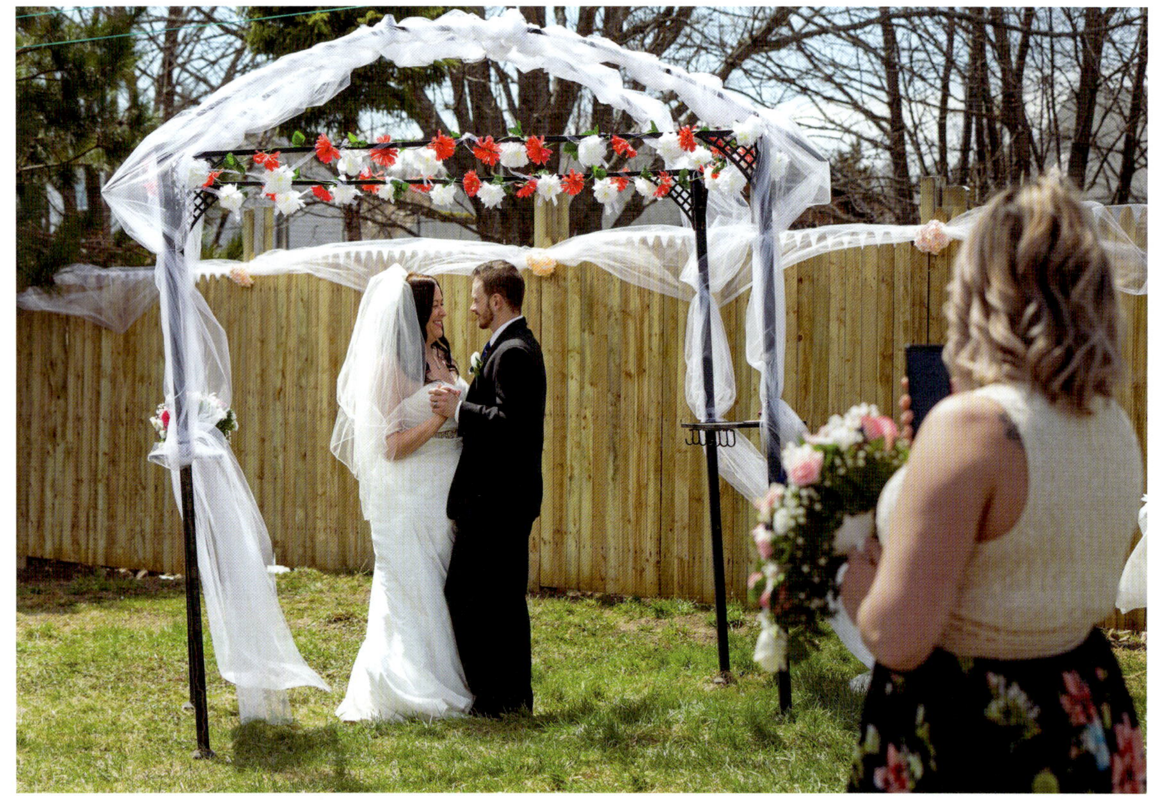

Shannon and Randy Krupp on their wedding day in May. (Steve Wadden)

there was no physical way for them to be there."

When the big day came, the couple had only the maid of honour, Jessica Spooney, the best man, Devon Paul, and a justice of the peace beside them as they said their vows under a decorated trellis in their backyard. Shannon's children, Michael, Rhiannon, and Xander, dressed in their Sunday best, watched from their doorstep.

Online, a multitude of family and friends watched as Jessica live-streamed the entire event on Facebook. Shannon's grandmother, who lives in Quebec, was particularly excited to watch online. A few friends messaged that they were crying tears of joy.

"Honestly, I'm really glad it happened the way it did," says Shannon. "We never really wanted a big wedding. We mostly wanted it just for our parents and close family, because they all wanted to be there, and we didn't want to exclude anyone. [But] this was more me and Randy.

"In thirty years we can look back on this year, not for the negative, but for the positive. We got married!"

SAYING GOODBYE: *Charlene Chiddenton*

Charlene Chiddenton didn't realize that when she hugged her father, Gerald Jackson, goodbye on March 7 and said "I love you," it would be the last time she would ever be with him in person.

Gerald, an eighty-four-year-old navy veteran and father of seven, had dementia and had been in nursing care at Northwood, a seniors' residence and long-term care facility in Halifax, for only ten months.

"Every time we left [his room], he'd follow us out," says Charlene. "We'd hit the button for the elevator; he'd give me a kiss and a hug and I'd say, 'Dad, I'll see you in two weeks.' He'd say, 'I love you,' and then he'd always go back to his room, to the window, because he could see where I'd parked our car. He'd go to the window and he'd wave as we were going out to our car. Same routine."

But when nursing homes across the province cut off access to visitors to curb the spread of COVID-19, Charlene had to have some difficult conversations with her father.

"Why aren't you guys coming to visit? You don't like me anymore," her dad would say when she called.

"I understand it; we were coming every two weeks and then all of a sudden—nobody, for three months. I'd explain, 'Dad, it's the government that's set down these rules because of this disease. We can't come see you,' and he would reply, 'Oh, yeah, sure; that's what you say.'"

After many unsatisfying phone calls with her dad, Charlene and her family decided to try a new approach. Charlene went to Northwood and stood outside in a red jacket, holding a red balloon.

She called her father from her cellphone and had the nurse bring him to the window. "I saw the curtains open and heard, 'Gerry, your daughter's down there. Can you see her? She's holding a red balloon and she's got a red coat on.' I could see Dad; I could hear Dad. 'Yes, yes; I see her!'

"Then he gave Dad the phone and I said, 'Hi, Dad!' I'm waving and holding the balloon. And he said, 'Hi! What are you doing here?'

"I said, 'Well, I'm not allowed in the building, but

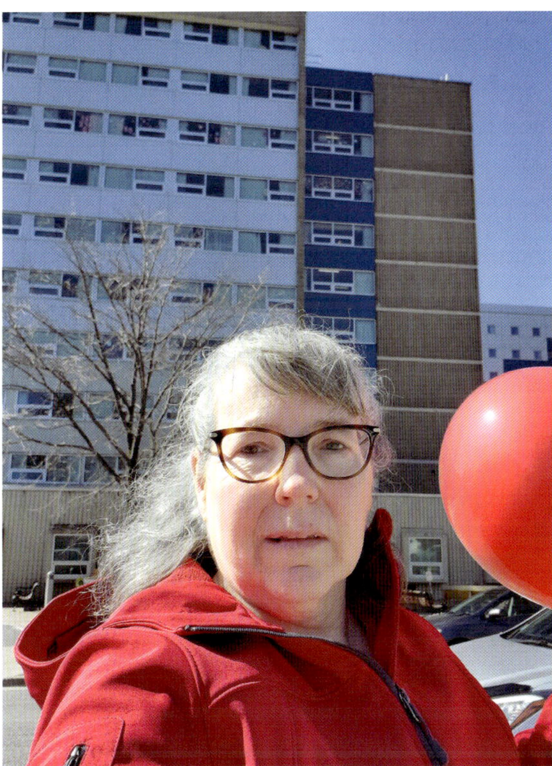

Charlene Chiddenton held this red balloon outside Northwood so her dad, Gerald Jackson, who lived at the complex, could see her. (Charlene Chiddenton)

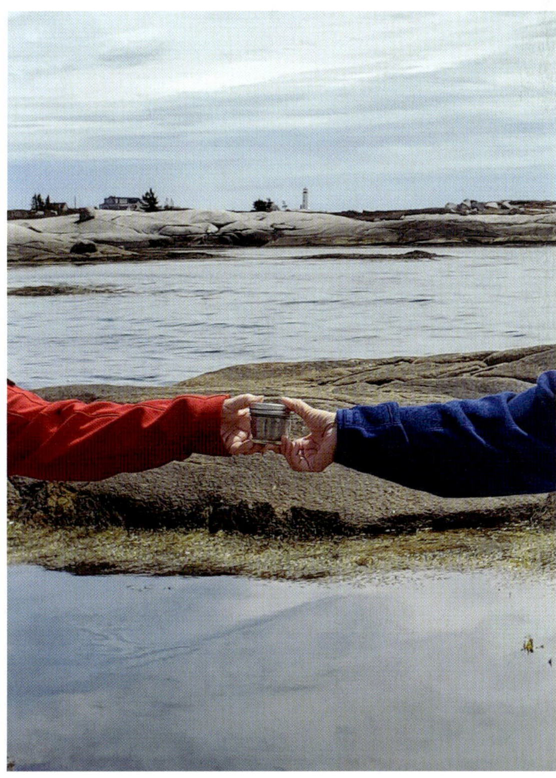

Charlene Chiddenton and her sister, Darlene Metzler, prepare to spread some of their father's ashes near Peggys Cove. (Charlene Chiddenton)

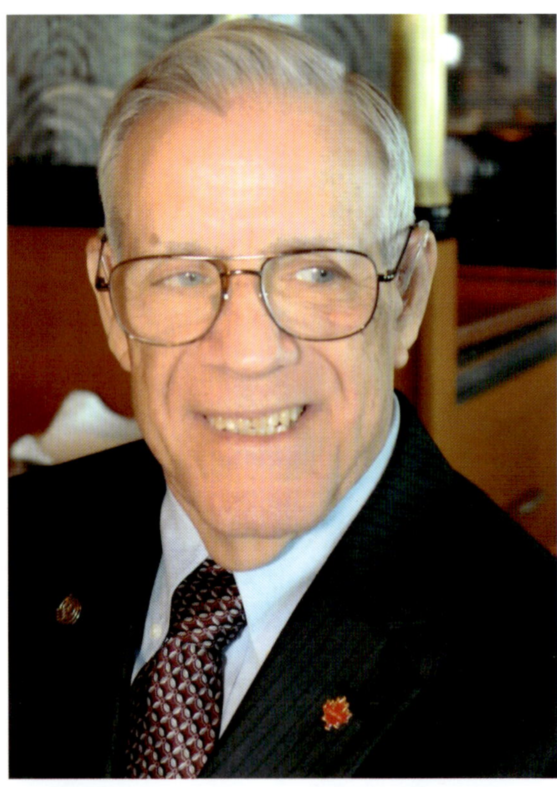

Gerald Jackson died at Northwood at the age of eighty-four from the effects of COVID-19. (Charlene Chiddenton)

I just wanted to come and let you know I'm thinking about you and I wanted to be here.' And he said, 'Oh, that's so nice!' And we chatted for a couple minutes and then he handed the phone back to the nurse.

"He says, 'Your dad's going to sit down now; he's tired.' I said, 'Okay. Well, tell him I said goodbye,' and then I saw him leave the window. I stood there for a couple minutes more holding the balloon, just in case he came and stood back up to the window, but he never did. That was the last time I [saw] him. And then I broke down and collapsed on the sidewalk, holding my balloon, and a woman passed by and said, 'Are you okay?'

"I said, 'I will be; I was just looking up at my dad in the window.' And she was a little heartbroken for me."

As the number of people at Northwood who had tested positive for COVID-19 began to rise, the family's worst fears were soon confirmed. Charlene's twin sister, Darlene Metzler, got a call telling her their dad had tested positive.

"Darlene immediately called me and we both cried," says Charlene. "We were heartbroken, but we were also not surprised."

As it had with her sidewalk visit, technology again played a part in Charlene's final goodbyes to her father. Staff at nursing homes all around the province were using iPads and cellphones to ensure that families who couldn't visit physically could have some kind of connection with their loved ones.

The nurse caring for her father asked if they would like to do a video call.

"I did mine first and then Darlene did hers, and we each got to see Dad. That was really nice, but it was heartbreaking to see him like that, because he had changed drastically from when I'd seen him in March," says Charlene.

"He was awake, and I kept saying, 'Hi, Dad! Hi, Dad!'... [The nurse] said, 'I think he knows it's you; he's trying to grab at the iPad.' I said, 'Dad, I love you, and I'm sorry that you have to die alone, but I love you."

That evening, eight days after he had been diagnosed with COVID-19, Gerald Jackson passed away. A funeral for the entire family was out of the question (the twins have another sister and four brothers) because of gathering restrictions under the state of emergency, so Charlene and Darlene took their father's ashes out to an inlet near Peggys Cove and spread them in the ocean as the song "My Way" played on Charlene's phone.

"That's just the way Dad led his life: He did it his way," says Charlene.

"I made a promise to care for him until he died, and I tried my best—Darlene and me. I guess that's my biggest regret—that I couldn't be with him when he finally died."

Part Four: THE NEW NORMAL

KEEPING OURSELVES BUSY

As Nova Scotians settled into the state of emergency, the guidance from public health officials was to stay home as much as possible. All that enforced togetherness led folks to find creative ways to pass the time.

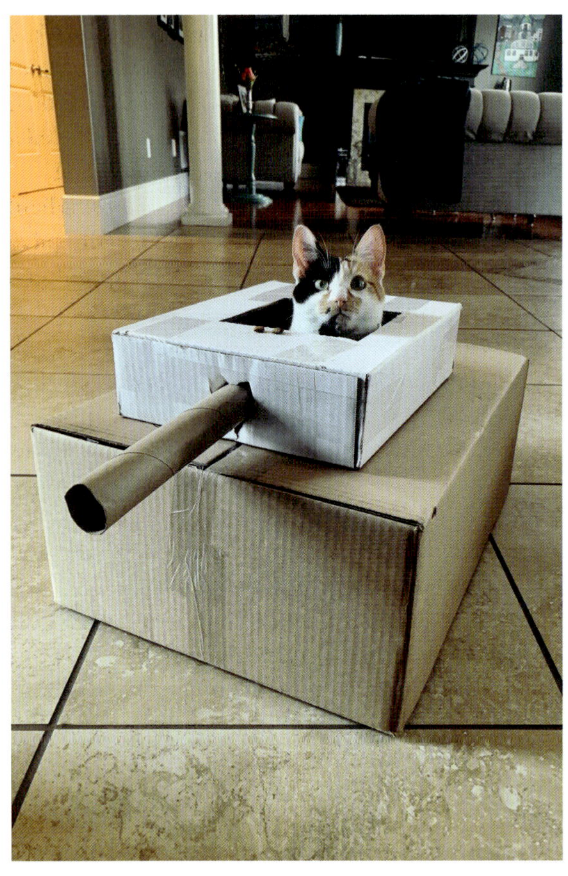

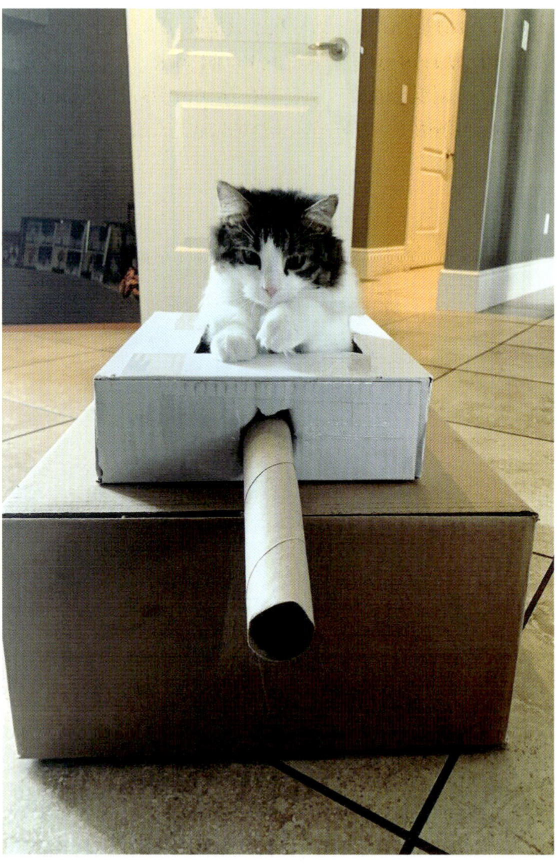

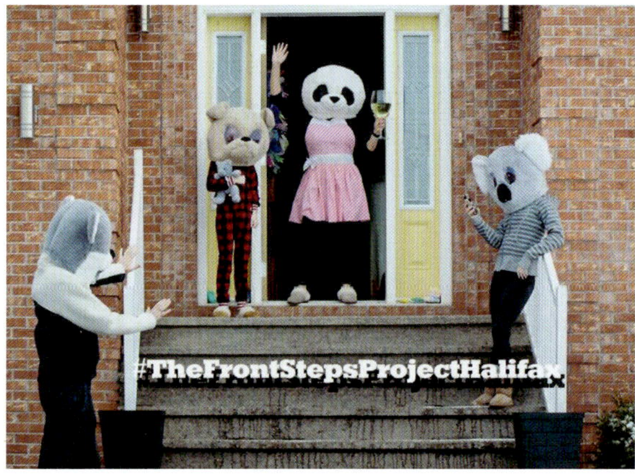

LEFT AND MIDDLE: *Jacquelynn Welsh of Halifax and her family got creative with some crafty (and hilarious!) cat tanks. (Jacquelynn Welsh)*

RIGHT: *Jacquelynn and her family also dressed up for The Front Steps Project, an initiative that invited families to come out to their front steps and take a photo that showed their "strength and resilience" during COVID-19. (Jacquelynn Welsh)*

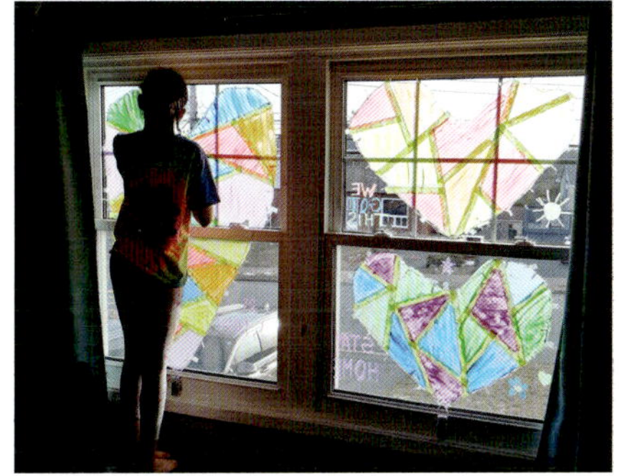

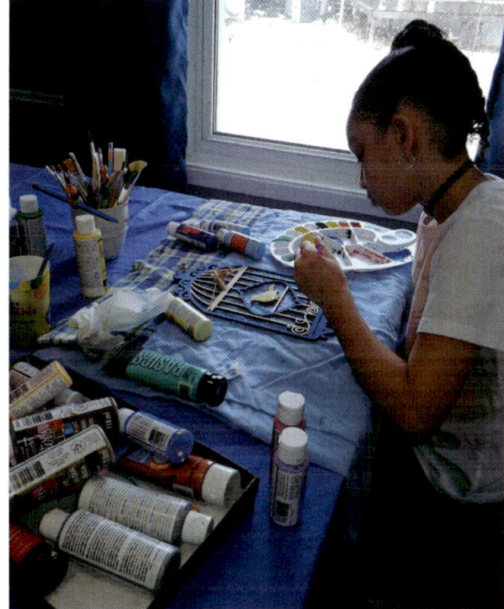

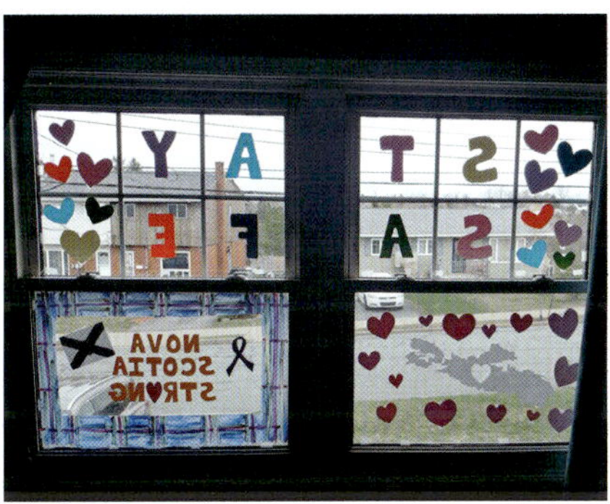

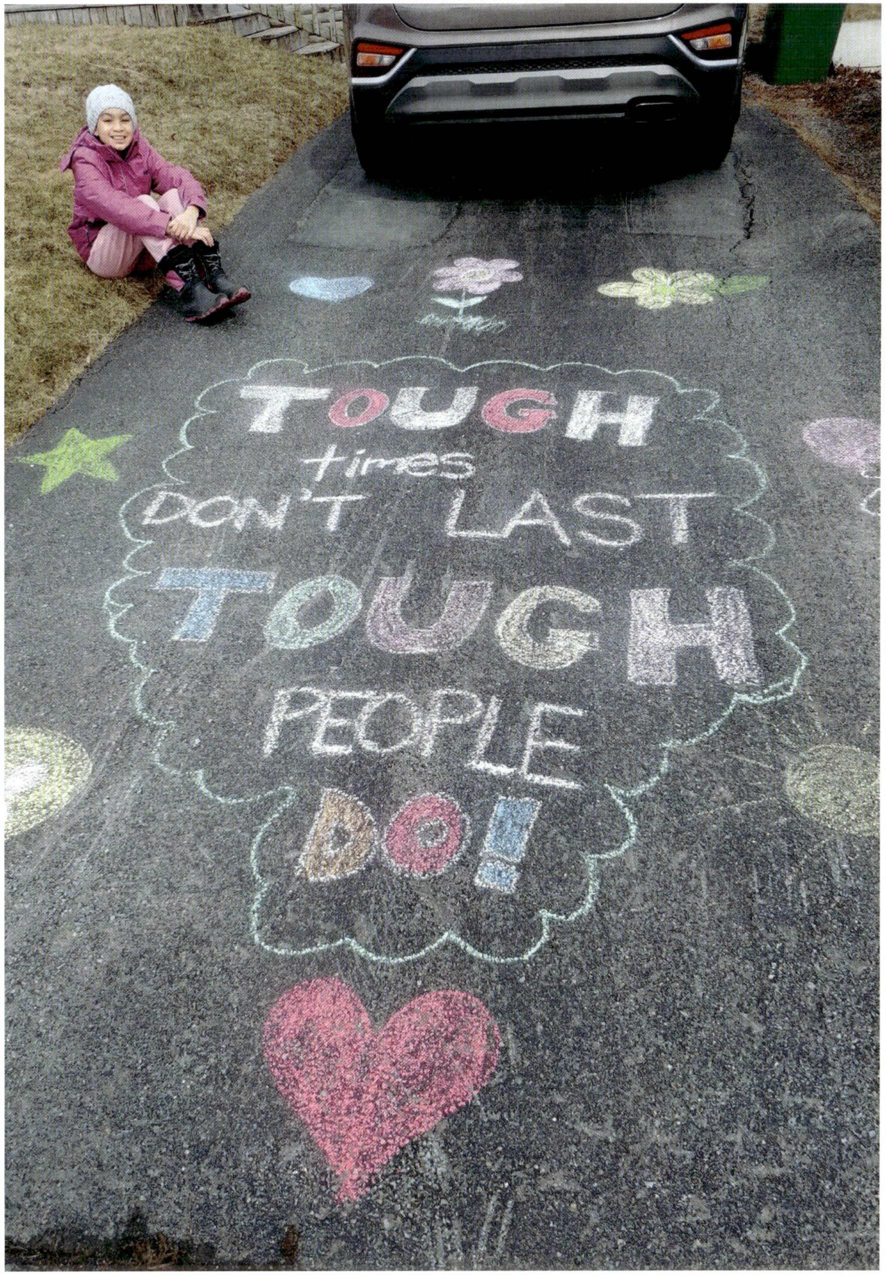

THIS PAGE: *Kelli Ross of Cole Harbour, NS, and her family kept busy making inspirational chalk drawings and doing creative crafts at home. (Kelli Ross)*

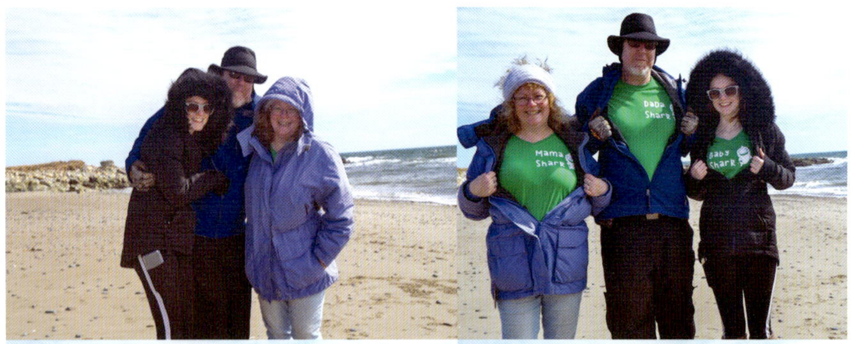

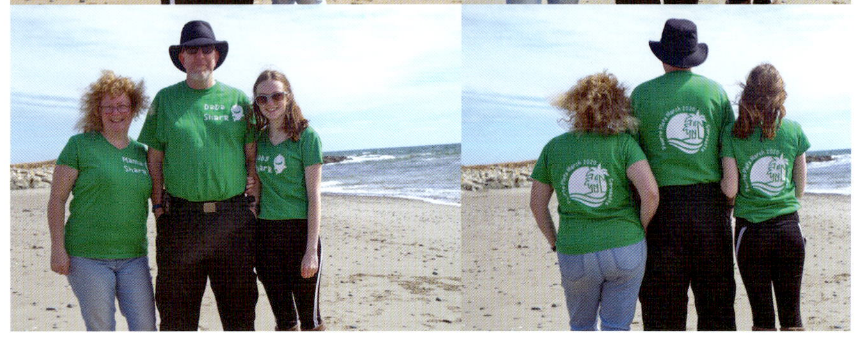

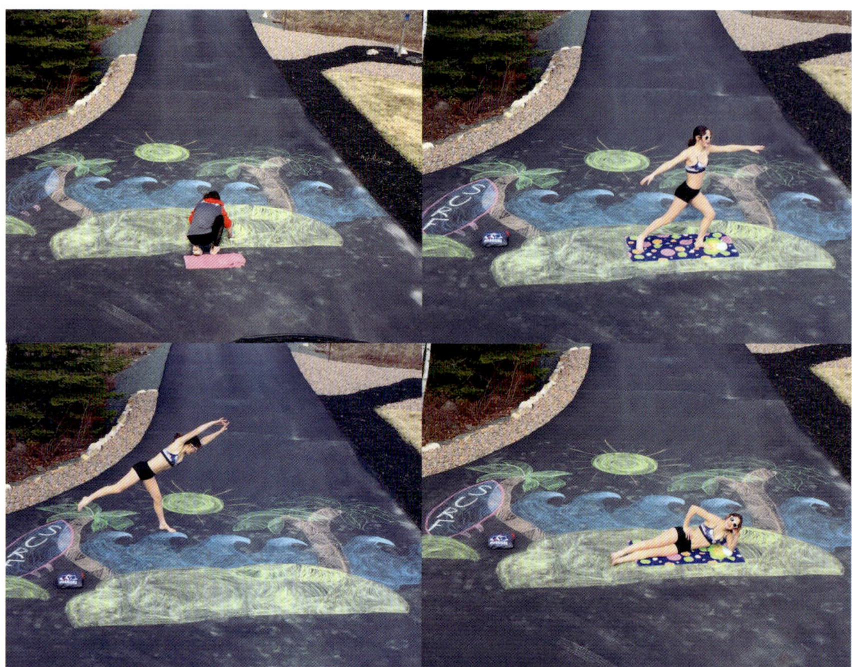

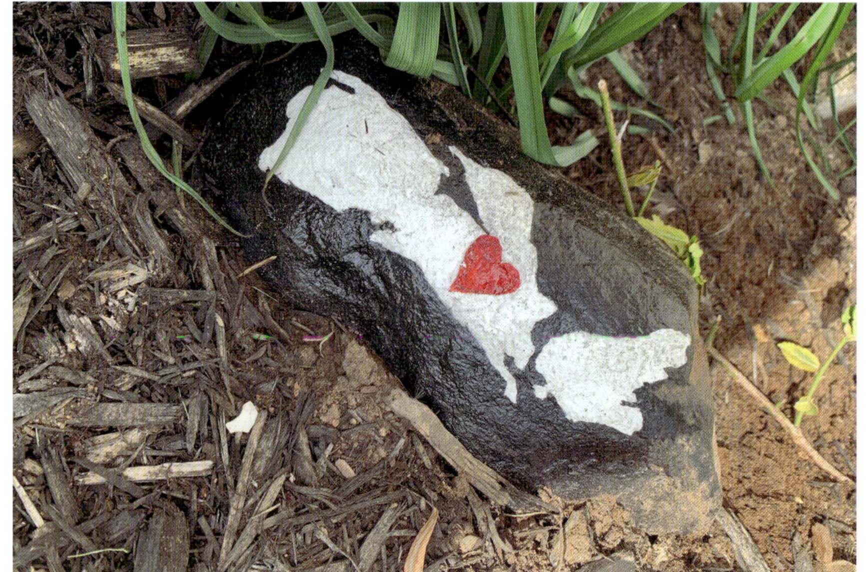

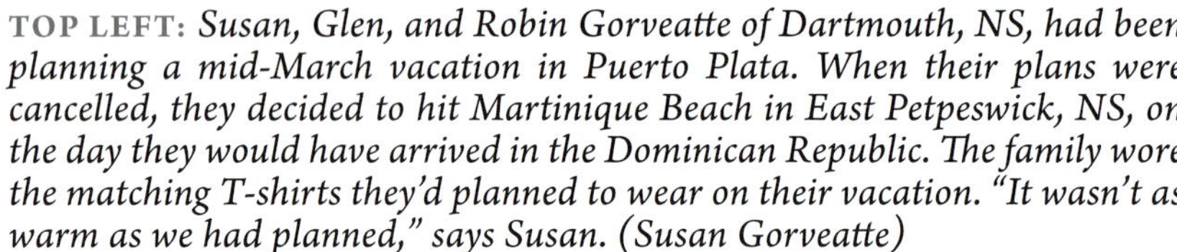

TOP LEFT: *Susan, Glen, and Robin Gorveatte of Dartmouth, NS, had been planning a mid-March vacation in Puerto Plata. When their plans were cancelled, they decided to hit Martinique Beach in East Petpeswick, NS, on the day they would have arrived in the Dominican Republic. The family wore the matching T-shirts they'd planned to wear on their vacation. "It wasn't as warm as we had planned," says Susan. (Susan Gorveatte)*

TOP RIGHT: *Fiona Day, thirteen, of Fall River, had some fun with sidewalk chalk in March. She wished she could be on a tropical beach, so she tried out some beach poses while her mom, Sophie Day, captured her sunny vacation day in photos (Sophie Day).*

BOTTOM RIGHT *Karen Brooking-Tinney of Fall River, NS, kept busy by painting rocks to brighten everyone's day. (Karen Brooking-Tinney)*

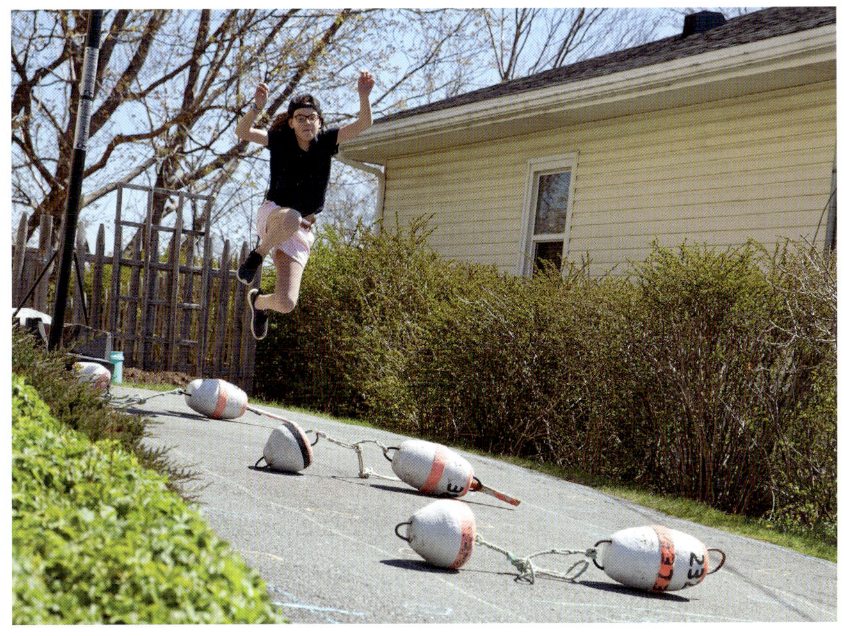

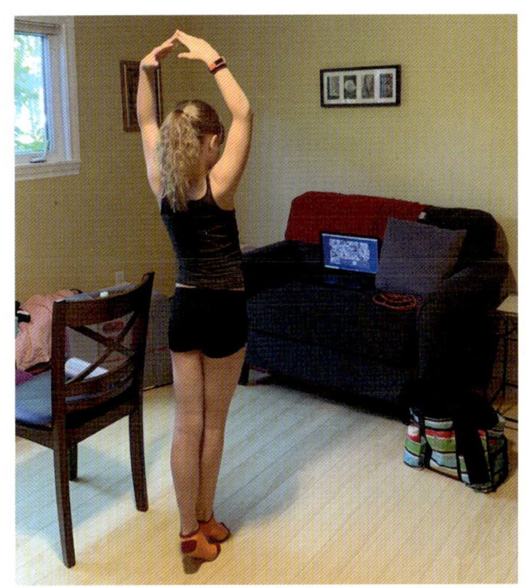

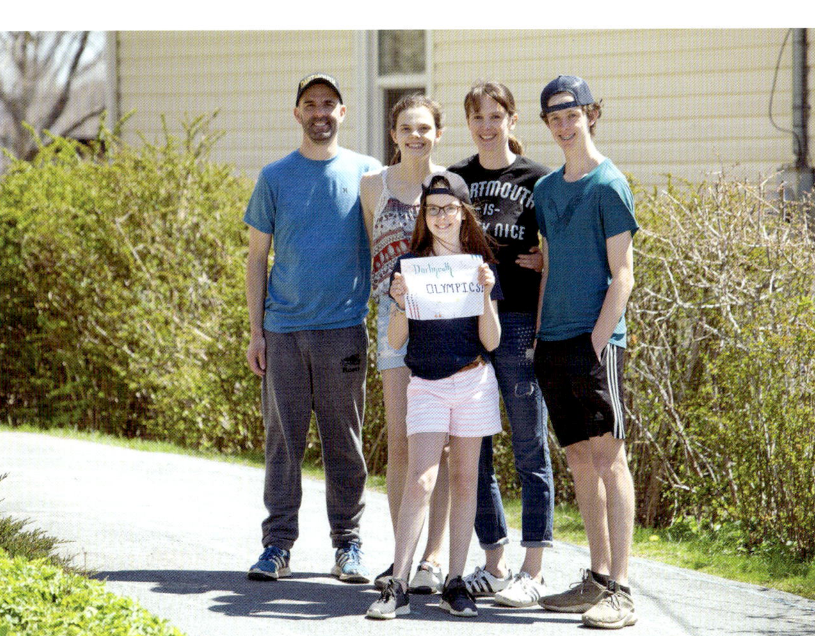

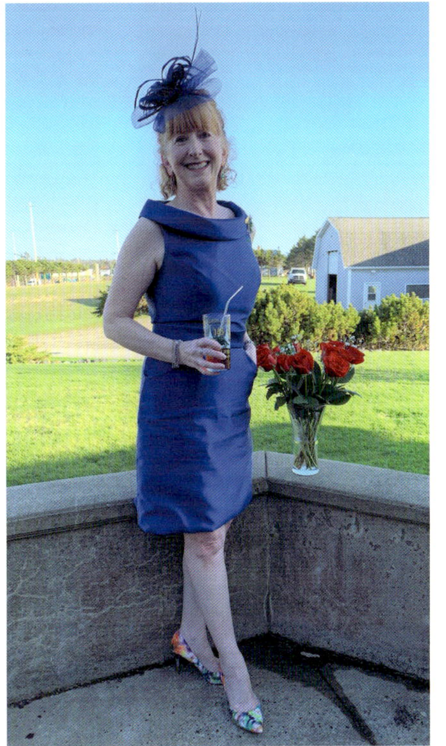

TOP LEFT: *Meaghan Ferguson, eleven, from Dartmouth, takes part in the "Driveway Olympics" organized in her community. (Nicola Davison)*

BOTTOM LEFT: *"Olympic" family, Pat and Erin Ferguson with their kids Meaghan (front), Claire, and Aiden. (Nicola Davison)*

TOP RIGHT: *Chloe Higginbotham, nine, participates in an online training session with Julie Jeffery, coach and technical director of the Illusions Rhythmic Gymnastics Club in Halifax. Many clubs came up with inventive ways to keep their members active and engaged.*

BOTTOM RIGHT: *Linda B. Deveau, of Salmon River, Digby County, had attended the Kentucky Derby with four of her good friends last year, so she was devastated when the race was cancelled this year. She and her friends hosted a virtual Kentucky Derby party on the first Saturday in May to make up for the loss. "We shared food and beverage recipes, dressed for the occasion, picked our historic Triple Crown horses and watched the virtual computer-generated race together ...a COVID Run for the Roses!" she says. (Linda B. Deveau)*

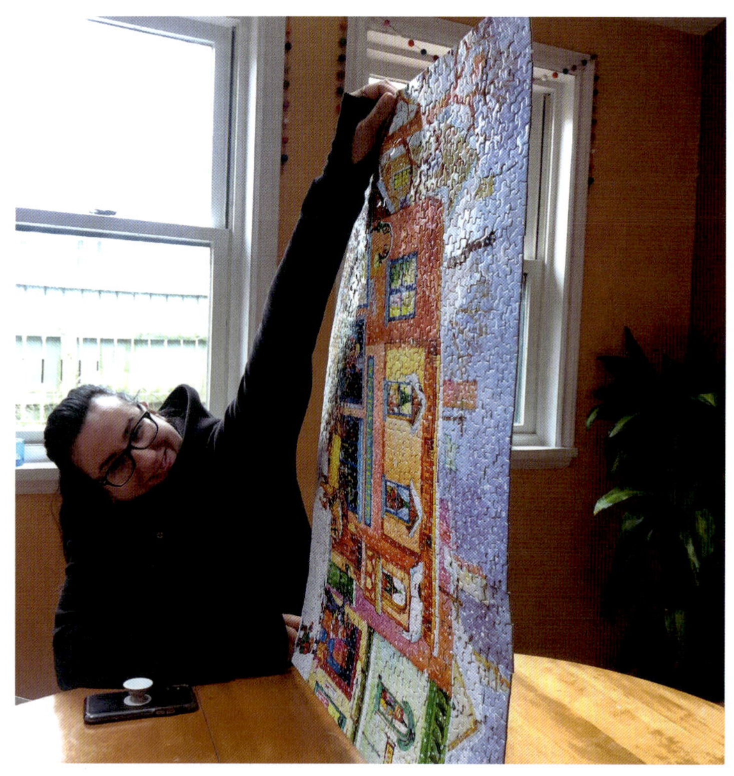

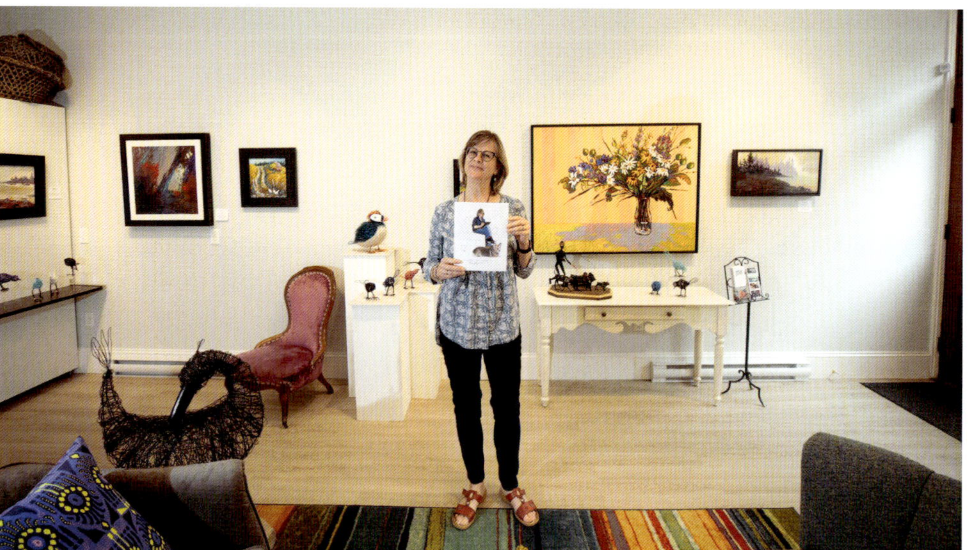

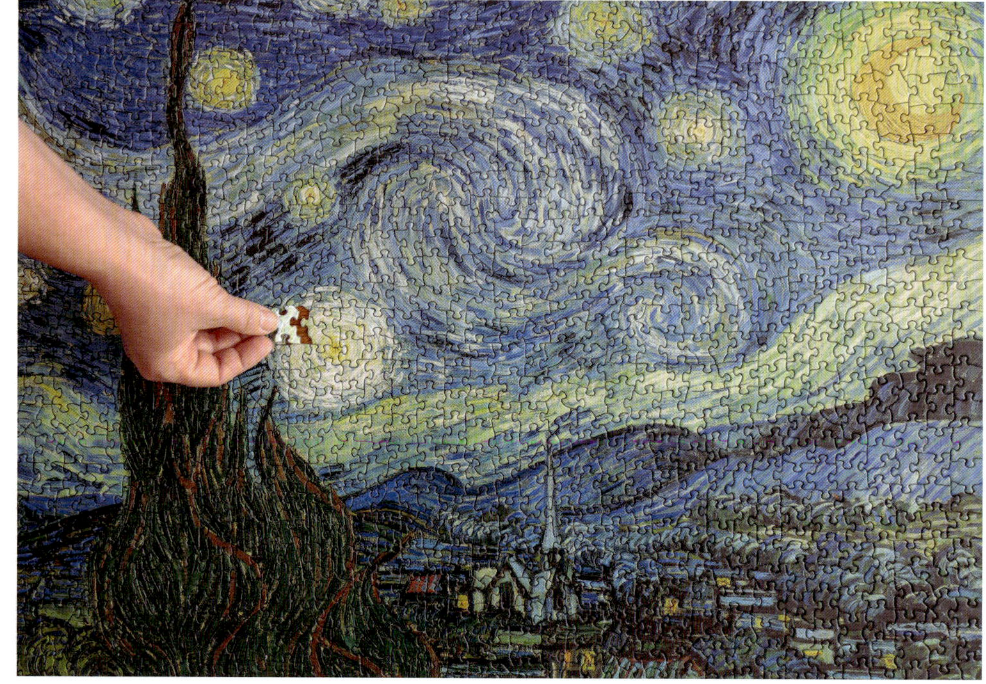

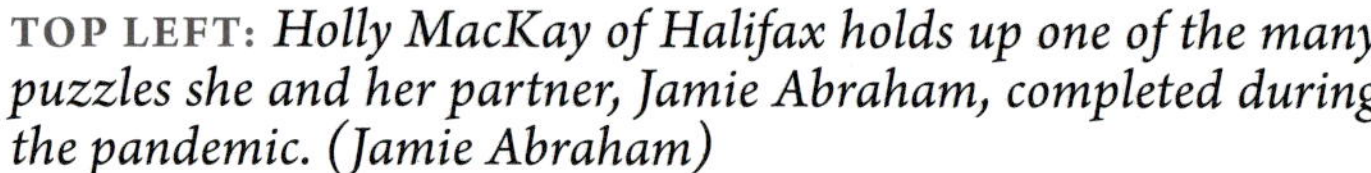

TOP LEFT: *Holly MacKay of Halifax holds up one of the many puzzles she and her partner, Jamie Abraham, completed during the pandemic. (Jamie Abraham)*

TOP RIGHT: *Artist Sharon Fox Cranston holds up a sketch of herself at Cranston Gallery in Lunenburg. When her studio closed down, she asked people to send in photos of what they were doing during the lockdown so she could post her sketches made from those photos online. She received an "overwhelming" number of photos, and for seventy-one days she posted a new sketch each night. On the final day, she posted this self-portrait. She hopes to publish the collection in a book.*

BOTTOM RIGHT: *Sandy Wagg places the last piece of a puzzle depicting Vincent van Gogh's* Starry Night. *Sales of puzzles soared during the lockdown as people sought creative ways to spend time together.*

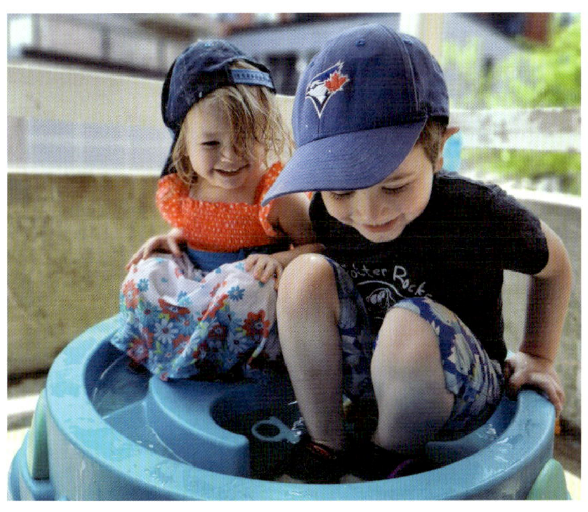

TOP LEFT: *Alicia Lee of Halifax says, "These are two of my three children: Hunter, four, and Rylan, two. Who says staying the blazes home has to be boring, even when you're cooped up in an apartment? We make the most of it and love all of the sunshine we have been getting." (Alicia Lee)*

BOTTOM LEFT: *Graham Walsh of Middle Sackville, NS, and his twelve-year-old daughter made these awesome "MOM Day" T-shirts for three-year-old Ava (right) and two-year-old Sadie (left). "Stayed the blazes home for Mother's Day!" he says. (Graham Walsh)*

BOTTOM MIDDLE AND BOTTOM RIGHT: *Angela Roach Fraser of Whites Lake, NS, says her family kept busy with hopscotch and living room family sleepovers. (Angela Roach Fraser)*

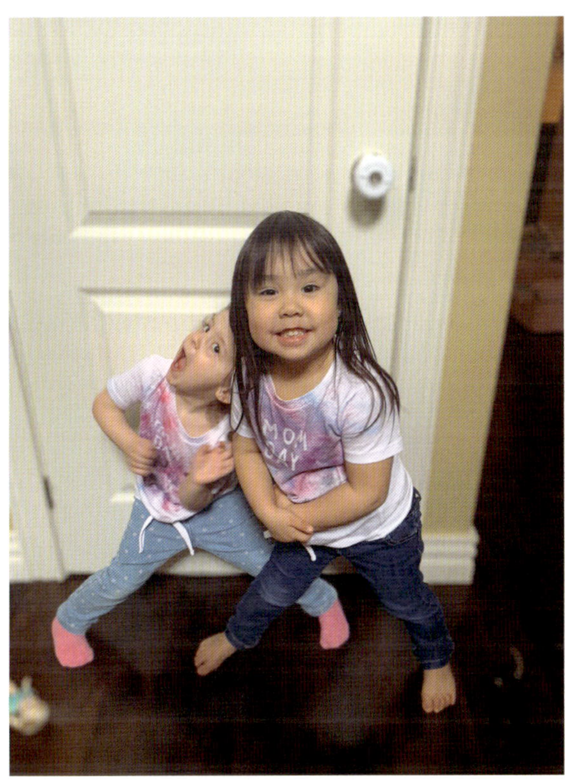

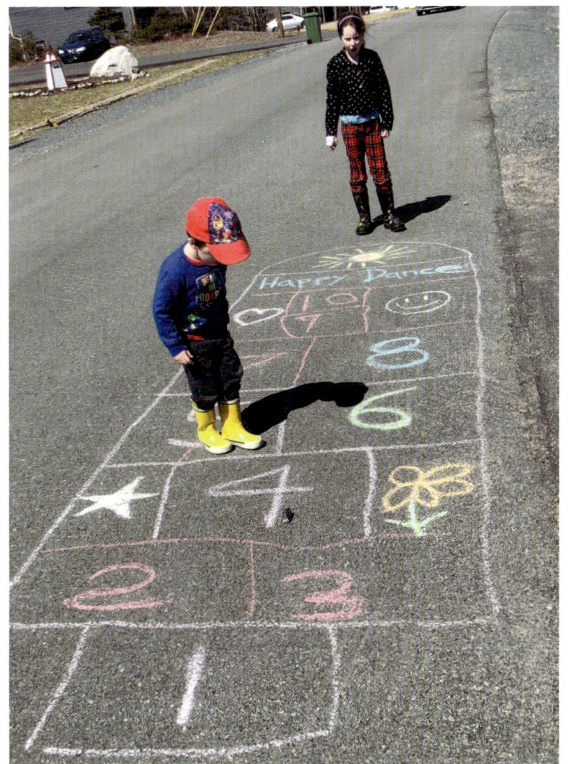

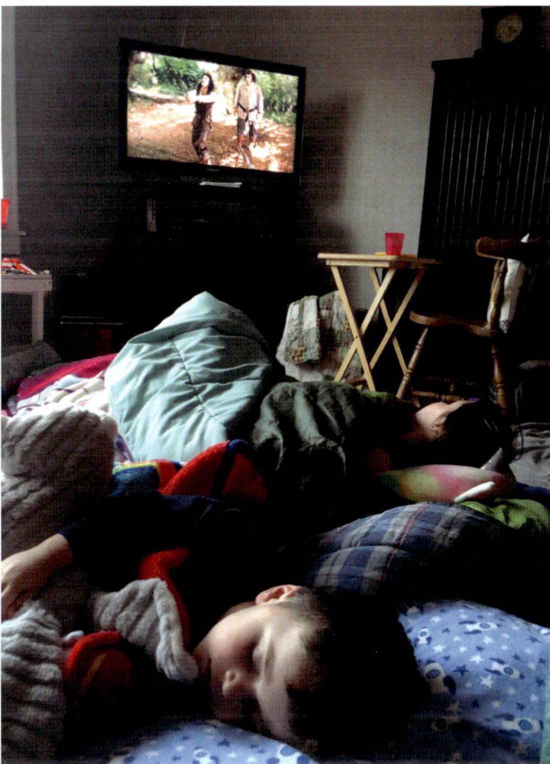

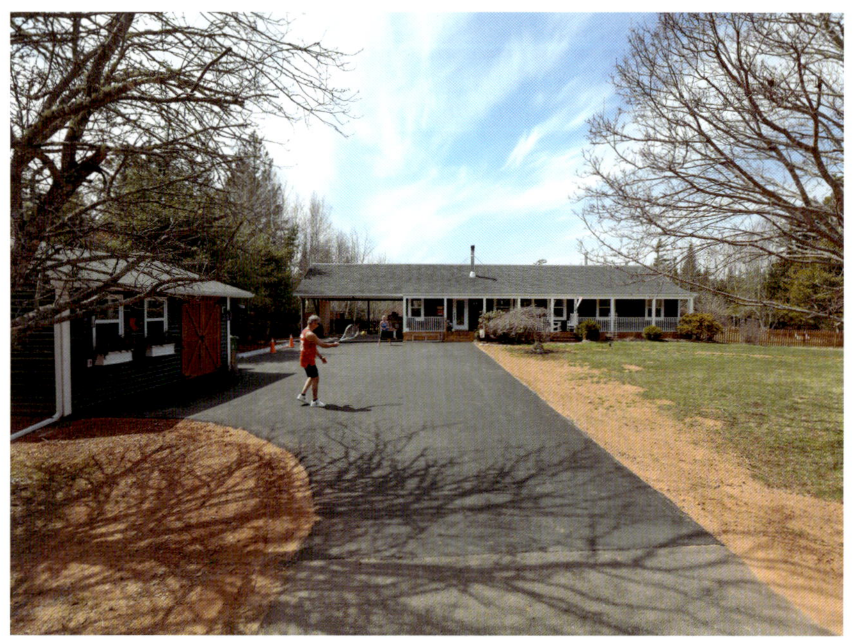

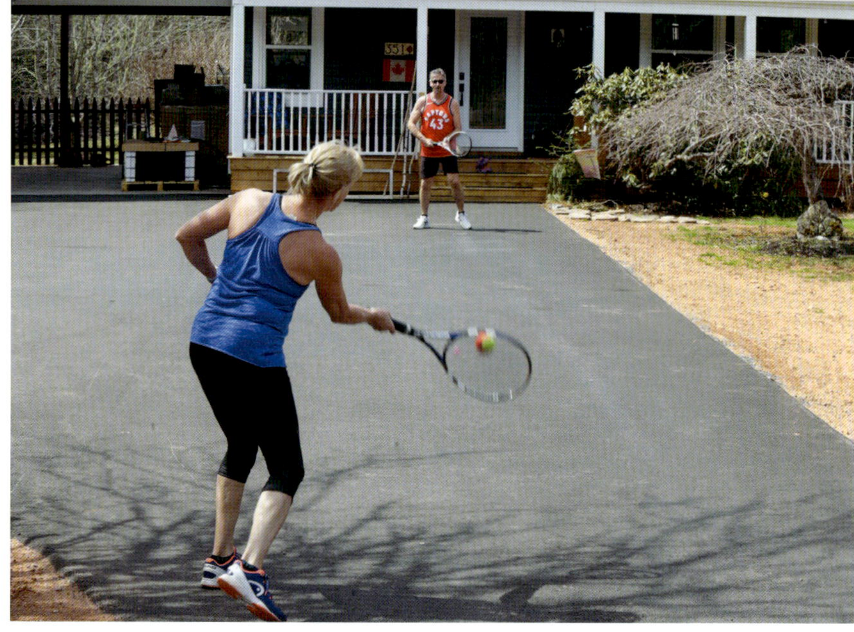

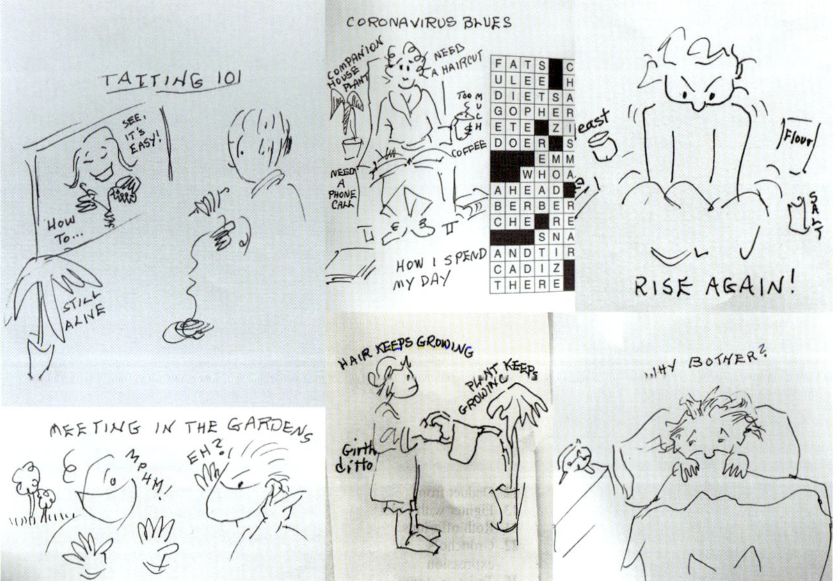

TOP LEFT AND TOP RIGHT: *Buck and Laura Wile would have loved to play at a tennis court on this warm April day, but because recreational facilities were closed, they improvised in the driveway at their home in Debert.*

BOTTOM: *Binnie Brennan sent these sketches made by her ninety-two-year-old mother, Mary Lou Payzant, an artist by training and trade. "She has been observing and capturing the essence of these strange COVID days in a series of ink drawings, finding expression through these simple, humorous, and thoughtful cartoons," says Binnie. "In the last few weeks she's amassed a good dozen or more, sketching on the back of crossword puzzles and scraps of paper as inspiration strikes." Her mother lives in Halifax. (Binnie Brennan)*

A SENSE OF PURPOSE

Contributed by Nadine MacLellan, Skinners Cove, NS

I am a lobster fisher out of Skinners Cove, River John, Pictou County. I fish with my father, brother, and eighty-year-old grandfather who is the operator. During the crisis in the fishing and fish-processing industries, we were not certain as to how to deal with the economic and occupational effects of the events we were facing. My family was preparing a new-to-us boat while the shutdowns brought a delay in our lobster season opening. We used the extra time to transition from an old wooden boat to something much more modern. We worked at things from a distance; my brother and dad handled the mechanics while I painted buoys and prepared ropes.

It has always a been a concerted effort to prepare for a lobster season, but preparing for it within the limits of COVID restrictions gave us a purpose and a sense of strength in our work. It was odd waiting out the season delay and there was a lot of insecurity along the way....

Like many Nova Scotians I tend to keep busy and work through tough times. Last fall I painted a mural on our new trap-house doors after Dorian had done some serious damage to the building. Now I feel like I have become a part of it as much as it has become a part of me. (*Photos: Nadine MacLellan*)

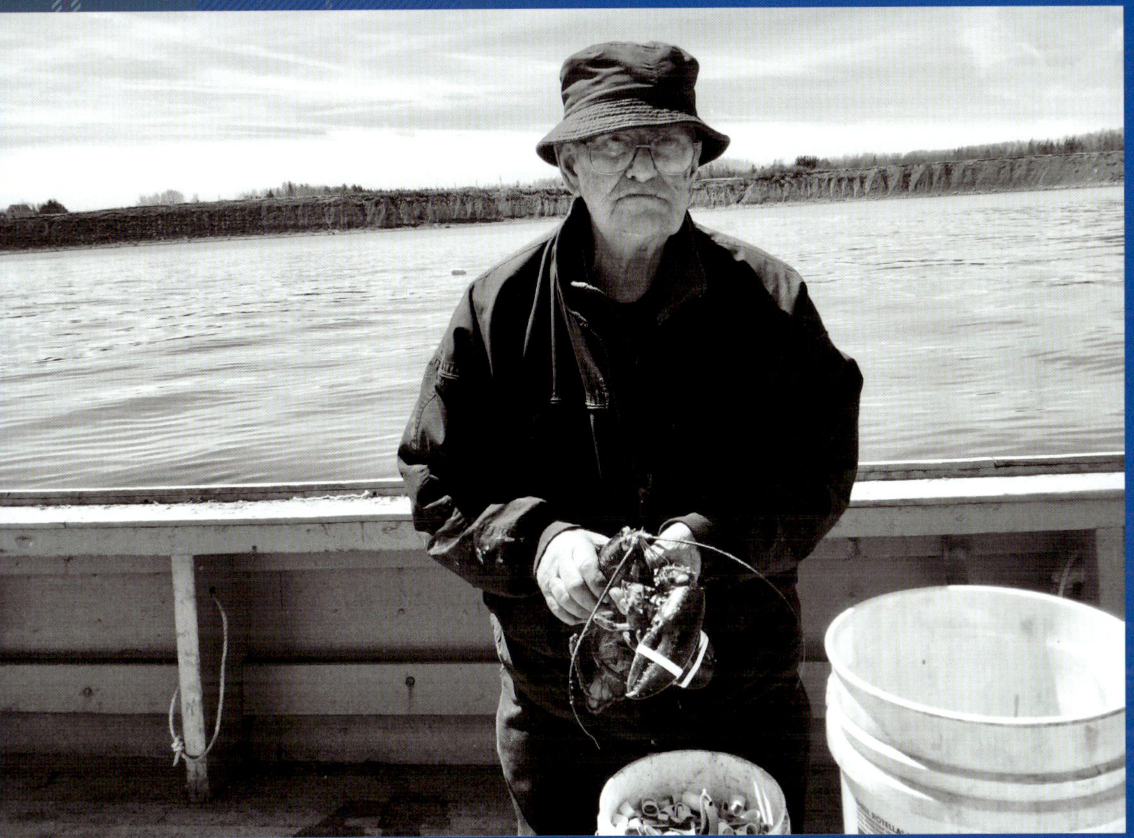

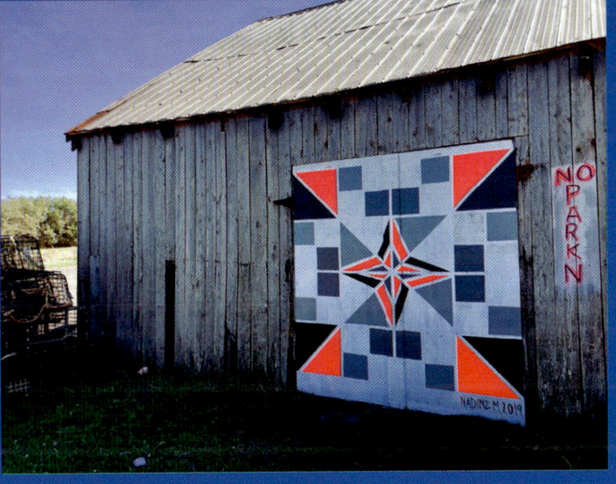

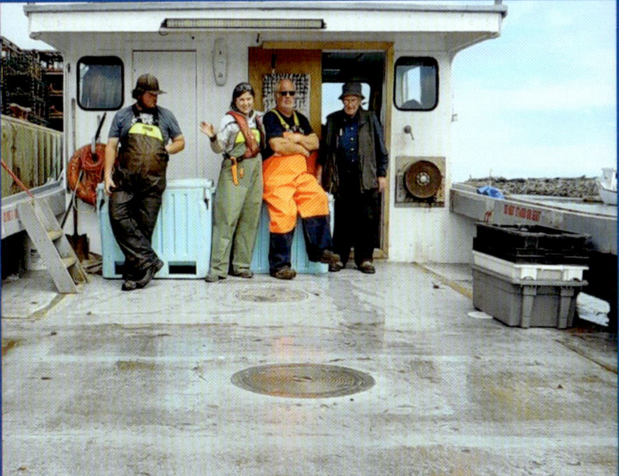

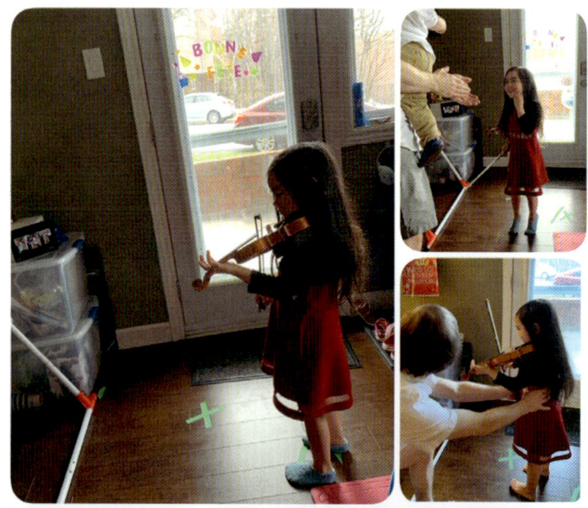

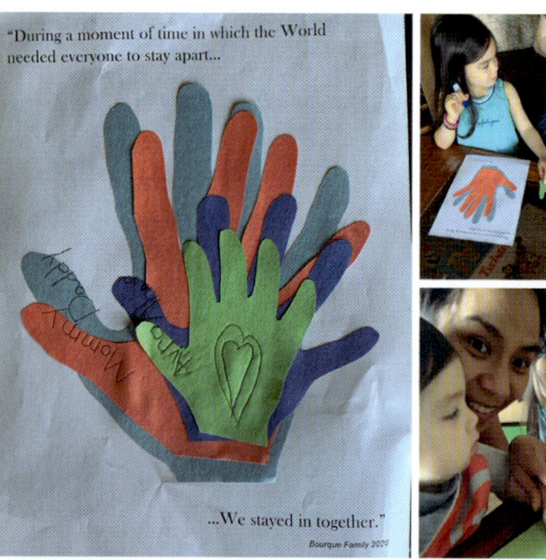

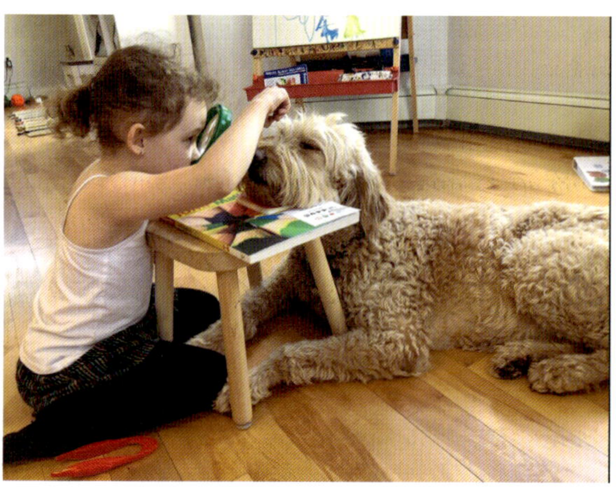

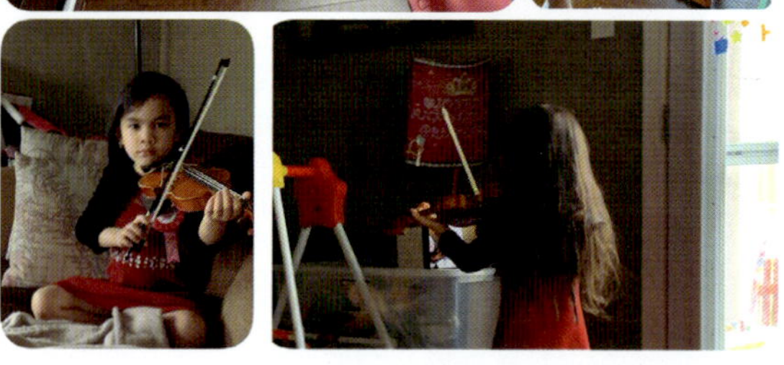

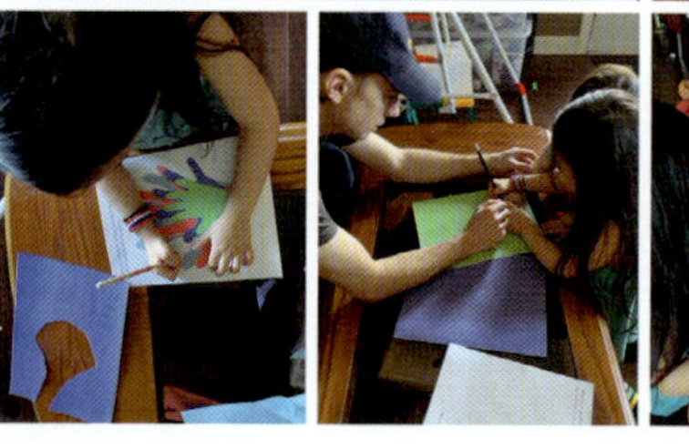

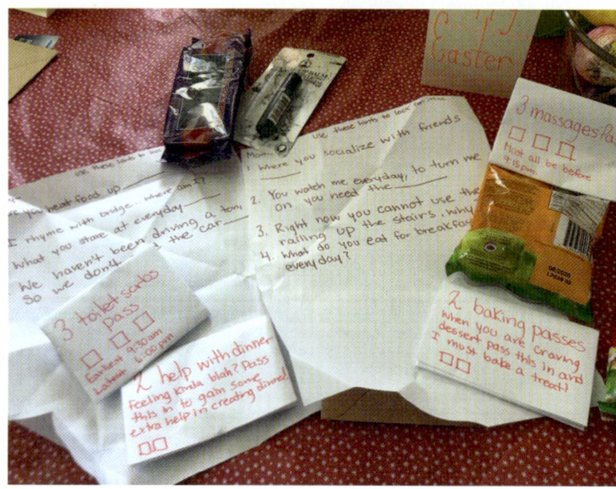

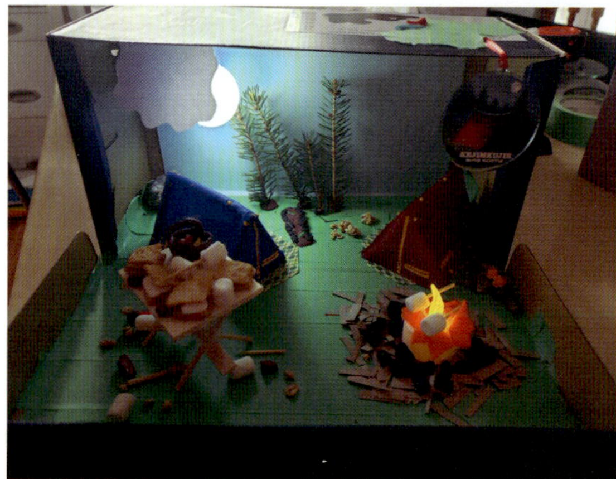

TOP LEFT AND TOP MIDDLE: *Alva Bourque of Halifax sent these images of her daughter attending her weekly online violin class, and of the family doing at-home crafts. "We will frame this and display it on our photo wall of our world travels," she says. Luckily, she says, her husband, who normally works in Toronto, has been home during the lockdown. (Alva Bourque)*

TOP RIGHT: *Five-year-old Charlotte Sweet, the daughter of Patrick and Vanessa Sweet of Halifax, passed some of her days playing vet. "Maybe," says her grandmother Sherma Versteeg, "she's influenced by the fact her Aunt Mere and Uncle Alex are vets." Here she examines her dog, Massey, for coronavirus. (Sherma Versteeg)*

BOTTOM LEFT: *Leanne Andrecyk of Halifax says the coupons pictured here were the result of her fourteen-year-old daughter's thoughtfulness; she wanted to provide her parents with an Easter–egg hunt, despite the fact that they had no chocolate. "We laughed until we cried!" says Leanne. (Leanne Andrecyk)*

BOTTOM MIDDLE: *Melanie Deviller of Hammonds Plains, NS, and her stepdaughter Miriam Joudrey made this diorama because they missed camping so much. (Melanie Deviller)*

SURVIVING COVID-19: *One Family's Story*

Kelly Marshall of Stellarton, NS, had one wish for her fortieth birthday: to have her father, sixty-nine-year-old Rick Cameron, home alive.

Rick and his wife, Faye, had travelled to Florida in February. In early March, when they were back home in Nova Scotia, Rick began to notice symptoms. At first, he passed it off as a cold—but then he had difficulty breathing. On March 19, he found himself in an ambulance on his way to the Aberdeen Hospital, and the next day he was transferred to the COVID unit at the Colchester East Hants Health Centre in Truro, where things escalated quickly. The attending physician asked Rick if he wanted to sign a "do not resuscitate" order.

"Fuck no, I'm too young to die! Do what you have to do to fix me up!" Rick told him. "He said he liked my attitude and he would be back later when the swabs came in."

Faye and Kelly, at home in Stellarton, soon received the bad news: Rick had tested positive for COVID-19.

"It was extremely shocking," says Faye. "[I thought], this can't be real. Rick's last words to me were, 'He said they have a plan.' He could barely get it out." Minutes later Rick, quickly failing, was moved to ICU and put into an induced coma.

Faye, Kelly, and Kelly's husband, Brian, who all share a home, realized they should also get tested—and all of their tests came back positive. The whole family had COVID-19. They would all have to self-isolate in different rooms of the house.

Kelly's part of the house included the kitchen and laundry room. She would "fully suit up" to do the laundry and then change her clothes to cook the meals she'd deliver to the other rooms in the house. Family and friends left food on their doorstep.

Because the family was not allowed to visit, Faye called for updates from the unit four or five times a day. Kelly took an online course in critical care so she could understand what she was hearing from the hospital. She also started a Facebook group to talk about her family's journey. The group received messages of hope from all over the country.

"That carried us through," says Kelly. "Plus, just how positive he is? I always thought of Dad as a fighter—no matter what, he never gives up." She also had a group of friends that she called every morning for support.

But April 1 was the scariest day of Faye's life. Rick had taken a turn for the worse. His kidneys were failing and his inflammatory markers were shooting up. As things went from bad to worse, Faye was given a choice; the doctors could try a procedure that required Rick to be flipped over to try to take the fluid off his lungs, but it came with dangers of its own. She was asked if she wanted them to try it.

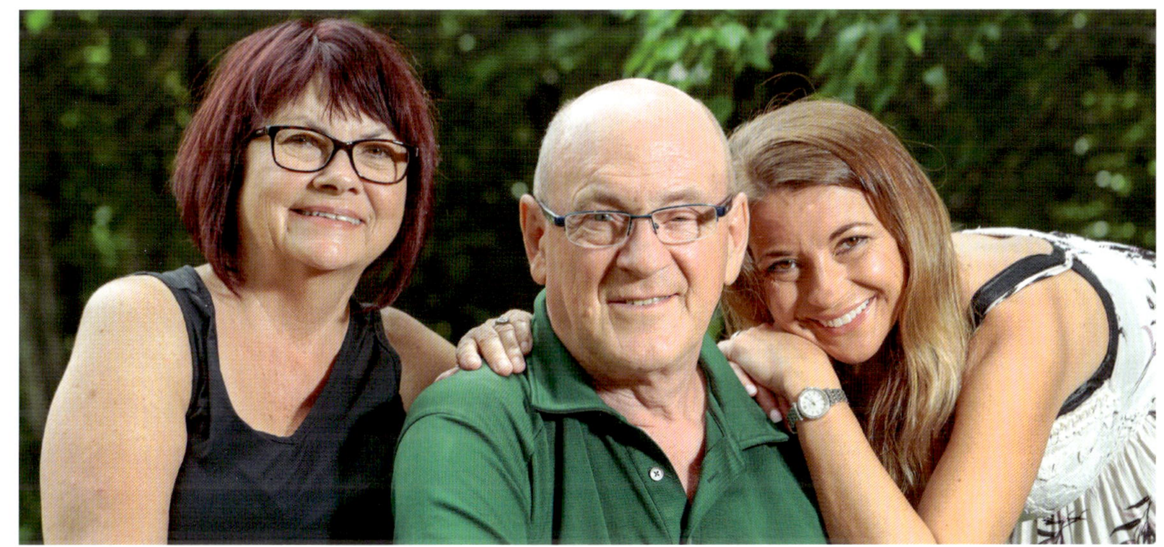

Kelly Marshall (right), her mom, Faye Cameron, and her father, Rick Cameron, all of Stellarton, share a light moment as they tell the story of their family's battle with COVID-19.

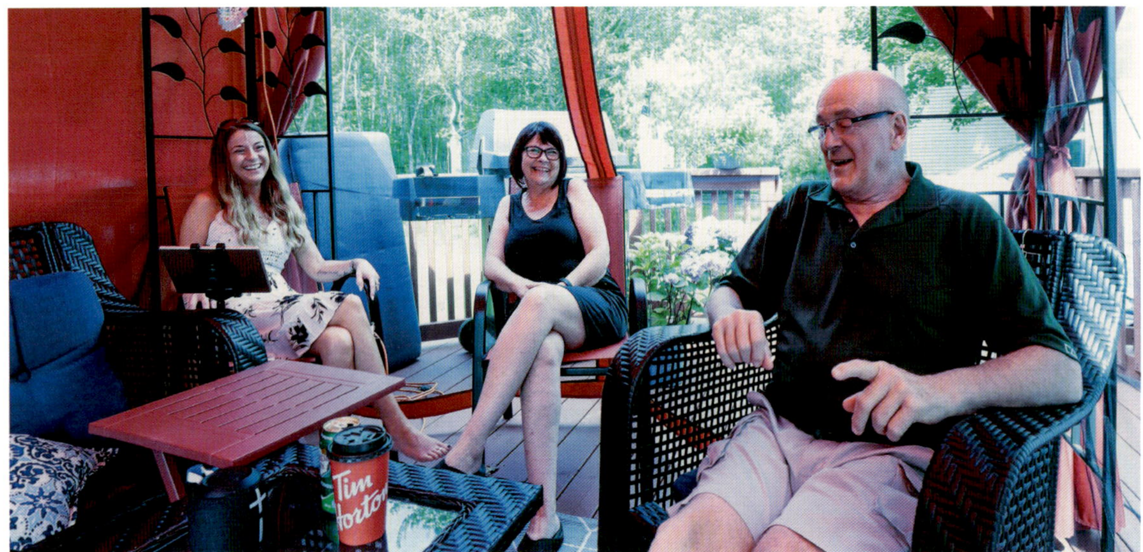

Kelly Marshall (left) and Faye Cameron smile as Rick Cameron recounts the story of his own months-long battle with COVID-19.

"I knew Rick wanted me to do anything that would keep him alive," says Faye, but she was worried about making the wrong decision. "I couldn't make the decision because I was too scared.... I told them I would do it the next day." By the next day there was no option; she was told they had to do the procedure or "that would be it."

It worked. Slowly, Rick started to get better.

On April 5, Faye's birthday, Rick's fever broke and his inflammatory markers dropped, signalling an improvement. On Easter weekend, he opened his eyes.

"I don't have a conscious memory of any conversation with anybody until May 2," says Rick. "I do remember vividly wanting a Heineken beer. I [also] remember that I wanted a ham and cheese sandwich."

He asked the nurse how long he had been unconscious, and she told him it had been thirty-seven days. "I said, 'Yeah, right! Who paid you to tell me that?'"

Rick struggled to speak because he had been intubated for so long. "He was getting frustrated.... We would try to guess what he was saying, and then he was like, 'Arrrrggghhh!'" Kelly says, laughing. He also struggled to move his fingers and toes, and to eat. He had lost forty-five pounds.

Eventually, after several weeks, the doctor told him it was okay to have that beer he'd thought about when he woke up—in fact, the doctor wrote him a prescription for it. "I remember leaning back, taking a swallow, and wanting to spit it out. It tasted terrible, like it had gone bad!" says Rick. COVID-19 had affected his sense of taste and smell.

Finally Rick, who had by then been transferred back to the Aberdeen Hospital for rehab, got the news he was going home. He had spent seventy-seven days in hospital with COVID-19, thirty-one of them in an induced coma, fighting for his life.

On June 3, an unseasonably cold day with rain and gusty winds—a day that happened to be Kelly's fortieth birthday—the staff at the Aberdeen hospital lined the sidewalk and applauded as he made his way to Kelly's car.

As she turned down their street in Stellarton, her father beside her, Kelly could not believe the scene. Family, friends, neighbours, and community groups lined the street to welcome Rick home. They held signs reading, "Welcome Home, Rick!" and "Happy Birthday, Kelly!" There were cakes, pies, Heineken, cards, flowers, and a specially labelled wine that read "F&*K COVID-19."

"I was in shock and overwhelmed. It was extremely touching and heartwarming to see such kindness from our community," says Kelly. "[It was] the best feeling in the world! It was like the end to our grief and our house felt whole again."

Sitting in their gazebo, the three of them recall their journey like comrades who have survived a battle together, finishing each other's sentences and thoughts. Faye says one morning she would wake up feeling great, and a few days later she would crash again with all the symptoms.

Rick, listening, asks, "Like the flu?"

Both Faye and Kelly laugh and shake their heads. Faye puts her hand on her husband's arm. "It was no flu!"

Most importantly, Kelly says, her birthday wish had come true. "His return was the greatest present I will ever receive in this lifetime."

WINDOW VISITS: *Tracy Dryden*

Tracy Dryden scrambles up the back stairs to her mother's room and looks through the window, giggling. It's Sunday, the day Tracy would normally take her mother, Betty Dryden, who is a retired nurse, to her home for dinner. Today, though, it means looking at her mom through the window at Sheldrake Lodge, a private long-term care home in Hubley, and having a phone conversation through the glass. Their conversations are often short because her mother has Alzheimer's.

She can see a home-care worker putting lipstick on her mother—the reason for the giggles. "One day I said something about how she'd never [ordinarily] be seen without lipstick, so now when I come to visit, they always have her lipstick on."

Tracy and her husband, Blaise Landry, blow kisses to her mother and she and her mom lock eyes as Betty brings her hand up and blows a kiss back.

Tracy, a nurse herself, knew trouble was coming late in February and into March. "They hadn't locked down nursing homes yet, but I didn't feel right taking her out of the protective bubble she was in," she says. She knew from news reports from around the world that older people with underlying health problems were being hit hard by COVID-19. She had seen the devastation the disease was causing in European cities.

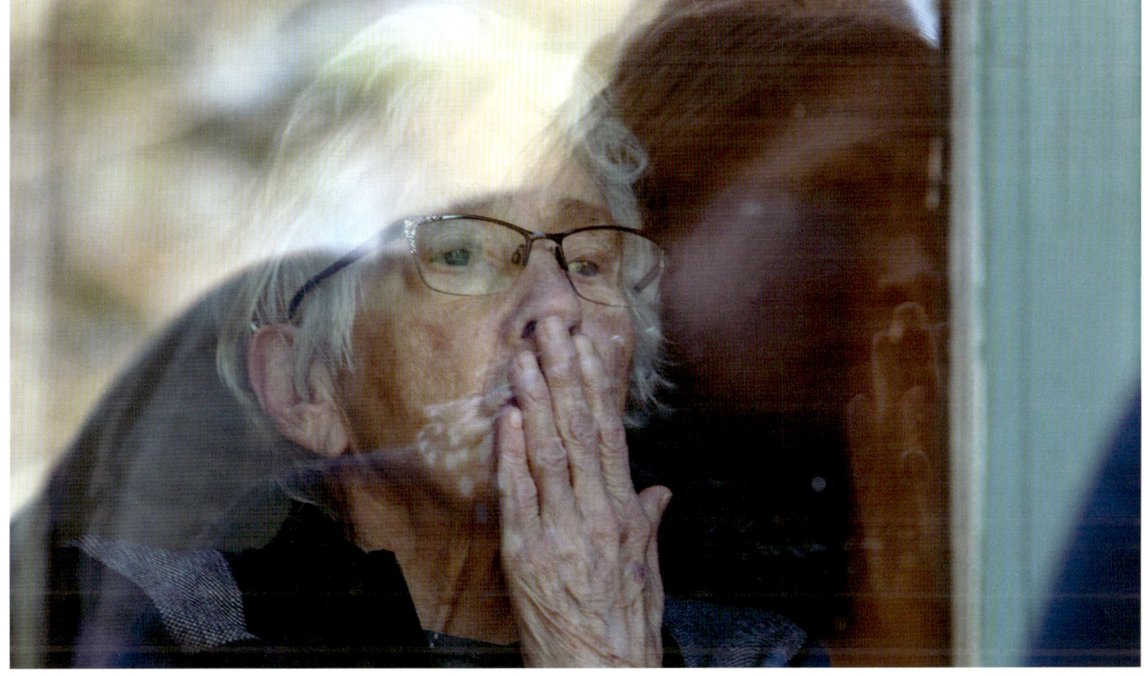

"I feel that she's safe in there, I really do. It's a very small staff. None of them work elsewhere, and they're very, very dedicated to the residents, so I'm not scared," she says. "I would be scared if she was in a public facility. My goal was to keep her [in her] home until she passed. But since her stroke, this is the best place for her."

Betty had lived at her own home in Hammonds Plains for over fifty years. She worked at the Grace Maternity Hospital (later the IWK Health Centre) and when she retired she volunteered at her community church and at some retirement homes. When Hurricane Juan shut the city down in 2003, Betty delivered meals to residents in a long-term care home. She was always there to help until medical problems of her own slowed her down.

"I think she would still see herself as a health-care provider," says Tracy. "She'd be an advocate for wearing masks, staying home, following rules. She'd be a champion. She was always outspoken about a cause, so this would have been a cause."

Tracy pauses and wipes away a tear. "I think knowing that [she] is receiving loving care ... makes it easier. I know they care about her. She's not a number. I see how they react with her. I see how they work to make her smile. To them, she's special," she says.

"I'd rather her here where she's safe."

Betty Dryden, a resident of a long-term care facility in Hubley, blows a kiss to her daughter, Tracy Dryden, as Tracy visits on a Sunday afternoon in April. To prevent the spread of COVID-19, visitors were not allowed inside long-term care homes in Nova Scotia.

SOCIAL BUTTERFLY UNDER LOCKDOWN:

Victoria Levack

It's mid-July and twenty-nine-year-old Victoria Levack hasn't left her home since early March.

Victoria has cerebral palsy and has lived for eight years at Arborstone Enhanced Care in Halifax. She says that, like her, none of her friends have been out since March either. "In terms of going where there are lots of people gathered, we're avoiding that," she says. "They're very fearful for their lives." She's also concerned about the possibility of bringing the illness home because she lives with so many seniors who may be more vulnerable than her.

She says she normally lives a very active life, but "the simple act of going to a store, seeing friends, often involves planning for days." Now, even that kind of planning is impossible, and the self-described social butterfly says she has been dealing with mild anxiety. "A lot of the problems I live with now are the same problems I had when we weren't locked down, but with COVID here, you know, I just can't get away from it."

Victoria realizes it may be awhile before her life gets back to what it was before the pandemic, but she hopes the crisis is giving people a chance to rethink some things.

"I just think while we have the time, if you're not a front-line worker and you're gonna sit at home, you should be taking this time to learn, so that when we do go out, we... don't actually go back to normal," she says, "because normal was not very good for all people."

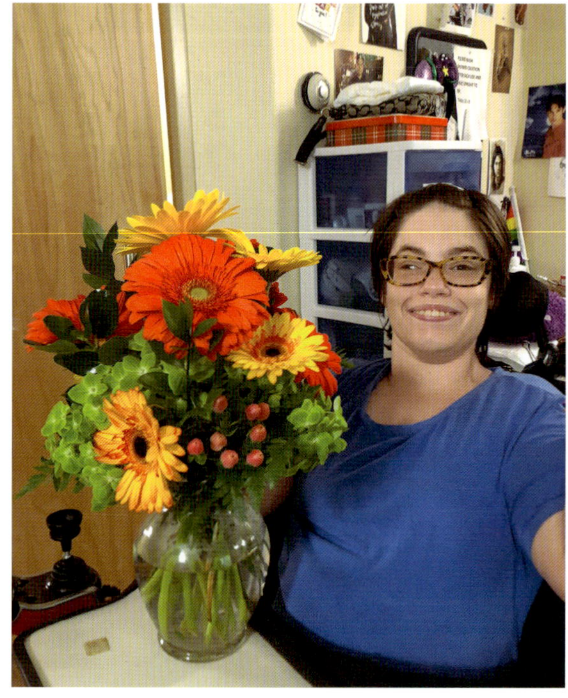

Victoria Levack, a self-described "social butterfly," says she's avoided going out during the pandemic because she lives among many vulnerable seniors at an enhanced care home in Halifax, and doesn't want to risk making anyone sick. (Victoria Levack)

TEACHING FROM HOME:
A New Model for Grade School

Sandy Wagg, a grade two teacher at Holland Road Elementary School in Fletcher Lake, is like most teachers: she can usually tell you when the moon is full without looking at a calendar. Throw in that full moon, a Friday the thirteenth, the March Break, and a global pandemic, and Sandy—who happens to be this author's wife—just knew it was going to be a week.

She recalls a staff meeting during that week early in March in which she and her colleagues had discussed their travel plans; they had raised the potential that students and staff who travelled outside the province might have to isolate upon return.

When the provincial government announced that schools would remain closed for at least two weeks following the March Break, the veteran teacher knew there were going to be many challenges as the transition to online learning started to roll out across the province. At that time, staff had no idea that there would be no physical return to the school for the rest of the school year.

"The first few days were filled with great frustration and tears," she admits, as she feeds Coral and Sparkle, the class fish that her students had named and taken care of—and who are now living at our home. "I did not think I was going to be able to do it. Google and YouTube saved me, along with colleagues from other schools and grade-level partners at my school—we all collaborated. We would share what we were doing and invite others to share what they would like to take from that. And if you came up with a good idea—we're all grade two teachers—we put it on a shared drive so everybody could have access to it."

It was that collaboration and teamwork that

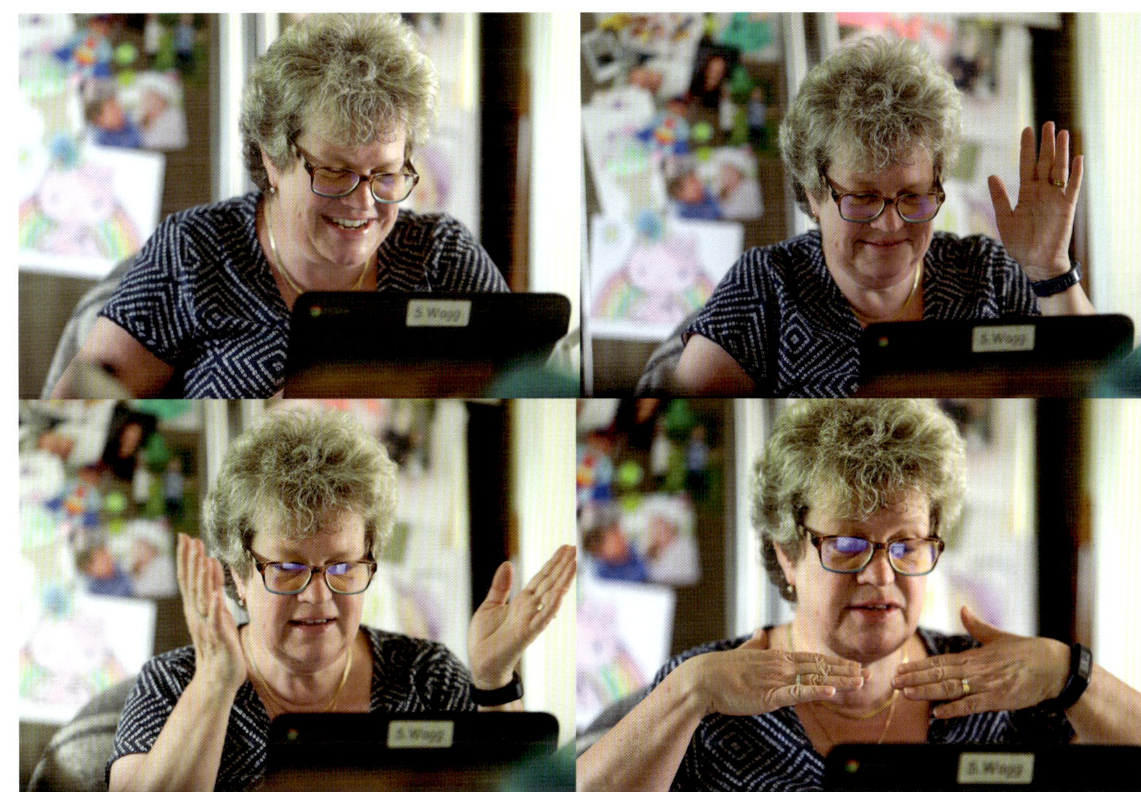

Sandy Wagg, a grade two teacher at Holland Road Elementary School in Fletchers Lake, goes through an online lesson with her students from her kitchen table.

enabled them to be ready to teach remotely as the announcement was made that schools would not reopen. Provincial learning packages were delivered to all homes across the province, and teachers would meet with their students online daily to try to give them some sense of normalcy.

"Initially, I was hesitant to do a Google Meeting," says Sandy. "We had one as a staff about a week into online learning and it was very chaotic, because unless you mute your microphone, you pick up on everybody's background noises—people moving their feet, people shuffling papers."

Before she held her first online meeting with her class, she laid out the rules to the kids. "I messaged them all that, just as we do in school, one person speaks at a time. There were a few glitches, but generally the kids were very supportive and accommodating," she says.

"It was just so great to see their little faces. And yes, you could tell a lot of them were still in their pajamas, and that was fine. You just focused on their eyes and their smiles."

Connecting with kids is why she went into teaching. "[I] love working with the kids, [I] love teaching them, and it's the connection that makes the difference. And that's what's been hard to maintain because, for our first online meeting, we probably had most of the students; [after that] we usually missed six or seven."

As it turned out, technology would play a huge part in the pandemic. While kids were supposed to be in an online classroom, parents were often working from home at the same time—creating challenges when it came to computer access.

One of the elements of the grade two science curriculum is "animal growth." Sandy reached out to parents to ask if anybody had found any frogs' eggs or tadpoles. "One parent volunteered to collect some for me," she says. Sandy collected them—without contact—from a sealed bag in a bucket on their front step. She kept them in an aquarium on our front porch until the end of the school year, photographing and documenting their progress so her students could follow along.

"One of the biggest things I heard from my families was that [the kids] missed [our] daily reading. So I started recording a book, a chapter novel at the grade two level, every day. In April it was *SOS Titanic* and in May it was *Charlotte's Web*."

She found out that not only were the children watching her videos and listening to the stories, but their families were watching, too.

"I feel that in the eyes of parents we have gained, because parents now have a greater appreciation for the job that teachers do. Parents are working with their own children—but imagine working with your own plus twenty-one others. That's a huge shift when you [have to] try and figure out how you're going to motivate your own child—and you think about how teachers have to motivate an entire group of children."

She says she's learned a lot about how to teach online and how to use new technologies, but says what she has missed most is contact with the kids. "You can see them on the screen; they wave at you when they'd like to say something, but it's just not the same as seeing them in person."

On the final day of the school year, many of the students came together online for their final Google meeting. They talked about their summer plans and said goodbye to their classmates.

"It was very sad to say goodbye that last day," says Sandy. "It was gut-wrenching to not be able to give the kids a hug on the last day of school."

HOME-SCHOOLING

As schools across the province were closed and education shifted online, families had to take on the responsibility for making sure their kids kept up with their studies.

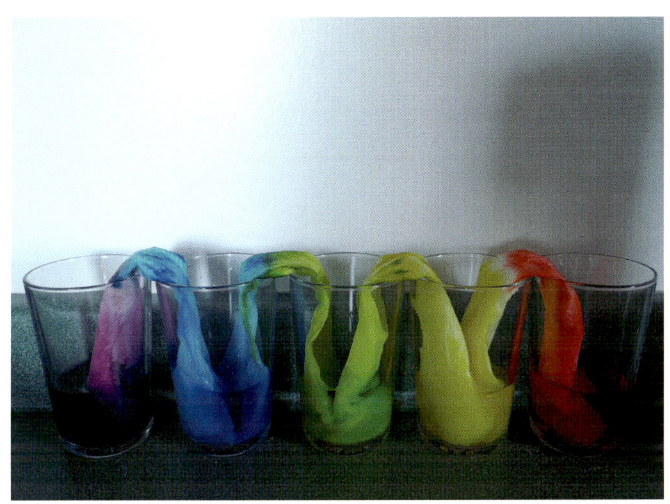

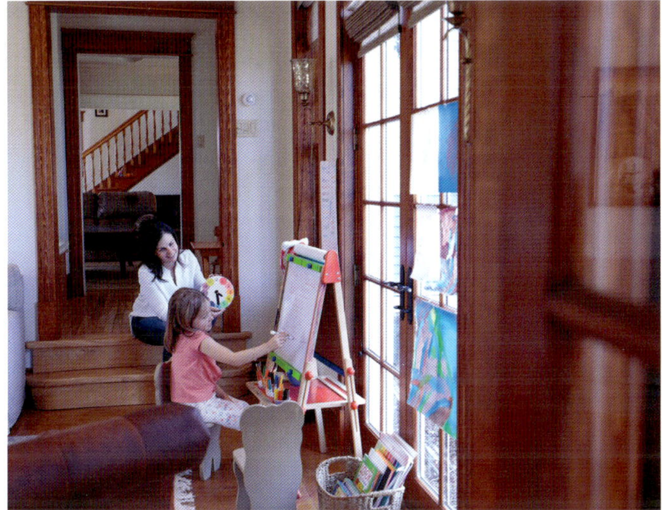

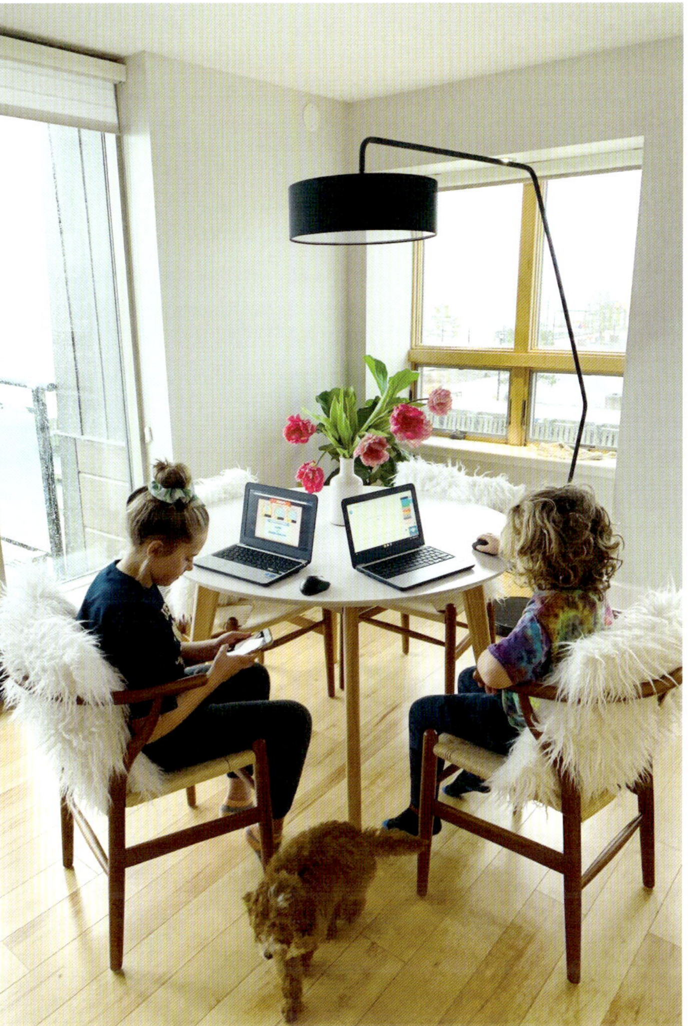

TOP LEFT: *A few science experiments sent in by Kelli Ross from Cole Harbour, NS. (Kelli Ross)*

BOTTOM LEFT: *Jocelyn Lightfoot and her daughter, Meadow, of Wolfville, go over some schoolwork in the family home. "Although these are [Meadow's] early elementary years, she is engaged in learning critical life skills, and that couldn't go on the back burner at a time like this," says Jocelyn. "She is learning how to read, how to write, how to add and subtract; learning the values of money and how to tell time. We have embraced this opportunity as a gift we got to share with each other."*

RIGHT: *Charlie and Oliver Boyle do their home-schooling homework in downtown Halifax. (Lindsay Watters)*

WORKING FROM HOME:
Balancing Kids and Career

*Rachel Boomer had been looking forward to March—*it meant a break from work, a vacation, and a chance to get away with her three girls, aged eight, ten, and thirteen. But she was also dreading the month: it would mean marking the first year since her husband—the girls' father—had died.

They were planning to head to Sunday River in Maine for some skiing, but the COVID-19 pandemic changed all that. Their trip was cancelled at the last minute; Rachel and the girls stayed home—and they haven't left home since.

Rachel, a communications director for the Nova Scotia government, says working from home and simultaneously home-schooling is a challenge. "I find it really stressful. I feel like working motherhood is always a balance between the guilt of not being with your kids, or not doing everything that you should be doing with your kids, and the guilt of not doing everything you feel you should be at work." As we chat, two of her girls run past and jump onto the trampoline in their backyard, jockeying for position. Rachel, meanwhile, pauses to take a work call.

"I could never have been a teacher," she admits. "I miss my adult time. I don't go to work for just for the paycheque—I go to work for the socializing and the adults."

She says working from home is very different than her normal workday. "I [would] go to the office, shut my door. People might knock on it politely," she says. Now, when she's video conferencing, her youngest wants to say hello to everyone on the call, her middle daughter wants to show people their dog, and her eldest doesn't hesitate to express her opinion on the subjects Rachel and her colleagues are discussing—while her mic is on.

One of the ways Rachel balances her home

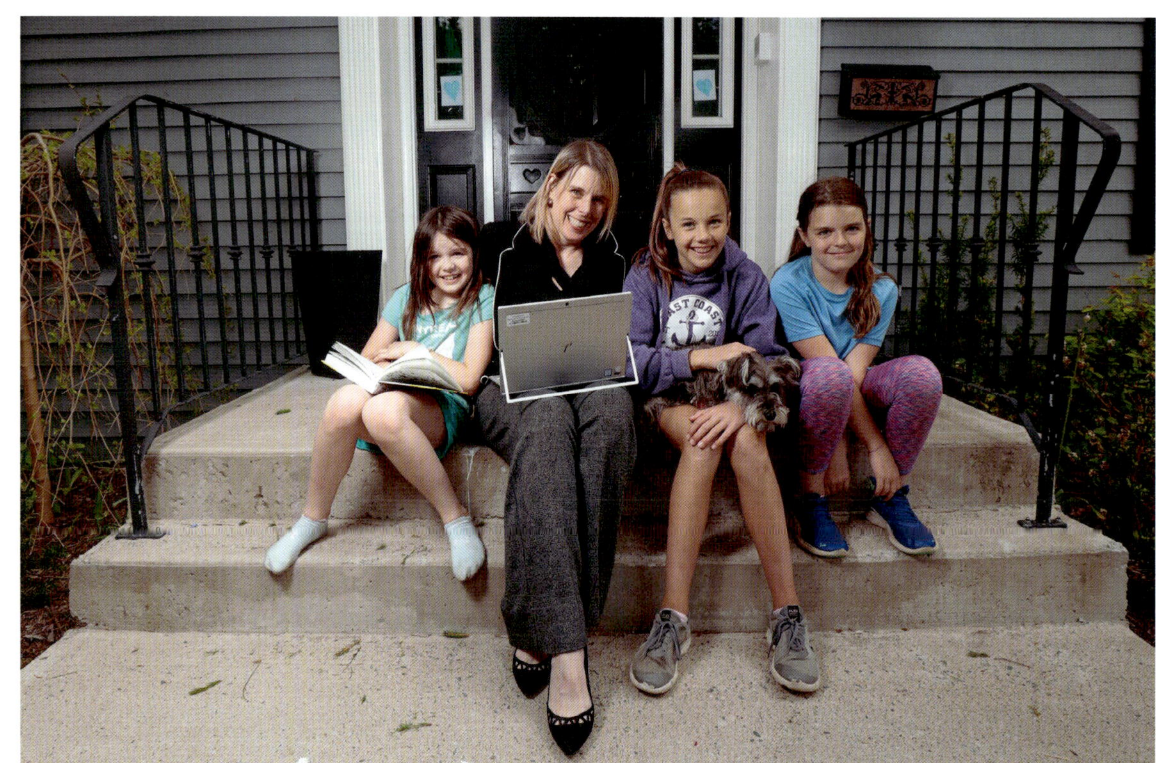

Rachel Boomer, who works from home these days, sits with her children, (from left) Claire Wilkie, eight, Julia Wilkie, thirteen, and Maya Wilkie, ten, in front of their home in Halifax.

and work lives is by sharing humorous posts on social media. She's assigned her kids positions in their "company;" she refers to one daughter as "Legal," another as "Comms," and variously refers to her kids as "Enforcement Services," the dog as "HR," and herself as "the CEO."

The posts have given her friends a laugh and have provided her with a chance to enjoy some adult company. "Friends chime in about their own struggles and it makes me feel less alone," she says.

"Working from home is hard. Sometimes I will take my phone and the dog and go for a walk during a call, which helps a lot because I find I can focus. Other times I beg, other times I bribe, and other times I threaten," she laughs.

But Rachel says she sees the upside. "I like not having the stress of having to run someone somewhere after work; I like being able to cook meals without stressing out about it. I like not having a commute. I love a walk with the dog and I love being able to take the kids with me. A certain amount of busyness and rush has gone from life, and I do quite enjoy that. My oldest said to me this morning, 'COVID isn't all that bad. I can finish school when I want; I can hang out in the yard when I want!'"

Rachel says her family has shown its strength during the crisis. "I feel a huge amount of pride in being able to continue on and keep things rolling with very little help, particularly in this time," she says. "I feel I am a pretty strong person and I am very proud, I guess, of keeping the kids on an even keel, and relatively happy, during this whole pandemic."

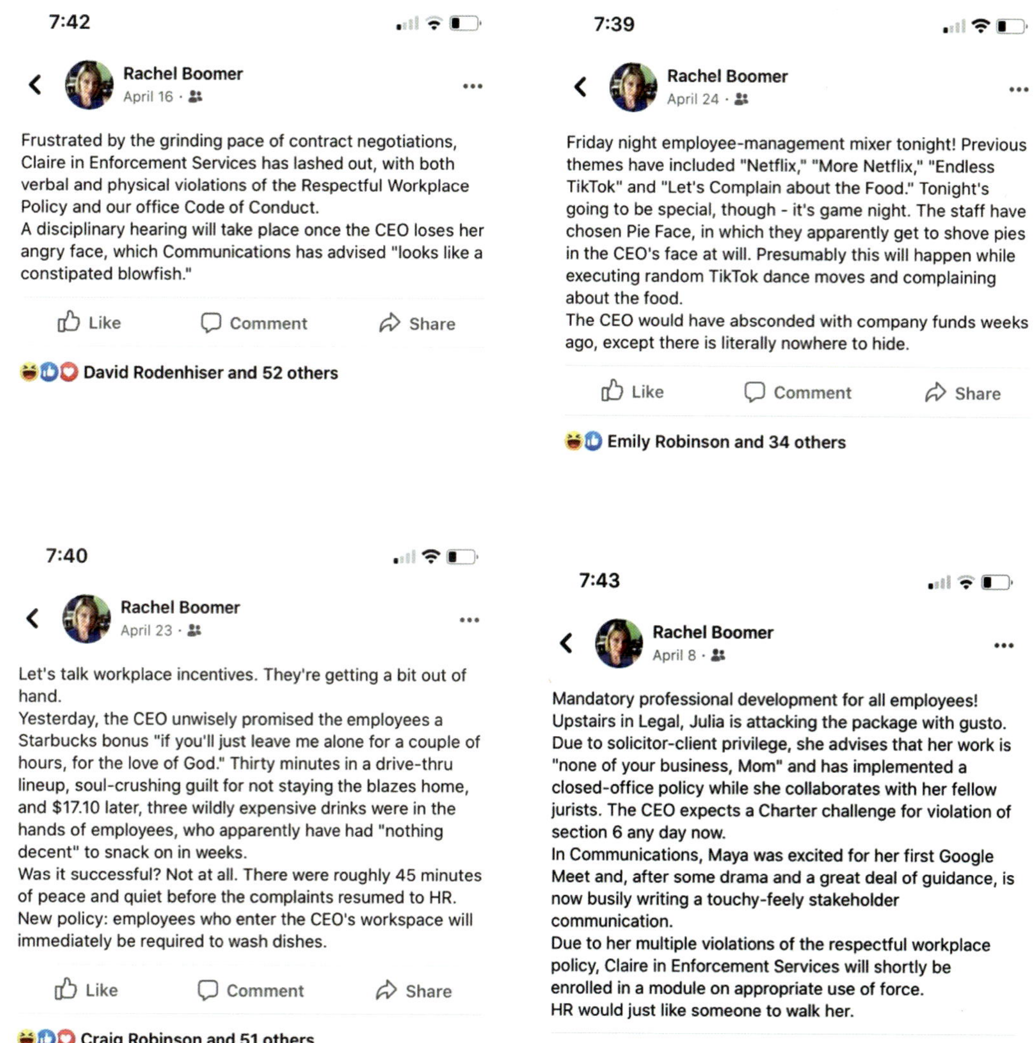

Screenshots from Rachel Boomer's Facebook page, in which she humorously refers to her kids as "Enforcement Services," the dog as "HR," and herself as "the CEO" as she attempts to work from home during the pandemic.

FINDING FAITH ONLINE:
Easter Sunday at Saint Benedict

Father Simon Lobo stands on the altar at the Saint Benedict Parish Catholic church in the normally bustling Halifax suburb of Clayton Park and gazes out toward the pews, but not a single pair of eyes looks back. Row upon row of pews sit vacant. In normal times, this Easter Sunday mass would have been attended by nearly two thousand people—a culturally diverse mix of middle-class and working-class families—but these are not normal times. It is Sunday, April 12, 2020, and a deadly pandemic has disrupted the world.

Lobo, a native of Ottawa and the pastor of this church, says he has mixed feelings about today's service. Along with the joy and excitement of celebrating Easter, there are other emotions. "It's sad, because our church is empty and we want to be able to celebrate with our community. This morning, even as I was praying before mass started, I was moved emotionally, just feeling the pain of all the many people who are part of our community who would love to be here, but who can't be here because it is the right thing to do to stay home and stay safe. And yet it is hard to experience it at the same level, because people are not physically in the church building with us."

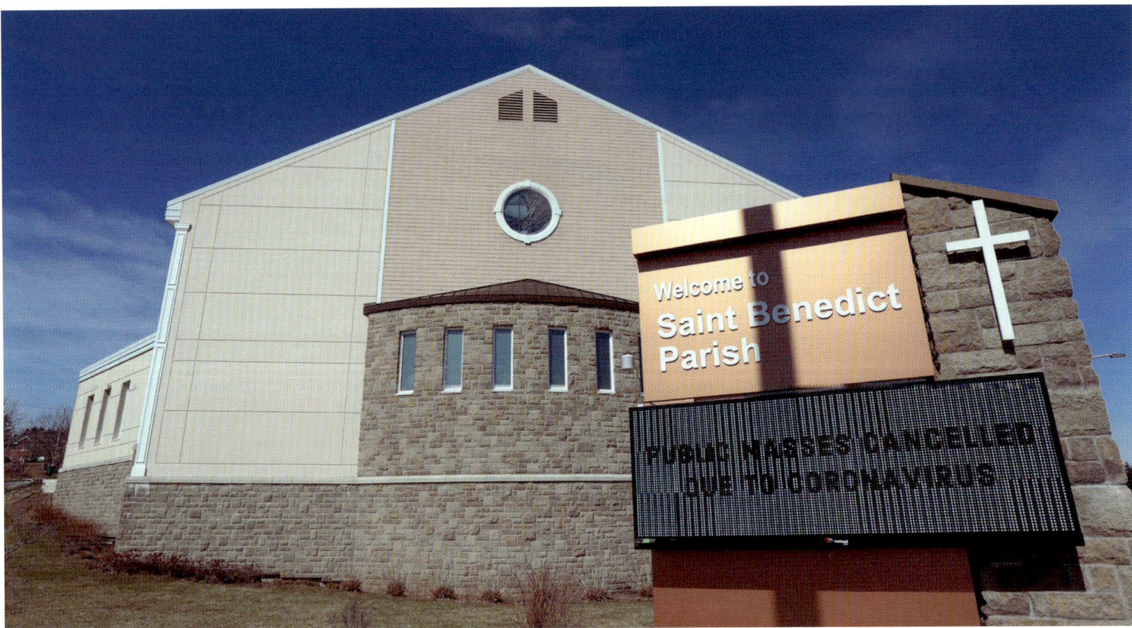

Associate Pastor Father Alex Colautti sees the positive side of this new reality. "The irony of this whole thing is that even though there's nobody here in the building, I just preached this morning—and I preached to the largest crowd ... in my life!"

That crowd was, of course, online. In 2014, Saint Benedict's leaders had seen the potential in reaching parishioners via the internet, and had installed cameras on the pillars to accommodate livestreams for those who could not physically make it to church.

"We always wanted to reach out beyond the walls of the church," says Lobo. "On the internet, you can watch from a safe place. It's the new front door for the church."

The viewing numbers for the parish's livestream and YouTube channel are now in the tens of thousands. "Last year on Palm Sunday we had 600 viewers online; this year we had 12,600," says Colautti, adding that two-thirds of those viewers were from Nova Scotia and the rest were from across Canada and beyond.

Saint Benedict Parish in Halifax.

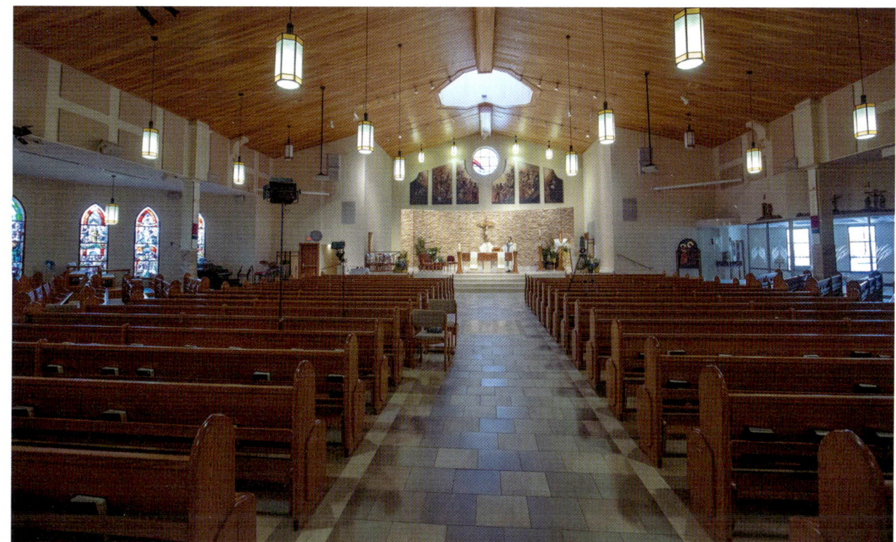

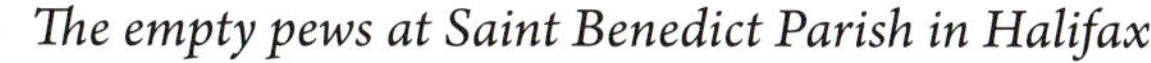

The empty pews at Saint Benedict Parish in Halifax.

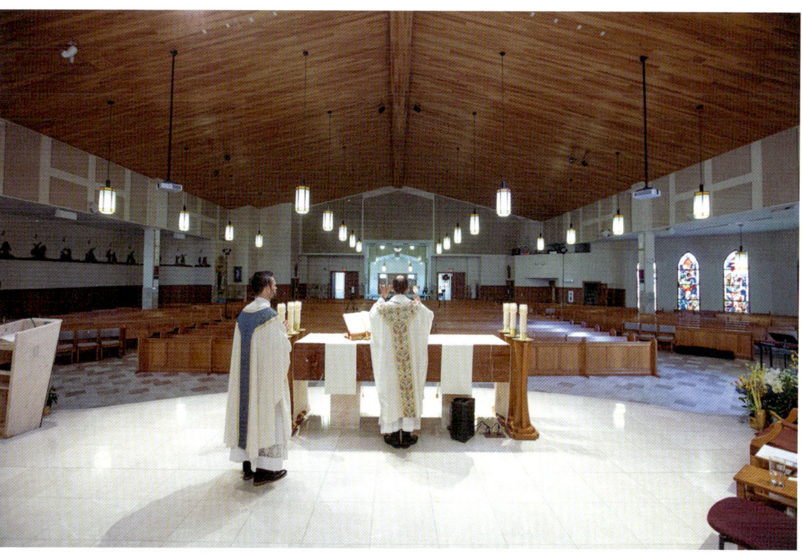

Father Simon Lobo (right) and Father Alex Colautti perform Easter mass at Saint Benedict. Because places of worship were closed, the parish live-streamed the mass to more than sixteen thousand viewers.

"People are afraid, and they are asking questions, looking for answers," says Lobo.

The numbers make Colautti feel the church's message is being heard. "When I see people's lives transformed with encounters from God, it gives me a high I can't find anywhere else. The church is playing the same role, but the impact during these times has changed."

His parish's ability to adapt is a source of pride for Father Lobo. "How do we react in times of crisis? We find creative ways to help people that are isolated, alone, depressed, afraid. We use phone, videos, livestreams. We have a kids' church online that our staff—working from home, but harder than they ever have—have expanded. Our members have set up food for families. People coordinate distribution for people, so they do not go hungry. I am blown away by the way this parish has responded, but there is more we can do."

When they first preached to an empty church on March 22, Lobo wondered how this time would be remembered. "This season would not be defined by COVID-19; it would be known as the time the church stepped up—when the church became the light when it was encroached upon by darkness."

Father Colautti leans forward. "COVID-19 is like a darkness, but we, as followers of Jesus, carry within us a light. It's not the darkness that defines the limits of darkness, it is the light that defines the darkness."

HELPING THE HOMELESS: *Shelter Nova Scotia*

Linda Wilson, executive director of Shelter Nova Scotia, knows about crisis. She has worked for over thirty years in the field of social work, mostly with women and children, until five years ago when she joined Shelter Nova Scotia, which oversees emergency shelters and provides supportive housing for homeless people in Nova Scotia.

Homelessness has been a problem in this country for well over two hundred years, she says—but the pandemic has added another level of challenge for those who are trying to help. Her organization's main shelter, Metro Turning Point, once housed fifty-five men, but they could no longer provide space for that number of people due to social distancing rules.

"We work in crisis. We've been trained to work in crisis, but this is crisis on top of crisis," she says, adding that because people have been ordered to stay home, the number of homeless people on the streets has become more obvious. "If you drive down Quinpool Road, it's just people leaning against buildings left and right. You can tell they have nowhere to go. I think before, they would get lost in the shuffle."

Shelter Nova Scotia launched initiatives to assist with issues of overcrowding in shelters. Metro Turning Point renovated its space and can now accommodate thirty men in socially-distanced "sleeping snugs"; Barry House, which used to have twenty beds, can now accommodate seventeen women.

But while the situation at Shelter Nova Scotia has been challenging during the state of emergency, many individuals and organizations have stepped up to help out. Miriah Kearney, owner of My Home Apparel, for example, raised a whopping $25,000 for Shelter Nova Scotia thanks to her wildly successful "Stay the Blazes Home" T-Shirt (see "The T-Shirt That Took Off," page 122).

"Since I've been in this business, I've never been surprised at the generosity of people that don't have much to give. That's Nova Scotia," Linda says. In fact, donations have increased in the past few months.

"[People] have dug deep because they know that we've had to cancel or postpone our fundraising events but we still have to have money because we're not fully funded."

As we leave her Gottingen St. office, Linda points to a group of men heading to the Brunswick Street Mission, where volunteers have been cooking three meals a day during the pandemic for those who don't have a home.

"We're all in the storm, but we're not in the same boat," says Linda, "and those experiencing homelessness are not [even] in the boat."

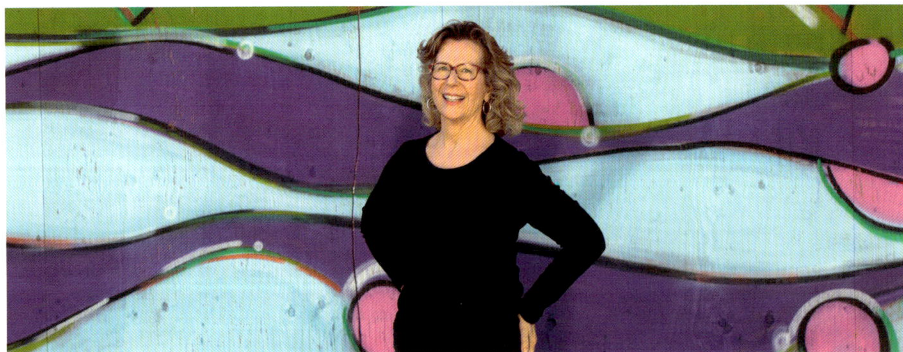

Linda Wilson, executive director of Shelter Nova Scotia, says staying home is tough when you don't even have a home.

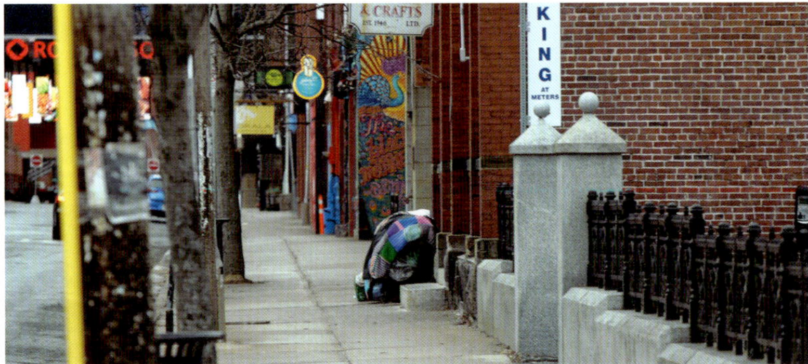

A homeless couple creates a shelter in the deserted downtown core of Halifax during the pandemic.

MASKING UP

As knowledge around the pandemic evolved, it became clear that wearing a mask would become an important part of the new normal in Nova Scotia.

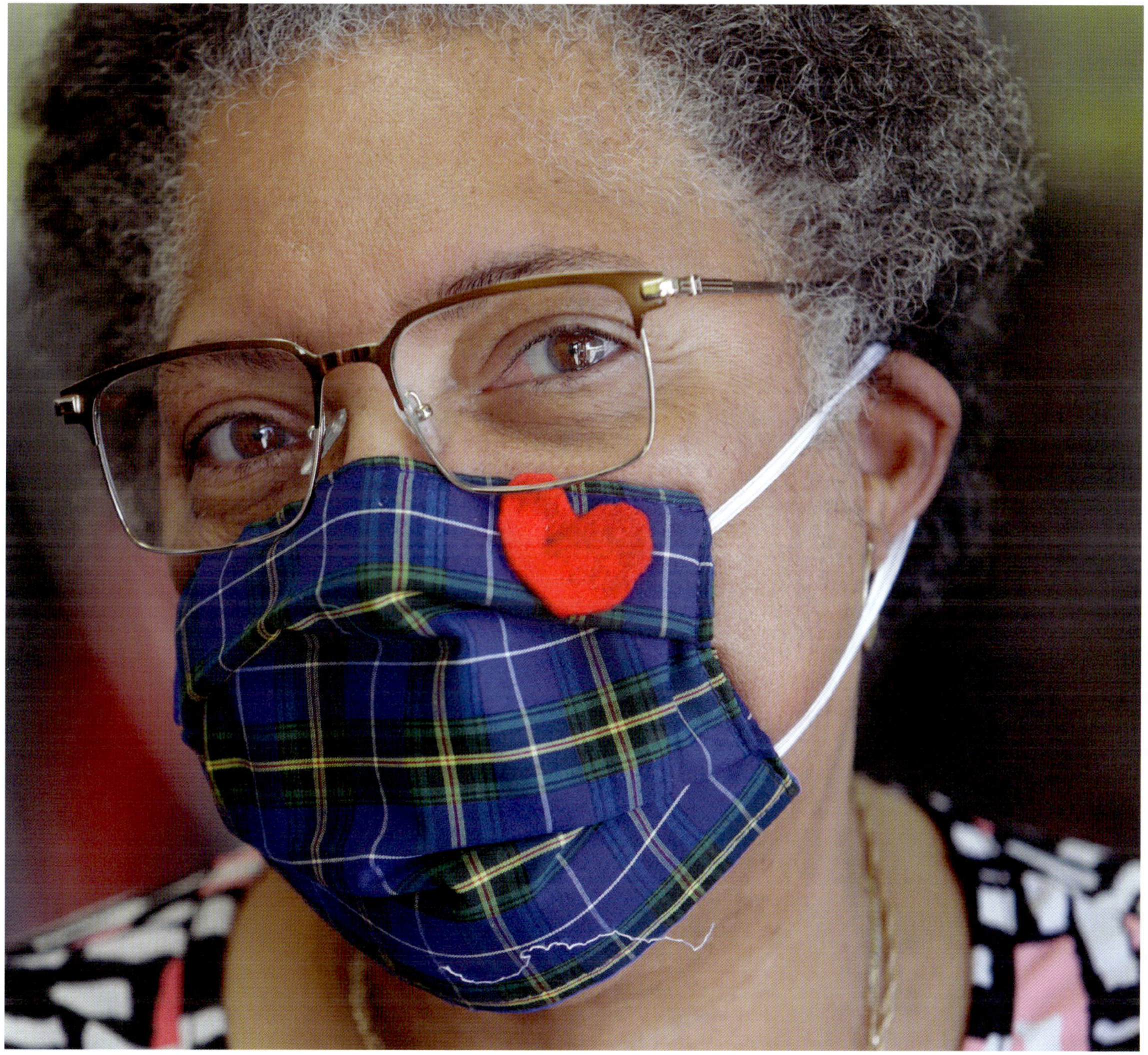

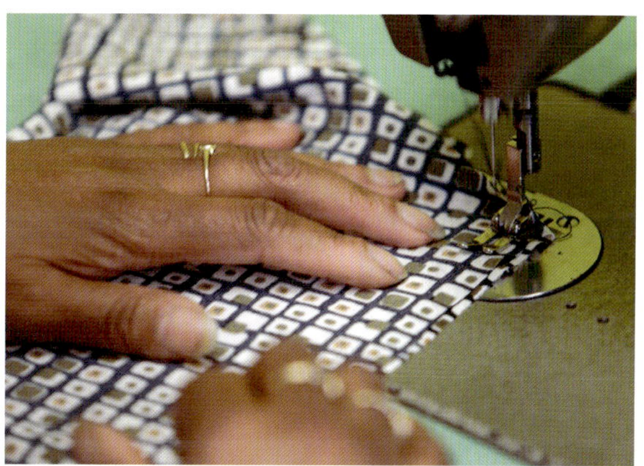

Paula Brown from Paula's Tailor shop on Farnham Gate Rd. in Halifax was one of the first people making masks, including this "Nova Scotia Strong" version, during the pandemic. Paula had been struggling to keep her business going with the prom and wedding seasons virtually decimated this year, but a brisk mask business has helped.

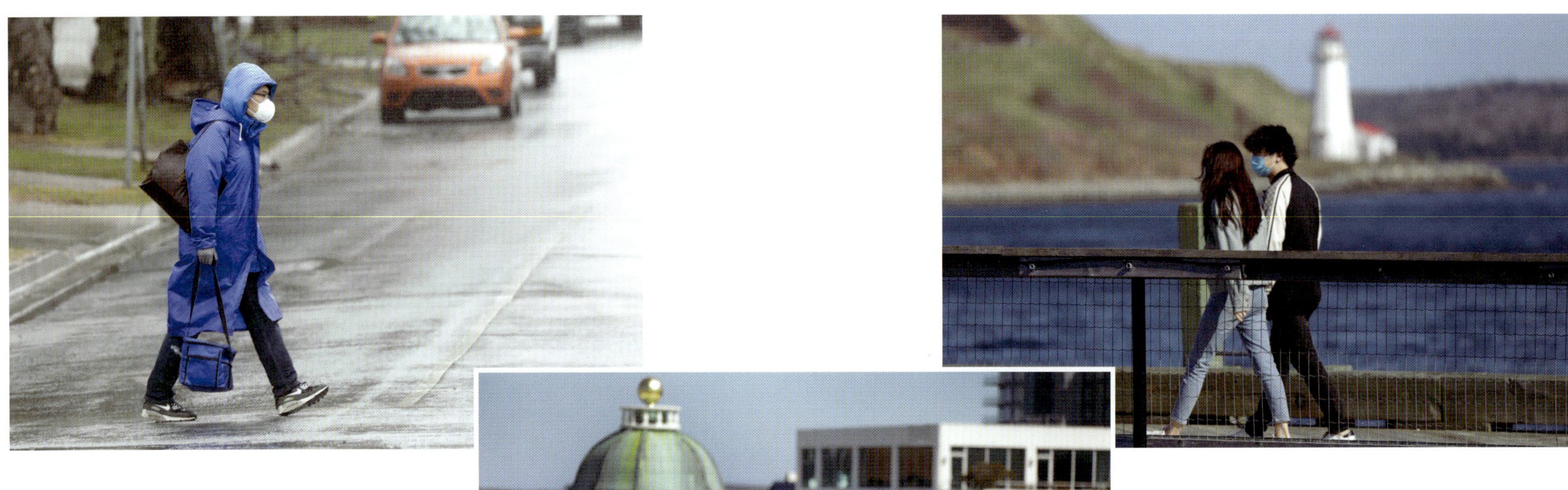

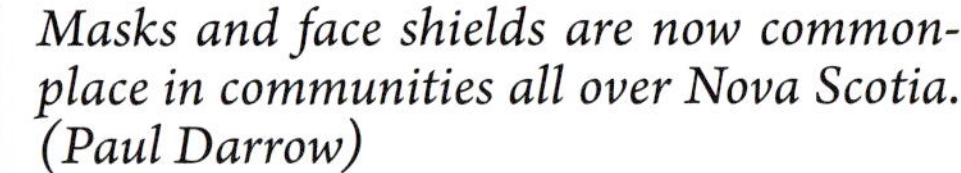

Masks and face shields are now commonplace in communities all over Nova Scotia. (Paul Darrow)

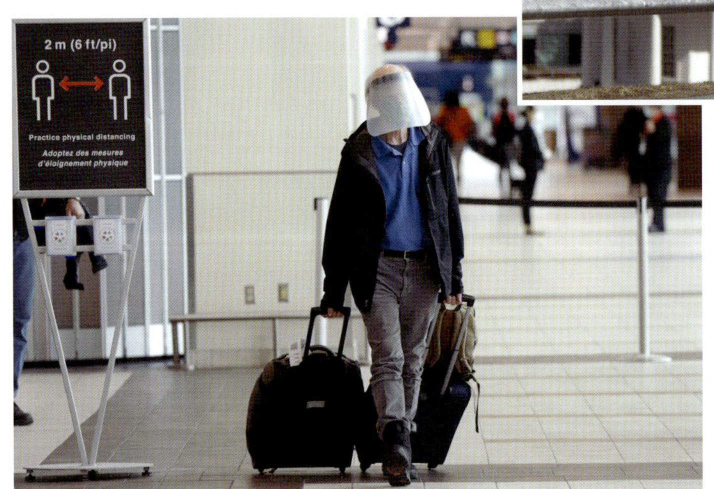

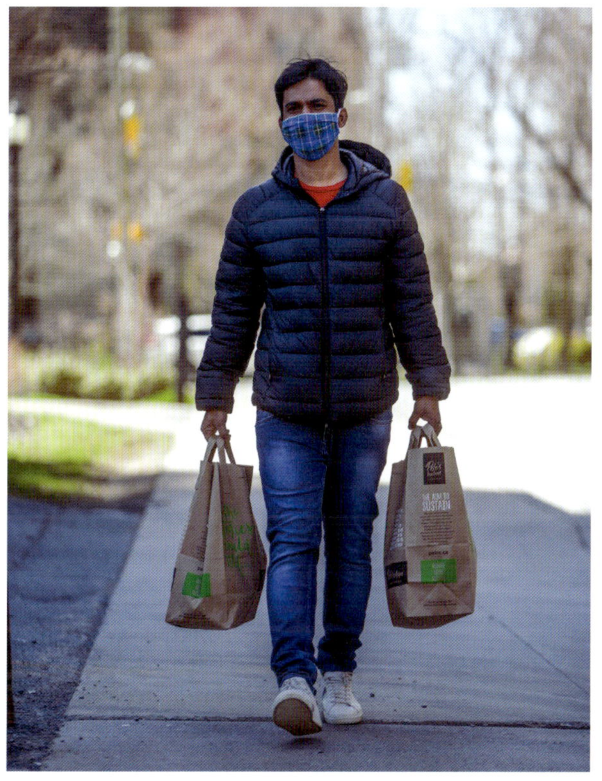

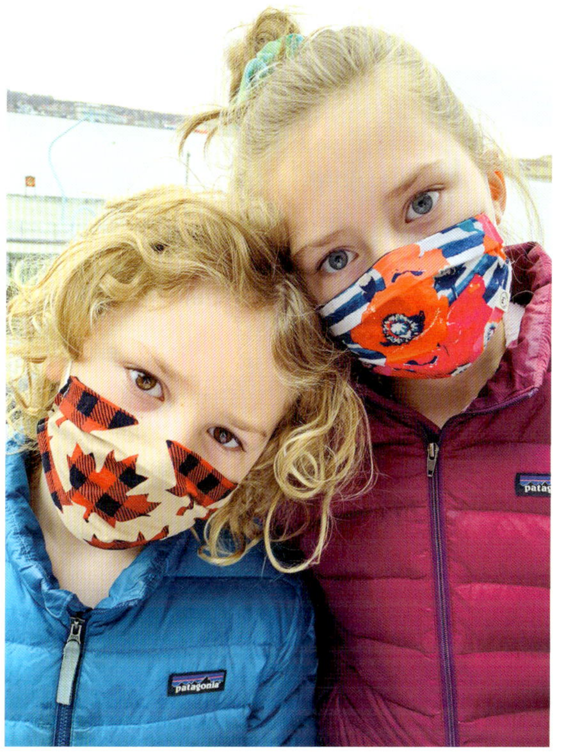

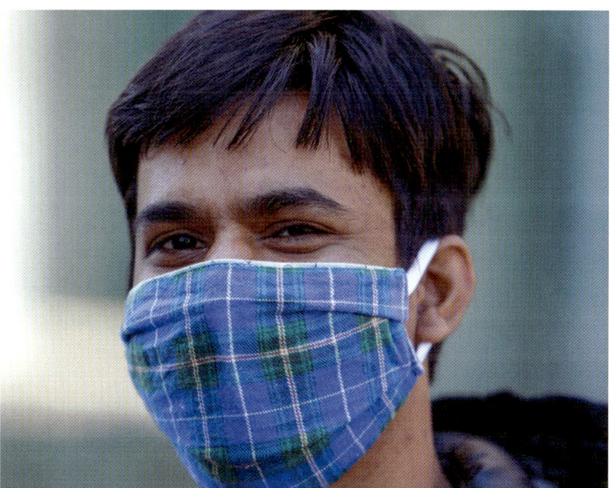

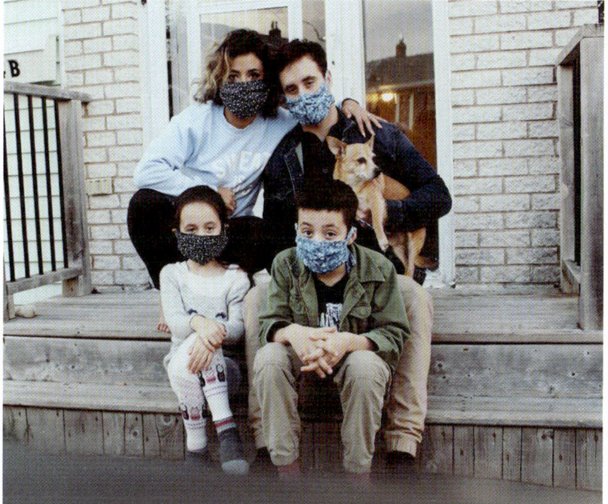

TOP AND BOTTOM LEFT: *Deepak Seku, a student from India who attends Dalhousie University, makes his way along South Park St. in Halifax wearing a distinctly Nova Scotian mask.*

TOP RIGHT: *Oliver and Charlie Boyle of Halifax really know how to rock a mask. (Lindsay Watters)*

BOTTOM RIGHT: *"We took the photo after coming home from a family member's funeral," says Savannah Webber of Cole Harbour, NS. "We had to watch the service from our vehicles, and four members of the family were able to stand six feet apart for the service at the gravesite. Once the service was over, we were able to go to the gravesite one family at a time to say our goodbyes. The masks were all handmade by my seventy-six-year-old grandmother. She has made close to four hundred so far and has donated many to Chebucto Links Senior Support Association and made sure all of our family members have some." (Savannah Webber)*

ADAPTING TO THE NEW REALITY:
Halifax Public Libraries

Karen Dahl, the senior manager of programming and community engagement for Halifax Public Libraries, is sitting in the reading lounge at the Halifax Central Library, a space that's usually a bustling community hub where people relax with a cup of coffee, children run and play on their way to story time, and adults beeline to computer stations for free internet access. Today, though, it's quiet, because this building, like all public library branches, has been closed to the public due to the coronavirus pandemic.

"I don't think we anticipated the scale of the impact of COVID-19," Karen says. "I don't think we really expected a global shutdown of businesses and recreation and schools and public spaces—and certainly not for so long.

"In the early days, we realized we needed to do something dramatic quickly—for safety, and in response to the health advisories. But I think it took us a few weeks to realize this wasn't going to turn around overnight."

Karen explains that this library—like most modern libraries—has always been about much more than books. "Care for our community is kind of the driving force for public library work." She says today's libraries are gathering places that provide "social seating opportunities" where people from different communities can bump into one another.

But the pandemic has meant that the library has had to figure out how to provide its services without the physical contact.

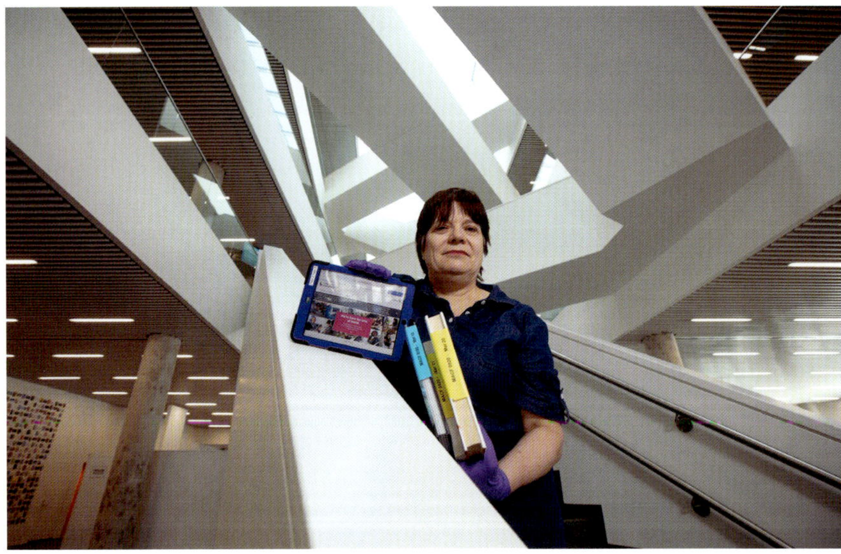

Karen Dahl, Senior Manager of Programing and Community Engagement for Halifax Public Libraries, says Libraries shifted quickly to provide services for people who were isolated during the pandemic.

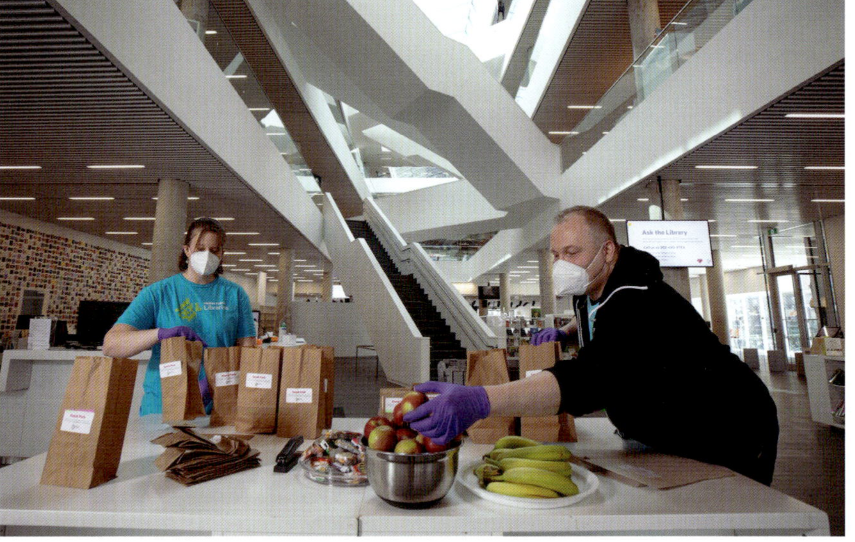

Library Assistants Siobhan Wiggans and Anders Balderston prepare snack packs that will be provided to six community partners and distributed to members of the vulnerable communities they serve.

"COVID-19 has been pretty transformative. It's thrown up a lot of challenges for sure, but it's also driven us into new areas of opportunity that we had been dabbling in or had thought about that we hadn't really explored fully," she says.

"We knew that community members would be hungry for reading and entertainment and interaction, so we started by making an online digital registration available, and that allowed thousands of people within the first few weeks to get library cards for the first time to access our digital collections. It was just phenomenal.... Suddenly [users could access] movies, music, books, audiobooks, stuff for children, databases, consumer reports, all kinds of newspapers and magazine articles—all for free and instantly."

And while the buildings were closed to the public, librarians shifted into high gear behind the scenes to create the collections that are now available online.

"We invested in way more e-books and bought a lot more copies of popular bestsellers to provide better access. We added on a new streaming film service called Kanopy, which opens up a world of international film, which is a gap in Halifax culture and in video collections from the past. So, it was just a wonderful way to say, 'Libraries can keep bringing it. We're just going to bring it differently.'"

The library has staff working at home doing virtual programming, creating content that focuses on health and wellness, writing blog posts highlighting community happenings, and creating video content—things like story times or yoga sessions.

"They're using Zoom and bringing newcomer groups together. Tutors and learners are breaking out into online breakout rooms and having their conversations. Leading readers are teens who work with young children to support their reading development; they are meeting in Zoom and doing one-on-one reading support with kids just as they did in the library. So there's a lot of shifting that's happening," says Karen. Library staff have also been maintaining personal connections with teens by phoning or texting them to check in on how they're doing. "With newcomers to Canada, we're calling and saying, 'How are things?' and 'Do you know about this resource or that resource?'"

One of the positives about the online shift has been the ability to bring together communities that might otherwise never meet. "Now knitters can get together in a facilitated Zoom meeting and share knitting tips and tricks, and laugh and enjoy themselves [with people] from around the globe."

She says the new approach eliminates the transportation and child-care issues that may have made it impractical for some people to get to the library in the past.

She also sees a role for the library to play in community issues like unemployment and food insecurity, which are magnified by COVID-19. "It's actually pretty exciting. Part of our role is advocacy for the priorities that our community needs in order to thrive. Internet access is one of those fundamentals. I think COVID has shown how deep that chasm is between the 'haves' and the 'have-nots.' When everything's closed, some people are in the dark. We've got a role to play there to mobilize our communities to look at the impact."

She says the library has a role in supporting people's transitions toward better health and economic success, and in providing access to education and opportunity.

"We absolutely will not stop doing this," says Karen, adding that she hopes they can also get back to doing in-person things soon. "That's our dream. There's a magic about face-to-face conversation and interaction that we would never want to lose. But I think this is more inclusive—and I think it's creating opportunities for people who might not otherwise have had those experiences."

TAKE WHAT YOU NEED:
A Community Food Drop Box

Jennifer DeCoste looks over at the tiny red schoolhouse replica that sits atop a four-foot-high post at the end of her lawn on Portland St. in Dartmouth. Masks hang from the sides. Inside, canned goods and other food items sit beside a sign that reads, "Take what you need. Leave what you can."

This little schoolhouse is a community food drop, and similar drop spots have popped up all over the province during the pandemic. This one came about when, about a month into the pandemic, Jennifer realized that there were a number of food-security issues in her community.

Jennifer lives just down the street from a recycling depot, so she often sees people in need going by her house. "The bus stops right in our driveway, so that makes it a perfect location," she says. Since she put up the food drop she's been re-stocking it five or six times a day. A local school parent association made a financial donation, enabling her to buy produce from Taproot Farm in the Annapolis Valley. "They're bringing fresh vegetables each week, so they drop off a box of food and we divide it out into little baggies and provide fresh fruit and vegetables out of the pantry," she says.

"What I think I've liked the most is when I see parents walking by with young children—because you can't go far these days—and they'll stop, and they'll talk about what the pantry is and what it means. I think it's been a really interesting teachable moment as well, "she says, adding that it's all about caring for the community.

As we chat, a car stops around the corner and a man gets out with a bag of canned goods. He places them in the schoolhouse and drives away.

She smiles. "You leave what you can and take what you need."

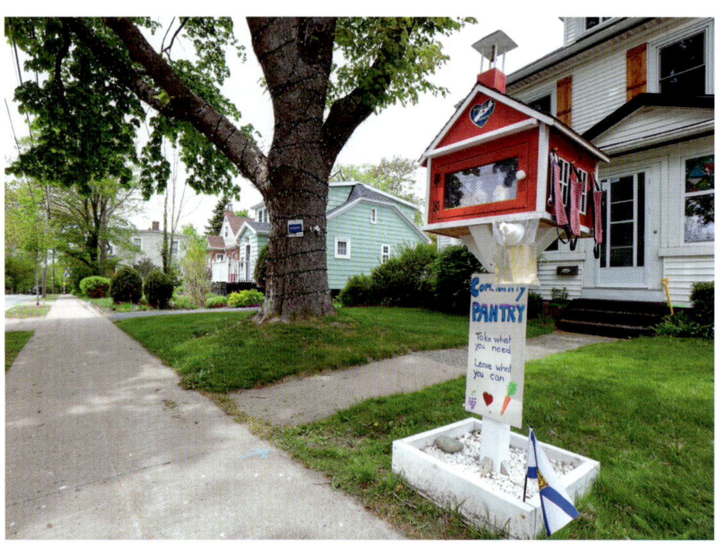

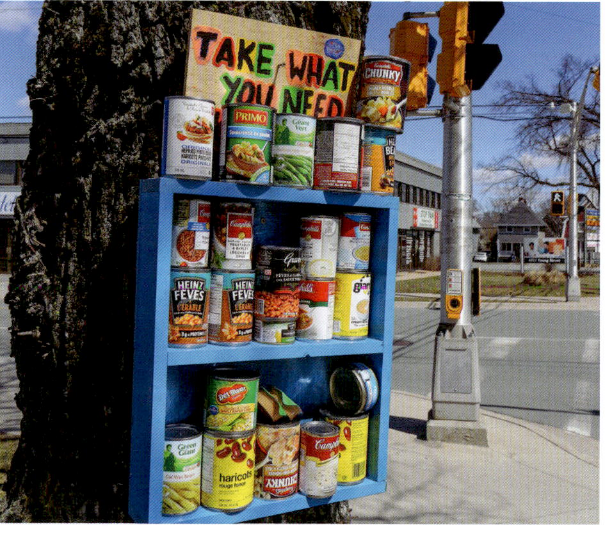

LEFT: *Community pantries like this one on Portland St. in Dartmouth popped up all over the province to provide items for people who could not afford them.*

RIGHT: *Take what you need, leave what you can. Young and Robie Streets, Halifax.*

A COOKING SHOW IS BORN:
Alain and Johanne Bossé

Spring is usually a busy time for Alain Bossé and his wife, Johanne Hulshof Bossé. The pair, who live and work from a farmhouse near Pictou, NS, run a consulting business in which Alain, known as The Kilted Chef, travels the world to promote Atlantic Canadian seafood and other Canadian food products.

That business, and the travelling that goes with it, came to a grinding halt at the start of March.

"Literally it meant that all our restaurant planning, all our shows, all our activities [were halted]," says Alain. "By this time of year, we would have done 75 percent of our yearly business, and that is down by 90 percent."

"It's the first time in our careers that something outside of ourselves has reached in and touched every single aspect of our lives," says Johanne. "Personal, business, financial, everything."

Fortunately, the pair had an "aha" moment.

"We didn't dwell on our sorrows very long," says Alain. "I've got to stay busy. I'm used to that public life."

Johanne looks up from the food she's prepping on the large butcher block in their kitchen. "We had an idea to entertain our friends and family. That's all it was…. It was meant for our immediate family and a few friends to say, 'Hey, we're going to do this live show just for a bit out of our kitchen.'"

And the show they're calling *The Kilted Kitchen* was born.

Each day, Johanne and Alain cook a different recipe and live-stream it on Facebook. They try to use what is in their fridge, keeping in mind the provincial directive to go out only if necessary.

Since the start, the two have done over seventy shows and counting. While Alain preps and cooks, Johanne takes questions from viewers and they answer them on the fly. The uptake has amazed them.

"We were reaching numbers of fifty or sixty people watching and we were going, 'Wow, this is pretty cool.'"

That number went up to more than four hundred

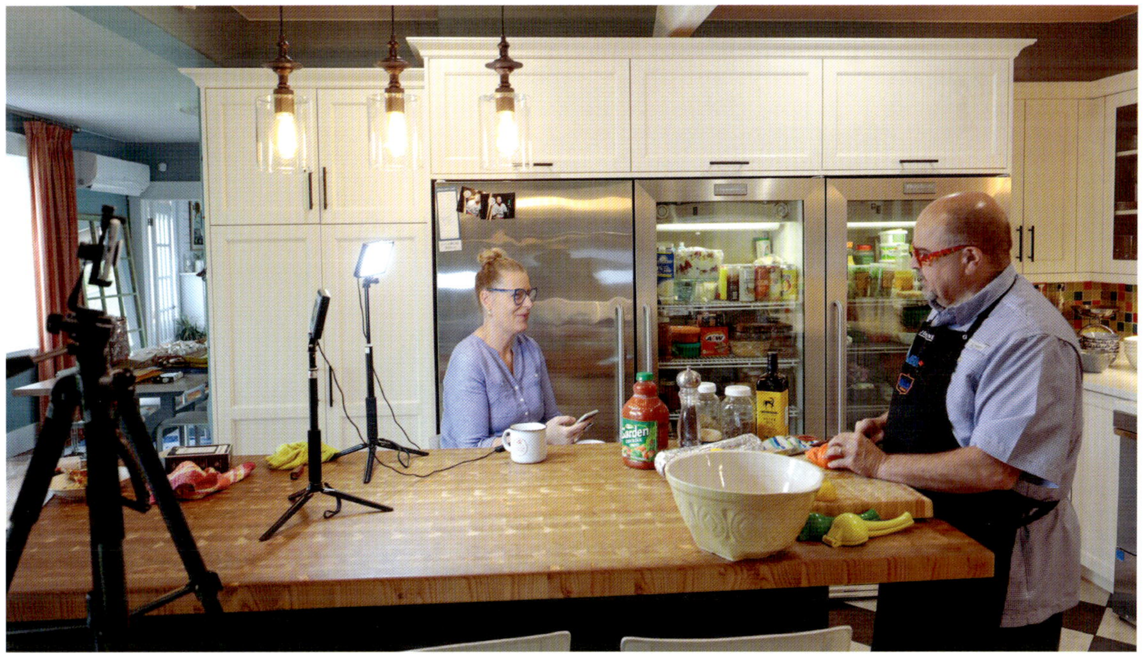

Alain Bossé, known as The Kilted Chef, and his wife, Johanne Hulshof Bossé, get geared up for another episode of the cooking show they live-stream from their kitchen in Pictou. The two started the show for friends and family and it has steadily gained popularity.

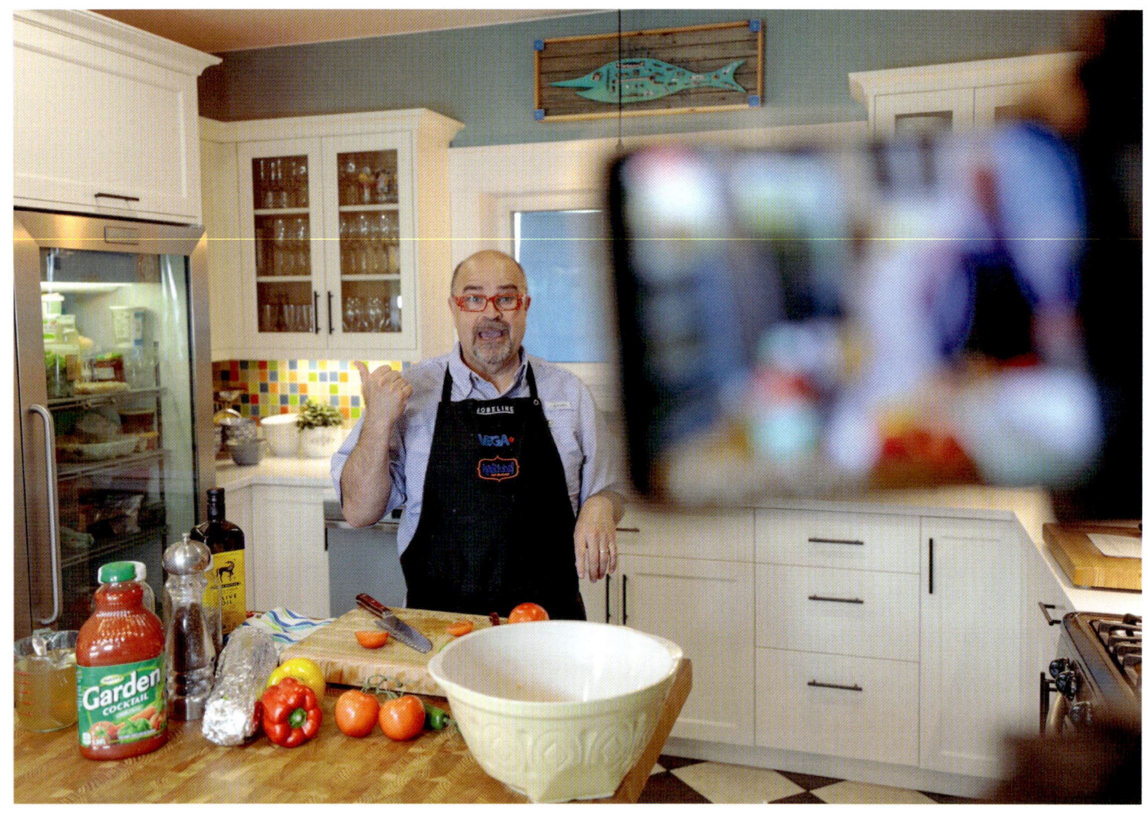

Alain presents The Kilted Kitchen.

live viewers, and they soon realized that, in combination with people who watched the shows after the fact, each episode was amassing around thirty thousand views. This thing they'd launched to give themselves an outlet and to help pass the time during the lockdown had turned their entire world around.

"Here's the funny part," says Johanne. "People think that we're helping them, [but] they're helping us. They've given us something to do. They've given us something to focus on. They've given us a purpose when really, other than loving our immediate family, we don't have a purpose right now."

"Exactly," says Alain. "It's basically turned our world around."

"Al has never spent this much time in our home since it was built ten years ago," says Johanne. "And here's the funny thing: this is kind of nice. We're liking this. We're living life."

Alain agrees. "I've gone from 150 miles an hour, constantly…travelling from one end of Atlantic Canada to the other, and doing that proudly. I love what I do," he says.

"Our little show is a purpose to wake up every morning. I mean, it's pretty amazing. And the three hundred, four hundred friends that are watching live every day and commenting, and the thirty thousand that view it, they have created a whole new fan base."

People have responded with appreciation. "Like, this nice lady just knocked on our door this morning and said, 'I left a treat—a bottle of wine,' and left. I don't even know who that person is!" laughs Alain.

"I go to the grocery store [now] and they're talking to me from three aisles down, you know? 'Is this the product you're talking about on the show?'

"It's very much humbling."

SURVIVAL BAKING

A lot of Nova Scotians worried that restrictions around COVID-19 might mean restricted access to basic staples—so they decided to learn the art of bread-making. Baking all kinds of sweets, including cakes and cookies, also proved to be an excellent (and delicious) way to pass the time.

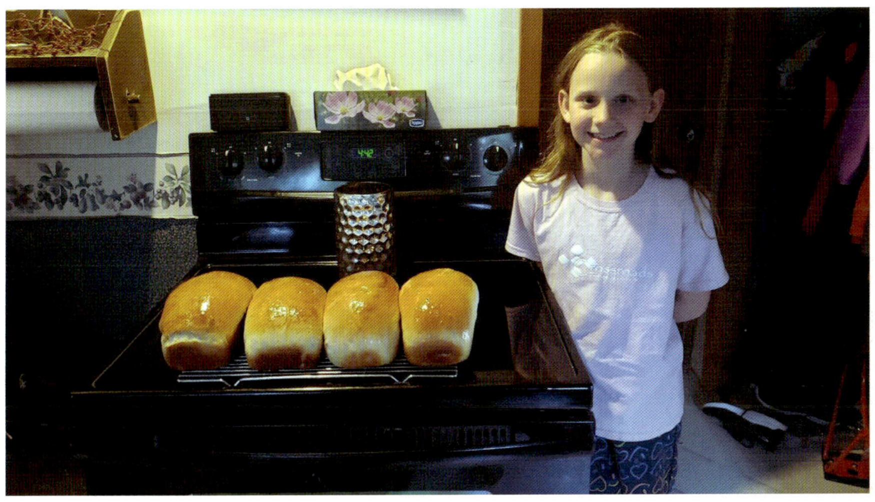

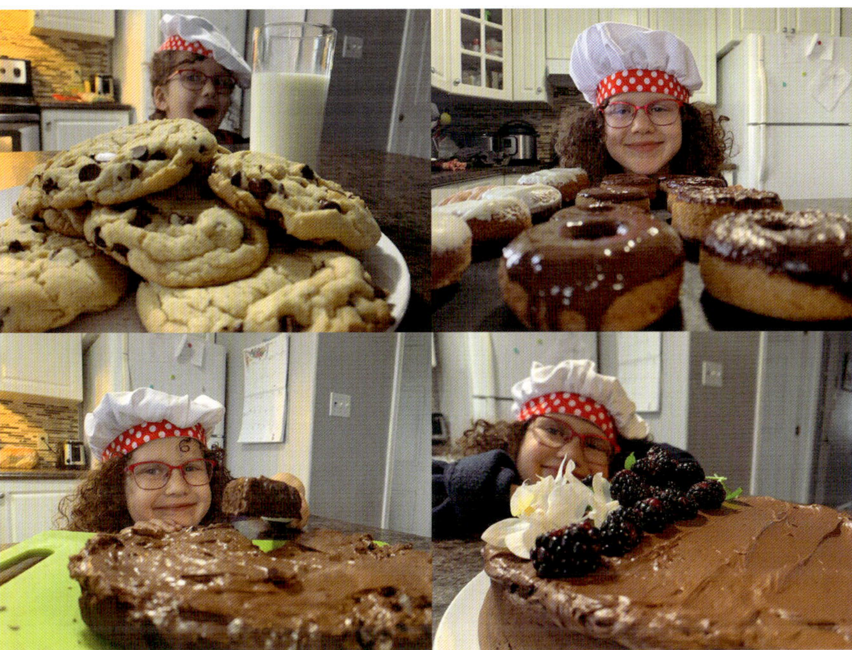

TOP LEFT AND BOTTOM RIGHT: *Isabelle Fraser, ten, and her brother Miles Fraser, seven, of MacPhersons Mills, NS, have enjoyed a bit of COVID baking. (Raylene Livingstone)*

BOTTOM LEFT: *Janice Smith's six-year-old daughter, Anika Gisler, of Bedford, NS, started a YouTube channel during the pandemic. (Janice Smith)*

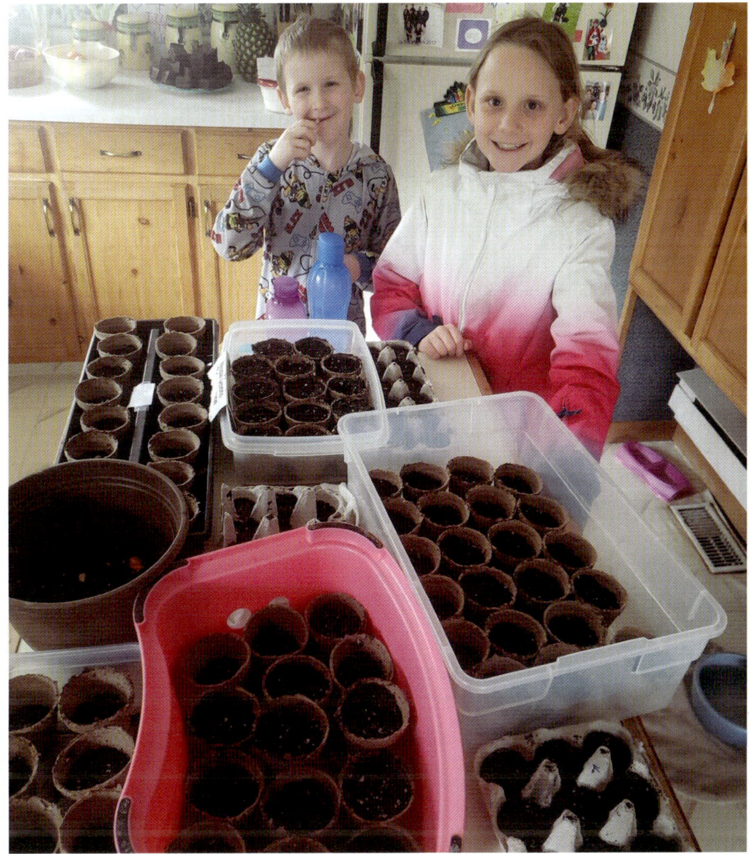

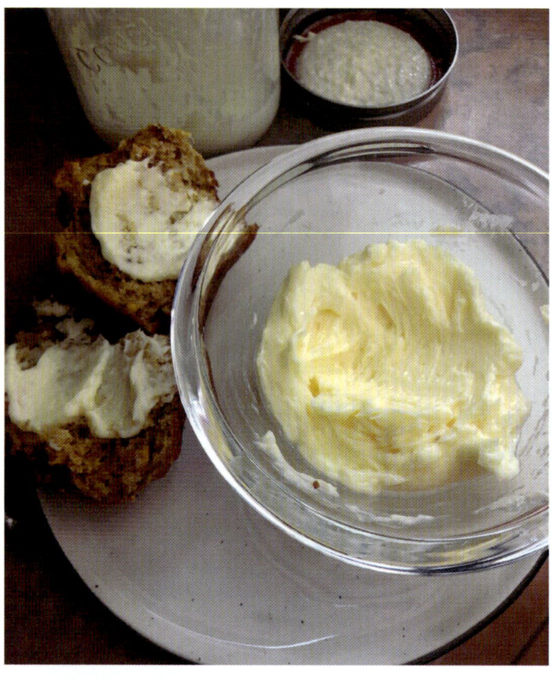

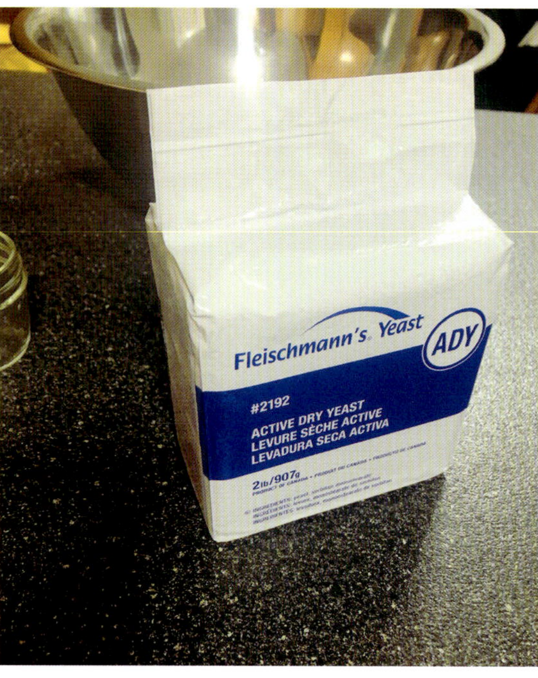

TOP LEFT: *Leanne Andrecyk of Halifax and her family explored the wonders of making their own butter during the lockdown. (Leanne Andrecyk)*

TOP RIGHT, BOTTOM LEFT AND RIGHT: *Allana Moore of Parrsboro, NS, took up a new hobby: collecting maple sap and making syrup. She says she also scored a huge package of yeast, which she shared with friends ("I was their yeast dealer," she laughs) and she tried lots of new recipes. (Allana Moore)*

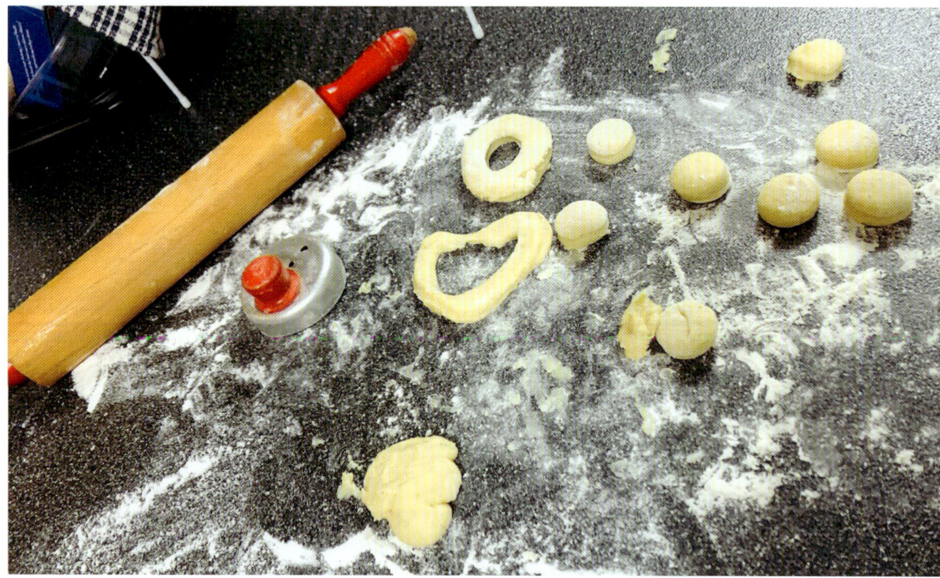

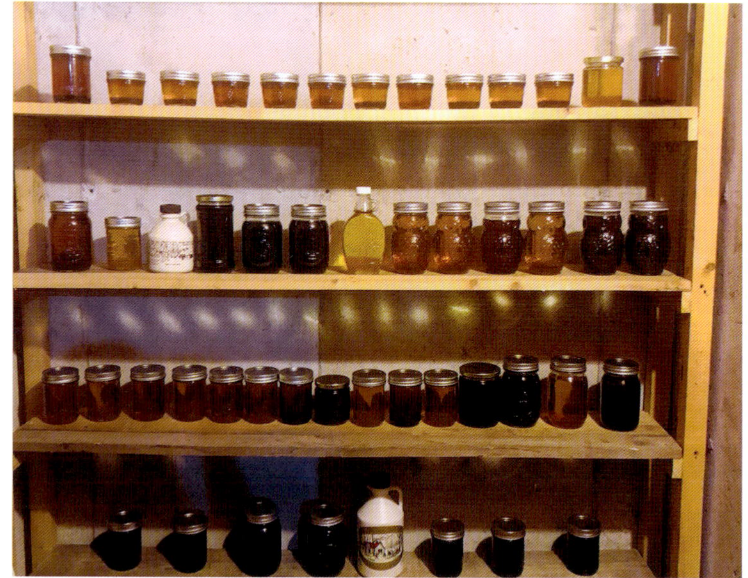

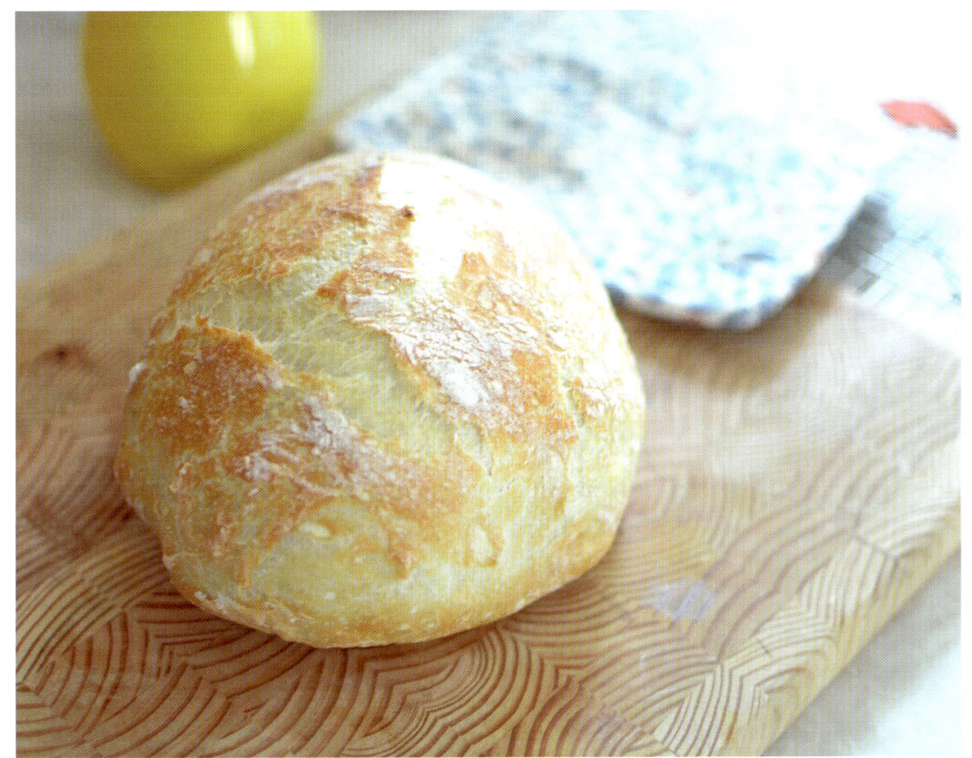

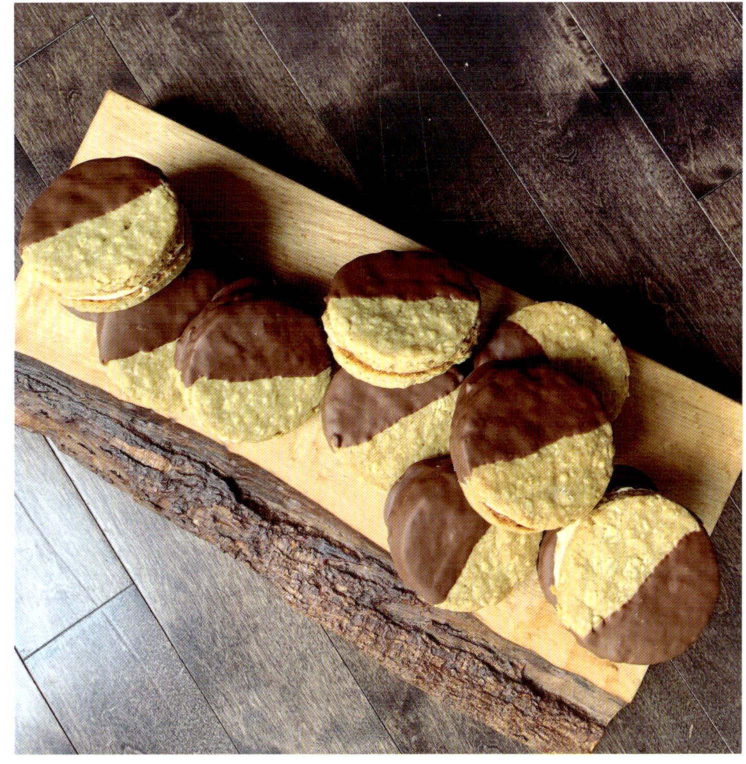

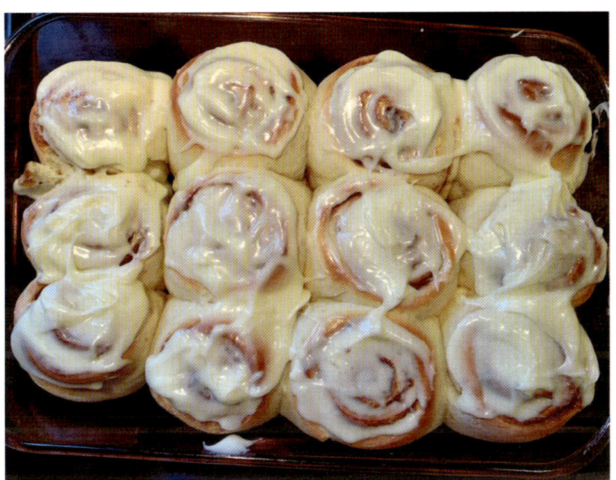

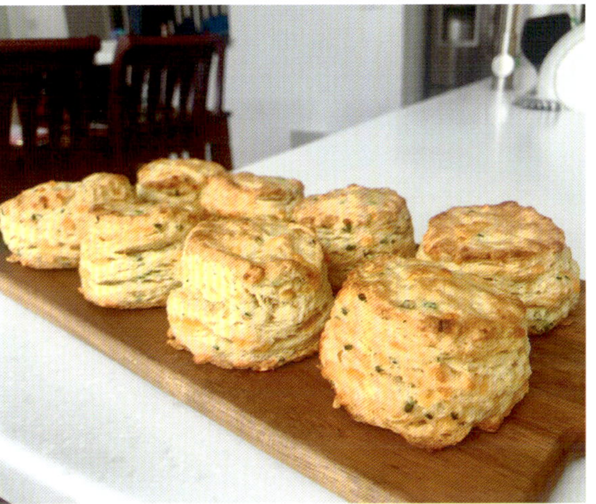

TOP LEFT: *Eight-year-old Violet Hirtle of Middle Sackville, NS, made her first loaf of bread during the pandemic. "It's a no-knead recipe," says her mother, Victoria Castle, "and it was delicious." (Victoria Castle)*

TOP RIGHT AND BOTTOM RIGHT: *Lindsay Cross of Bedford, NS, says trying new recipes made surviving the pandemic much easier. (Lindsay Cross)*

BOTTOM LEFT: *Catherine Williams of Dartmouth had to cancel a trip to Turks and Caicos because of the pandemic. Upside, maybe? Plenty of time to make these delicious-looking cinnamon buns. (Catherine Williams)*

CROSS-COUNTRY CHIN UP:
Adam Baldwin

"I needed to connect with other human beings," says singer-songwriter Adam Baldwin of Cross-Country Chin Up, his series of weekly live-streamed concerts that was born out of the COVID-19 lockdown. "I don't know how I would have gotten through this whole thing. I would have gone berserk."

It was early March when Adam started to see the bottom dropping out of his means of making a living. Restaurants, bars, and festivals were cancelling his appearances. Typically, he makes the bulk of his income from May through August; this year, the plan was for Adam to do solo gigs all over the Atlantic provinces, to perform with Matt Mays, and to perform with his band for the first time as an opening act for The Glorious Sons at Halifax's Scotiabank Centre.

"I just panicked a full-on panic," he says, when he realized his upcoming gigs were going to be cancelled. He called around to make sure his outstanding invoices were paid, then turned his mind to figuring out how he could continue to connect with his audience. "The only thing to do was to go on onto the internet," he says.

"You can either sit around and whine about it or figure out a way to feed your family. I got on my computer and tried to figure out ways to make broadcasts sound good—and that turned out to be way harder than me describing it," he says. "There's been a real learning curve. I'm still tinkering with stuff. I spend less time these days working on music and more reading about HDMI cables and all kinds of weird stuff," he laughs.

"But you know, I don't see my career going back to normal until there's a vaccine for this thing. I don't want to play in a building stuffed full of eight hundred

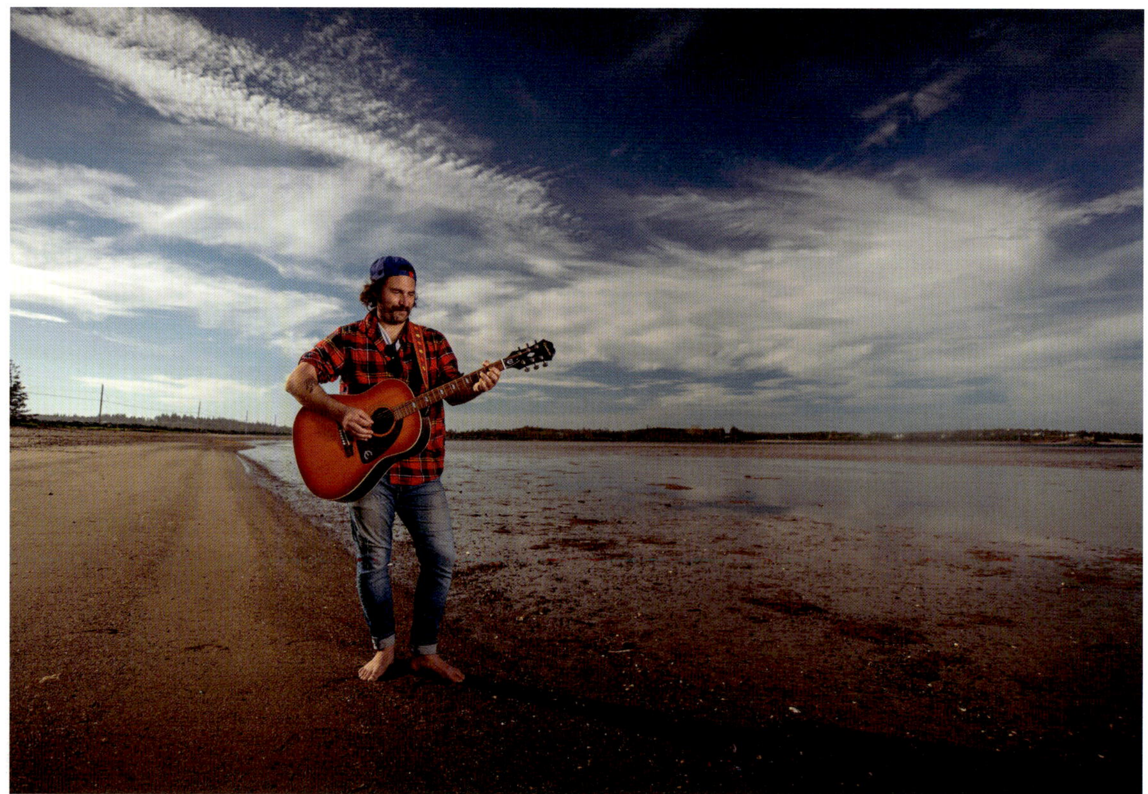

Musician Adam Baldwin created Cross-Country Chin Up to reach out to his audience and give them an "evening out" like they used to have.

people, and I wouldn't expect any of my fans to want to do the same thing, either."

Fortunately, Cross-Country Chin Up has turned out to be an excellent way to connect with his audience. Fans started tuning in to his YouTube channel every Friday night.

"I feel the same togetherness doing this weird thing on the internet that I feel in a room full of people," says Adam. "It's like a sixth sense or something—honest to God, I can feel everybody out there watching and engaging with it. They call their friends and they watch it together. It feels really good, and it feels normal to me—and everybody is looking for some semblance of normalcy."

Adam has been receiving positive feedback about the series since it began—messages, and even pictures of people dressed up for date-night during the lockdown. "It's really cool, man," he says. "I'm used to playing every weekend and, you know, I need this; it's not about the money really anymore. I'm feeding my family and I really love doing it!"

Adam says he's struggled over the years with drugs and alcohol, and now that he's not performing in bars every night, he's experiencing much less anxiety. "I don't have that general discomfort all the time now... because the choice has been made for me," he says. "That said, I miss the excitement of a live audience and that immediate response that only a bunch of people can give you."

The pandemic has had other upsides. "I have so enjoyed the time with my children and my partner, Jesse. It's been fantastic to have my kids around all day, every day, and... to teach them about what it is exactly that's happening. My parents never had to sit down and tell me why the entire world was shut down. It's given me an opportunity to teach them about empathy. The reasons we're not going out are not necessarily so that we don't get sick—it's so that we don't get other people sick," Adam says. "That's a big lesson for any anybody to learn, and not just a child."

He says if the pandemic has taught him anything, it's that we all need to connect with other human beings—and he's happy to keep doing his part with Cross-Country Chin Up.

"I feel like my duty is to kind of convene every Friday at nine and give folks a little bit of what Fridays used to be like."

A KITCHEN PARTY FOR ALL NOVA SCOTIANS

Like a lot of people living through the COVID-19 pandemic, Heather Cameron Thomson, who works as a residential counsellor at a group home in Pictou County, often relaxes after a long day of work by tuning in to musical performances online.

One day, while scrolling through Facebook, she happened upon a video of a friend of hers performing a song in his living room. "It made me feel a little bit better, and I scrolled a little bit further and came across another couple of friends of ours doing same thing," she says. "I thought, 'You know what? Why don't I just create a little group where we can all do that, and we can refer to it if we're … a little bit stressed and want a break or a distraction.'"

That distraction became a Facebook group called The Ultimate Online Nova Scotia Kitchen Party (Covid19 Edition), which now has 280,000 followers in over a hundred countries.

"It was never my intention that it would get to the point where it is," Heather says, adding that the group's success tells her a couple of things. "Number one is the power and the magic of music. [Number two is] that I wasn't the only person feeling … overwhelmed and stressed [about the] bombardment of negativity that was in the media and on social media."

As it grew, the group became a way for people to connect and come together. People danced, rapped, sang opera, and performed all kinds of music from their kitchens, living rooms, and front porches, and even from the great outdoors. Some spoke about their lives, their music, and their struggles. And just like a real Nova Scotia kitchen party, where friends

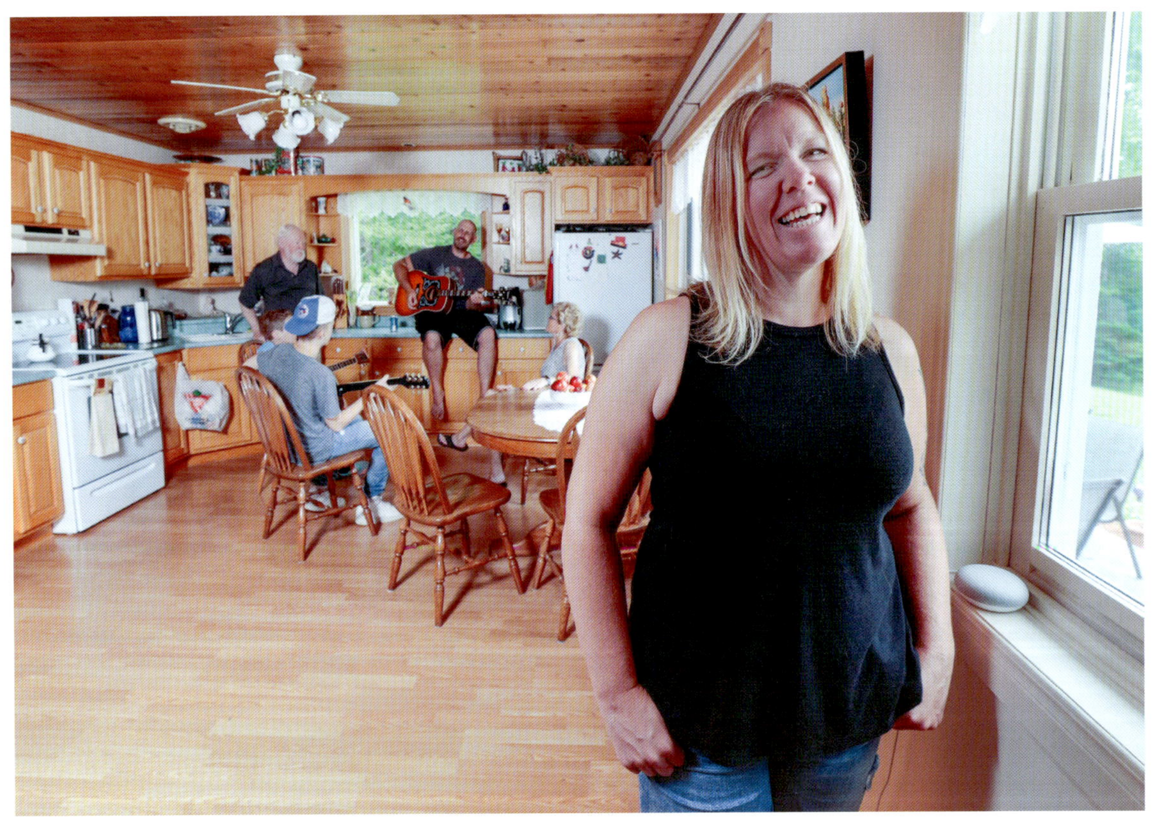

Heather Cameron Thomson shares a laugh as her family has a jam session in the background. Her creation, The Ultimate Online Nova Scotia Kitchen Party (Covid19 Edition), now has 280,000 followers in over a hundred countries.

might talk about their problems and others might chime in with advice, the people attending the online party did the same.

"There are people who are using this group to find support through their music, or even through commenting after they've listened to somebody perform or dance or whatever. They're supporting people who are going through some really, really hard times," Heather says, pointing out that some group members are dealing with the stresses around isolation, while others are dealing with substance abuse issues, PTSD, depression, or anxiety.

"We have one gentleman... he performs a song and he talks very openly in the preamble about what his struggle is for the day or if he's feeling good that day. And thousands of people are cheering for him. And that gives me goosebumps." Heather says there have been thousands of instances of people coming together to support others they have met through her page. "I find that the power of kindness has no boundaries," she says.

The Gillis family of Yarmouth has earned a sizeable following on the site. Barbara Gillis, her daughter, Catherine, fourteen, and son, John, eleven—no strangers to the "real" kind of kitchen party—first posted their rendition of "Big Yellow Taxi" at the request of relatives.

"I thought maybe we'd do one song. Maybe we'd do two, " says Barbara. "But then it started.... I literally now have a book with pages of requests and birthdays and anniversaries and memorials." And the requests have been coming in from all over the world.

"A lot of them are [from] Canadians who can't get home. [There are] people who are alone, who are stuck in isolation; they don't have a large family around them, they don't have a bubble like we have in this province," says Barbara, "so when they write to somebody and they write back, it just opens that door, and it's been really lovely. I've got a lot of pen pals."

And while there are thousands of performances on the page, one, in particular, stands out. It features Emily Tuck, the seventeen-year-old who, along with her parents, was senselessly gunned down during the mass shooting in Portapique, NS, just three weeks after her performance was posted to the page.

Dressed in plaid pyjama bottoms and a cropped top and standing in her family's living room, she plays a mournful air. Her performance ends with a flourish as Emily grins at the camera.

"There's some fiddle for ya," she laughs.

The post has more than five thousand shares.

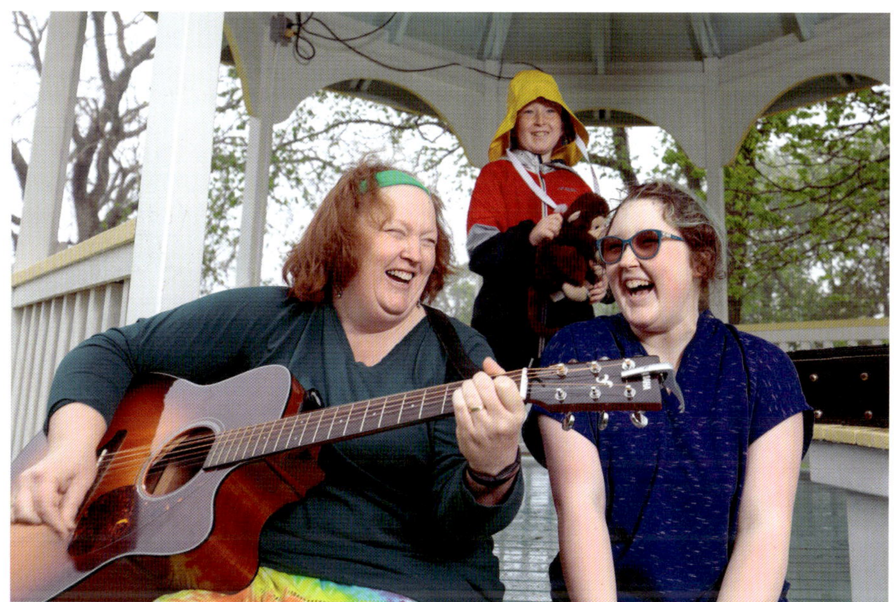

Barbara Gillis (front left), her daughter, Catherine, thirteen, and son, John, ten, play a tune at Frost Park in Yarmouth. Barb and Catherine's singing, and John's cameos, have made them a popular act on the Ultimate Online Nova Scotia Kitchen Party (COVID19 Edition) on Facebook.

COVID HAIR

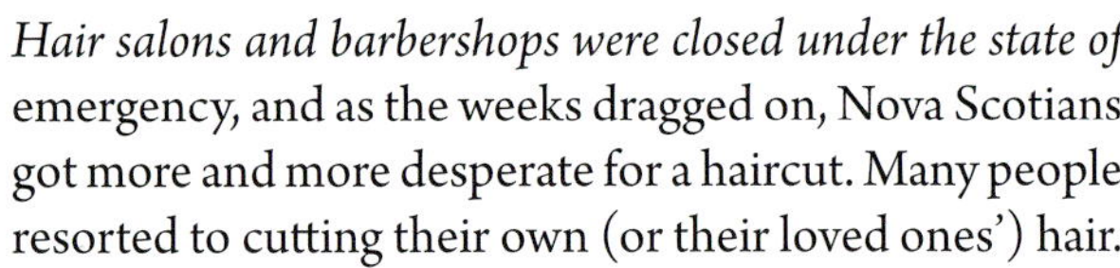

Hair salons and barbershops were closed under the state of emergency, and as the weeks dragged on, Nova Scotians got more and more desperate for a haircut. Many people resorted to cutting their own (or their loved ones') hair.

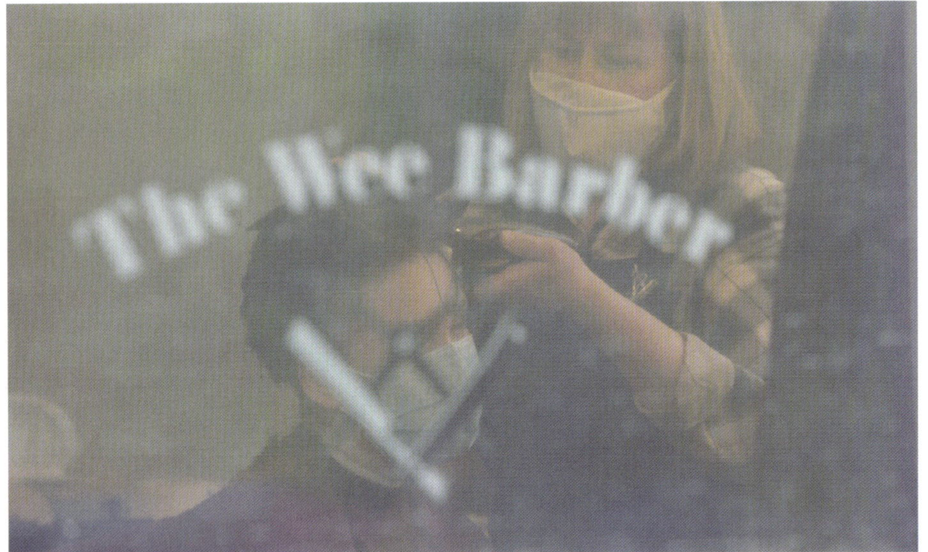

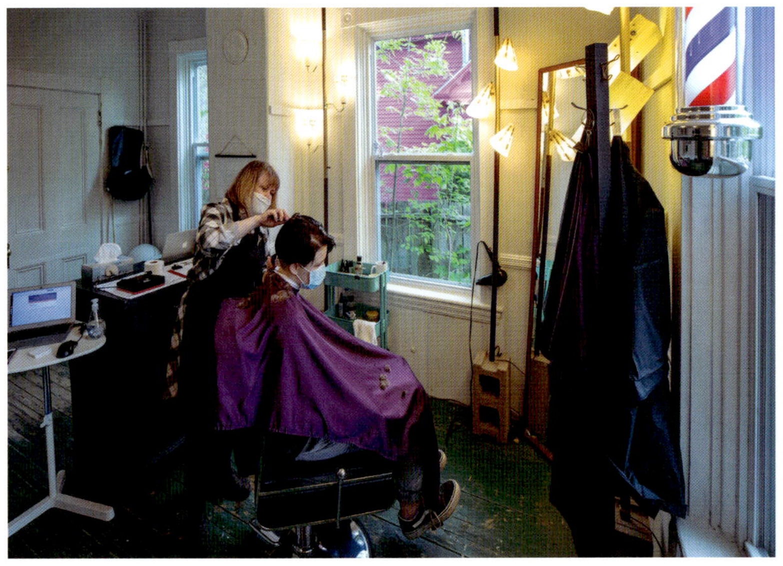

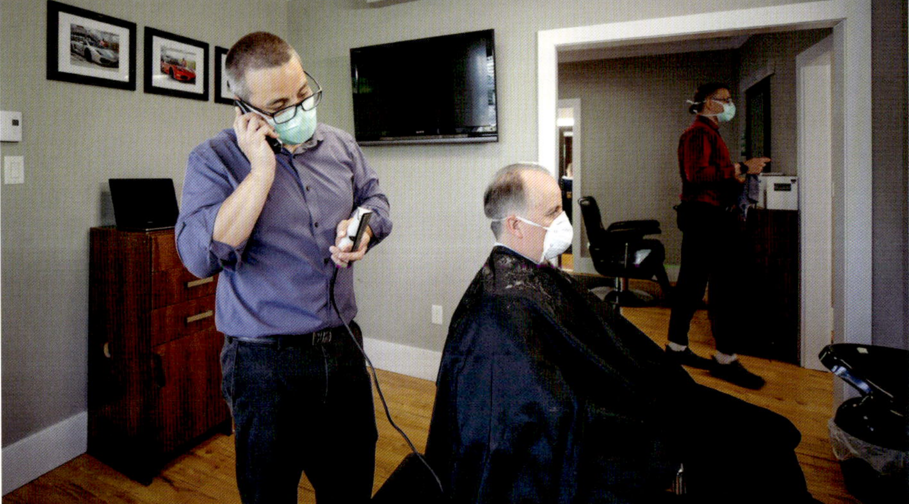

TOP LEFT AND TOP RIGHT: *Mahone Bay Barber Cheryl Stenstrom went back to work on June 5, when restrictions were eased, but discovered that she couldn't make a go of it under the new social distancing regulations. She made the decision to shut down the Wee Barber on July 31. She hopes to open in another form in the not too distant future.*

BOTTOM: *People were desperate to get a haircut after the shops had been closed for three months. John Skanes, owner of Tony's Barbershop in Bedford, multitasks cutting Barry Mason's hair while he answers his phone, which rang non-stop on June 5, his first day of reopening.*

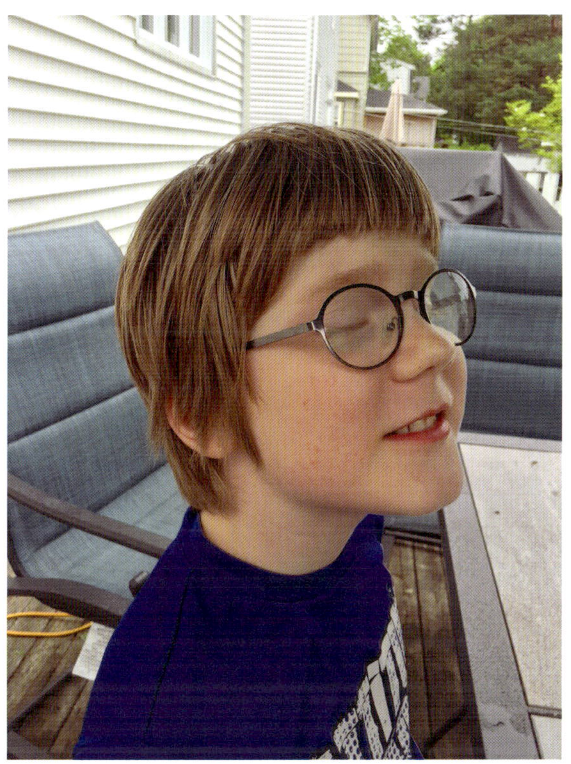

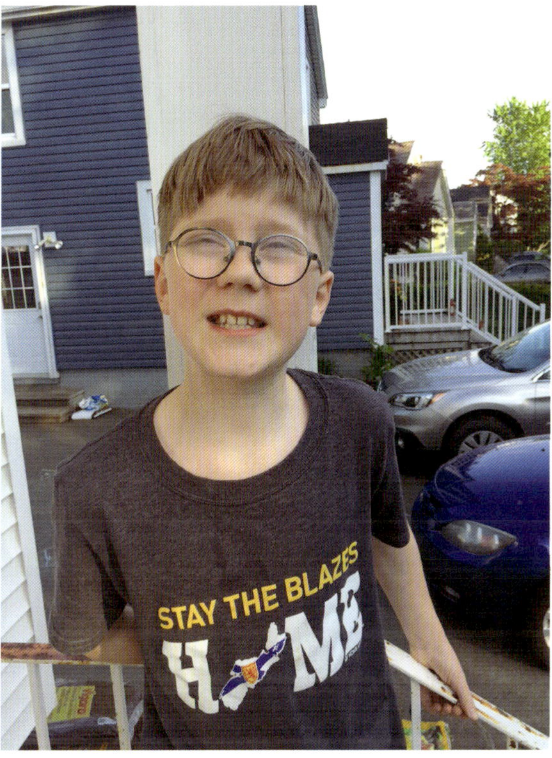

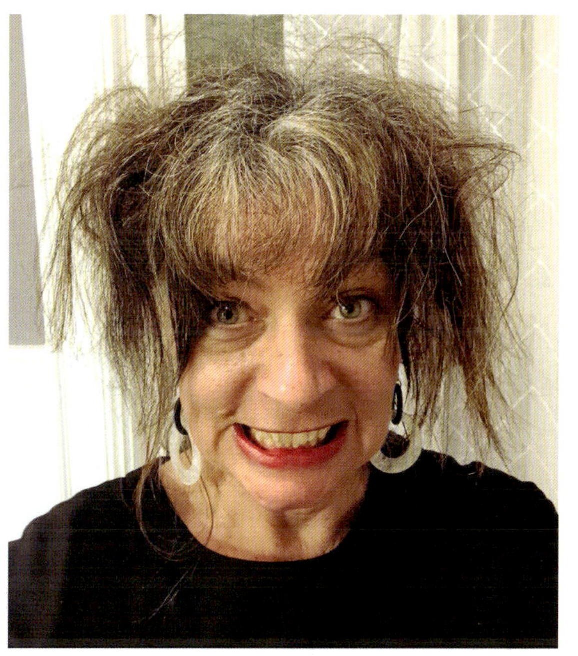

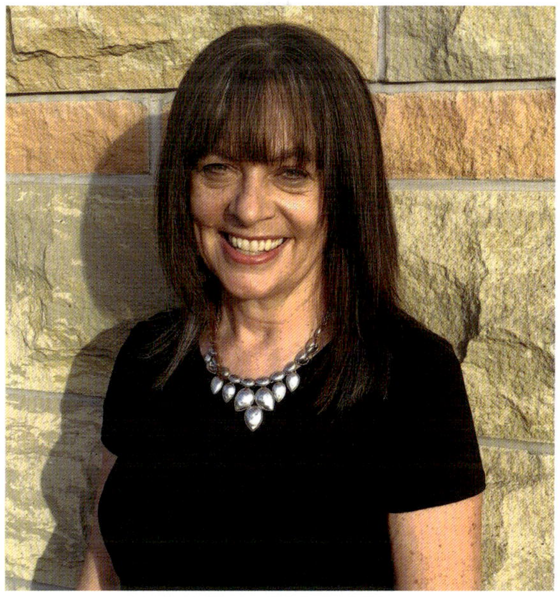

TOP LEFT AND TOP MIDDLE: *Eleven-year-old Owen Gillis of Halifax, pre- and post-haircut. His dad, John Gillis, cut his hair. "He'd grown pretty shaggy after a couple of months of COVID-quarantine," writes his dad, "and without the prospect of going to a barber at the time, he asked me to cut his hair—so I did that on the back deck, with clippers and scissors. [It was] the first time I'd attempted to cut hair." (John Gillis)*

TOP RIGHT AND BOTTOM RIGHT: *Terri McCulloch shows off the "before and after" from her haircut. Barbershops and hair salons were closed during the lockdown and had waiting lists to get back in after they reopened on June 5. Terri had to wait until late July for her appointment. (Terri McCulloch)*

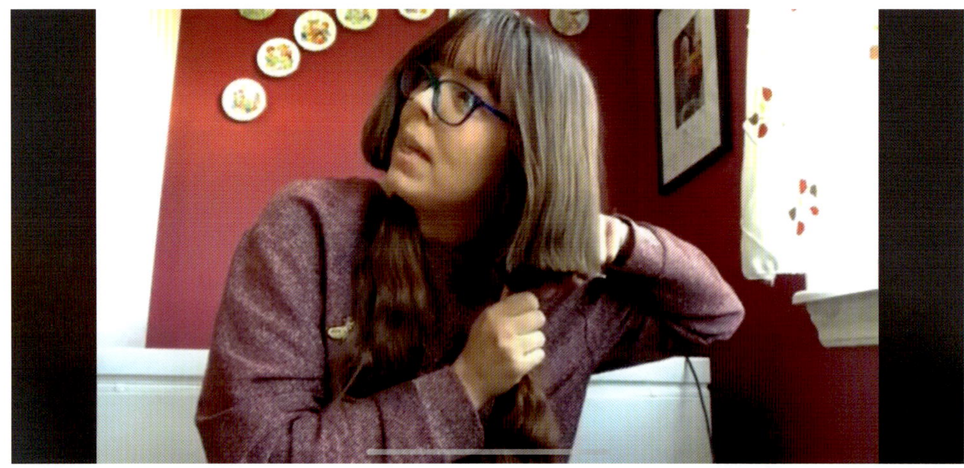

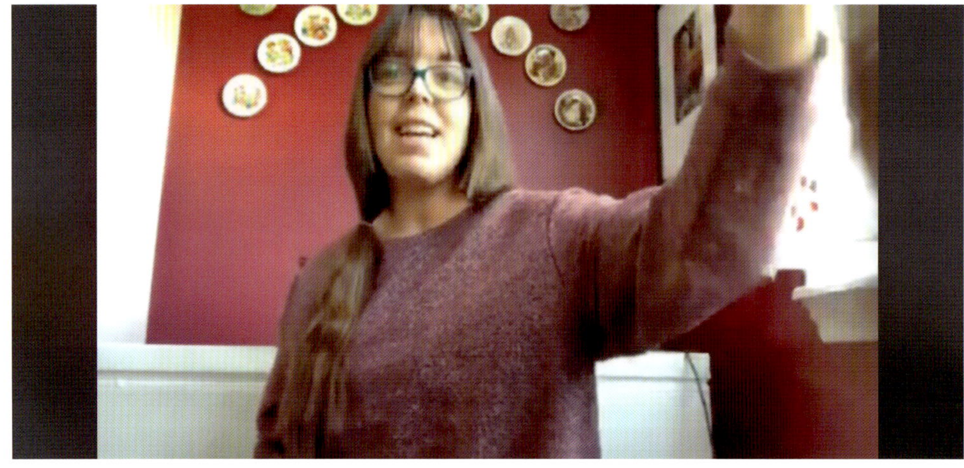

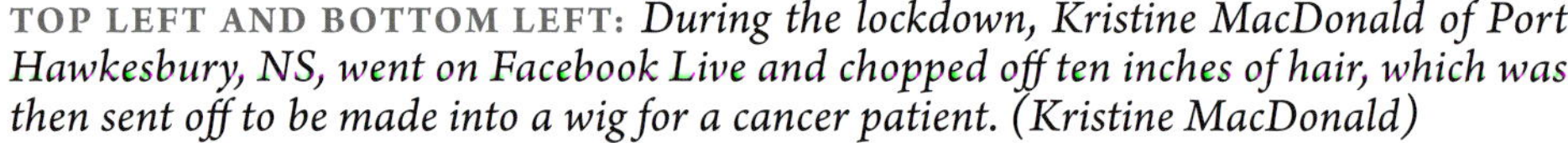

TOP LEFT AND BOTTOM LEFT: *During the lockdown, Kristine MacDonald of Port Hawkesbury, NS, went on Facebook Live and chopped off ten inches of hair, which was then sent off to be made into a wig for a cancer patient. (Kristine MacDonald)*

TOP RIGHT: *A COVID home haircut by Lindsay Watters of Halifax. (Lindsay Watters)*

BOTTOM RIGHT: *Lindsay Watters even dared cut her dog's hair. (Not sure how the dog felt about it!) (Lindsay Watters)*

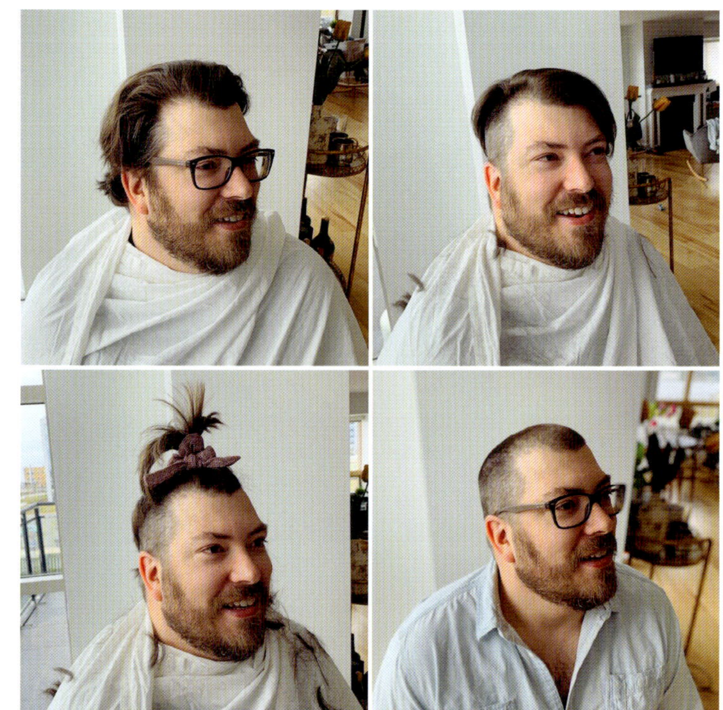

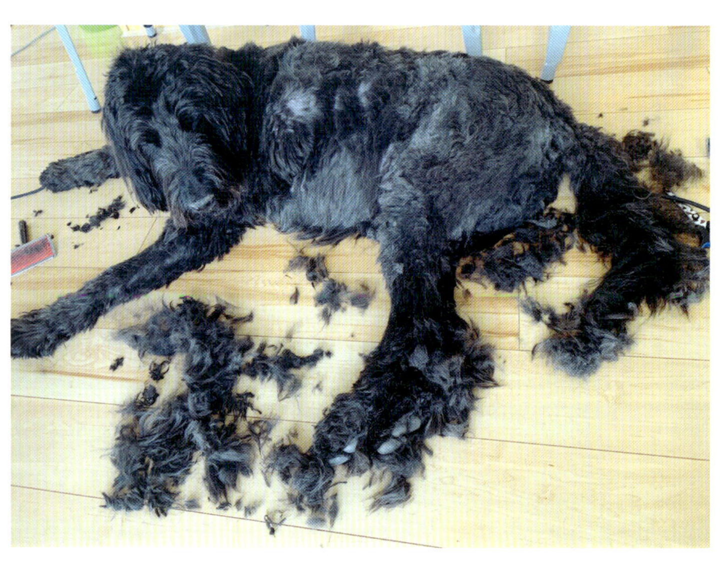

TO SAIL OR NOT TO SAIL:
Bluenose II

Captain Phil Watson has always set his internal calendar by the activity around the waterfront in Lunenburg, NS. Every year, from April 1 to mid-October, seven days a week for thirty years, he has been aboard the famed schooner *Bluenose II*, either as a member of the crew or as the captain. That schedule went out the window this year because of COVID-19.

With the global shutdown, the work of getting the ship rigged and ready to sail had come to a halt. Normally, the crew would have been sanding, varnishing, and learning how every inch of rope works on the schooner before they set sail at the end of May, just as the lobster pots were coming out of the water.

That hadn't happened—until the crew devised a plan to create a crew "bubble" that would allow the twenty-person crew to come together for training, maintenance, and to sail the vessel this season. Visitors would not be permitted aboard and there would be no cruises with passengers. That meant the ship could still visit communities along coastal Nova Scotia, where the significance of the ship is larger than the ship itself.

And they made it happen: *Bluenose II* departed Lunenburg in late July and visited twenty-six Nova Scotia communities. The ship also sailed along parts of the coast of New Brunswick and Prince Edward Island but did not dock in any ports.

"A schooner is an end product of the people of the province. It doesn't just show up at the end of

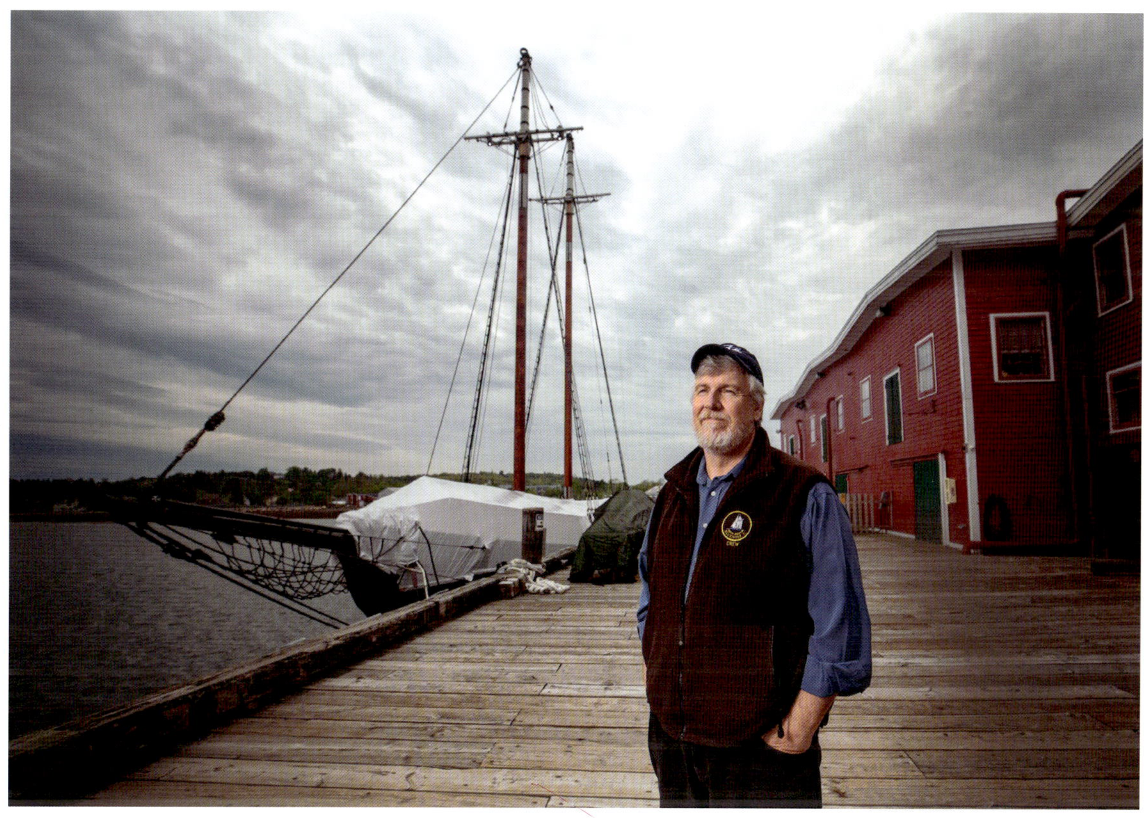

Captain Phil Watson stands in front of the Bluenose II. *The schooner was still docked in early June, a time when Phil and his crew would normally have been getting ready for a busy season. Fortunately, a plan was created in July that allowed the ship to safely sail along parts of the coasts of New Brunswick, Nova Scotia, and Prince Edward Island.*

the wharf," Phil says. "I absolutely feel that I've been entrusted with this piece of Canadian history... and that's not just the sailing; that's Ross Farm, where the lumber came from. It's Sydney, where the coal came from. It's the blacksmiths who made all this stuff," he says.

"A place like Lunenburg or Whitehead or Canso—that's their community history, right there. They just know that [for] their grandfathers or great-grandfathers... it was the way of transport, it was the way of gaining food, it was the way that goods came and went; it was everything to those communities."

And as important as the ship is to people in coastal communities, it also plays an important part in the lives of the crew.

"They don't all go on to be mariners, but... if you succeed on the ship, then you're going to be good at whatever it is that you choose to do," Phil says. "They'll take that [experience] and that'll be part of their life story."

In July and August 2020, the schooner once again become a part of the life stories of Nova Scotians.

"This Canadian icon, it's incredible—and to be captain of that?" says Phil. "I always say that [my job is] equivalent [to] driving the Statue of Liberty around."

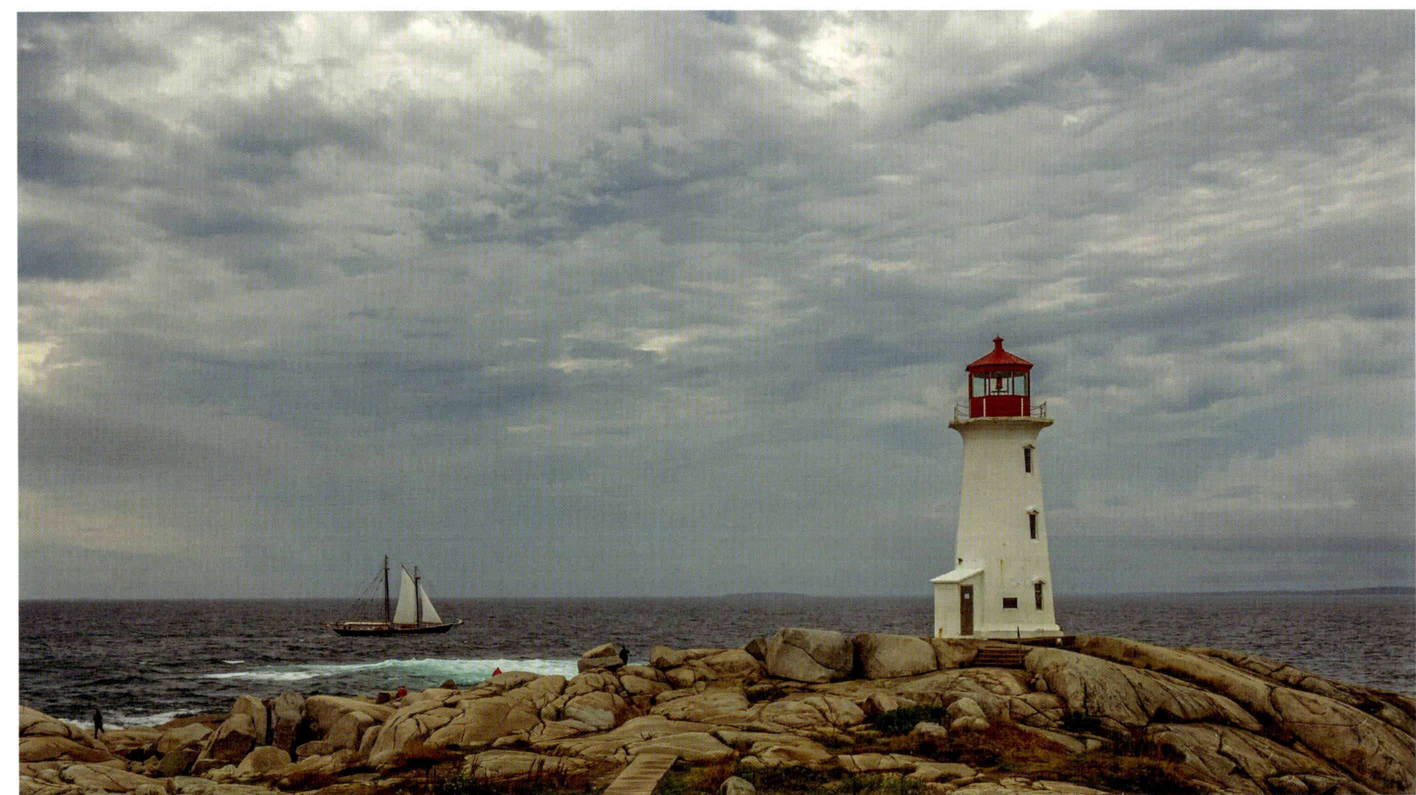

Bluenose II *under partial sail at Peggys Cove on its way to Lunenburg, September 2020. (Marleigh Leaman)*

A GUEST HOME WITHOUT GUESTS:

Bailey House, Annapolis Royal

Suzan Hebditch was enjoying a celebratory birthday lunch with friends in January 2020 when it dawned on her that something big was happening in the world. Hebditch is the innkeeper at the Bailey House Bed & Breakfast, a guest house situated in a classic Georgian home in Annapolis Royal.

"We were talking about how only in China could you lock down a city larger than the size of Canada—at least, population-wise—and build this hospital that they were building," she recalls, referring to the Huoshenshan hospital, which was reportedly built in just ten days in Wuhan, China, to treat coronavirus patients. "It was amazing and impressive."

By February, Suzan began to see a decrease in reservations at her business—an indication of the storm that was about to hit the hotel industry. She was growing concerned that the pandemic might have an effect on Annapolis Royal, a historic town with a huge stake in the tourism industry because of its wide, tree-lined streets, artisans' shops, bistros, and massive multi-century homes, many of which have been turned into tourist accommodations.

"Friday the thirteenth, that was it," she says. "I stopped everybody after that, or they stopped themselves. I haven't taken any guests since the night of March 14."

Over the next two months, with travel restrictions in place, a state of emergency, and news of a worsening pandemic in the United States, her business virtually shut down.

"Nobody was calling; that was it. Anybody that had a reservation was cancelling, and if they hadn't

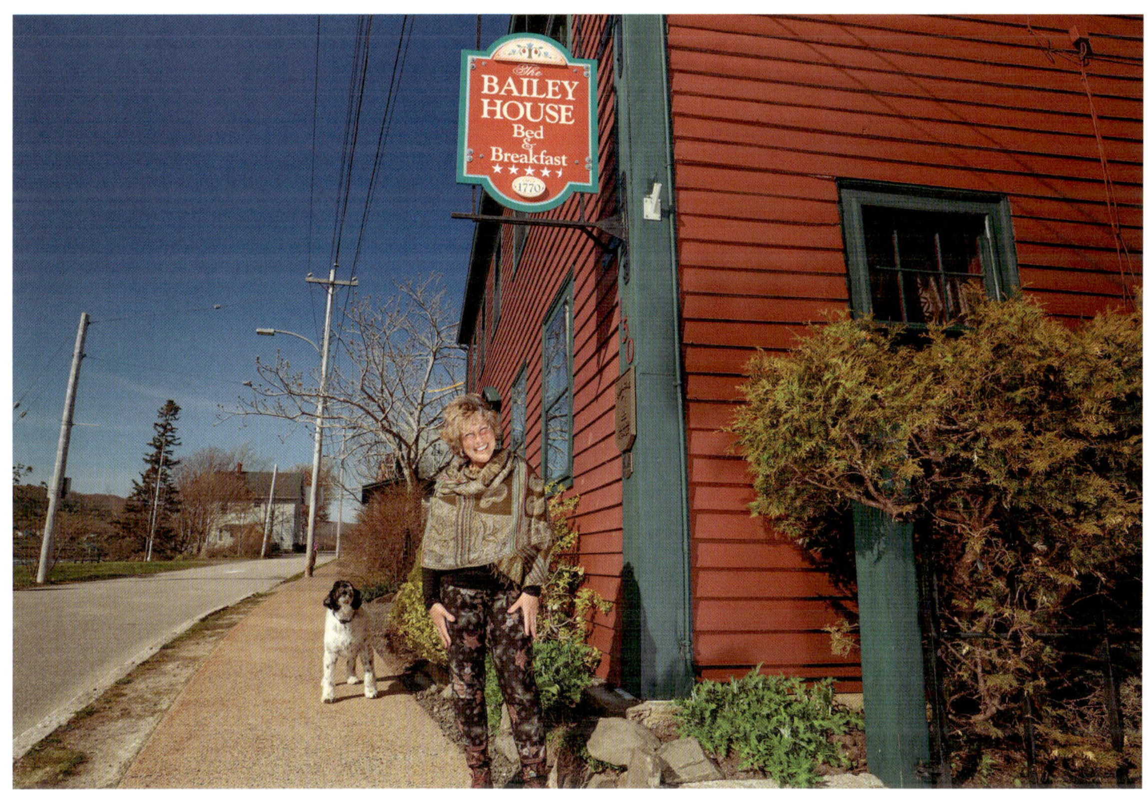

Suzan Hebditch and her dog Lucy stand in front of The Bailey House Bed & Breakfast in Annapolis Royal. Suzan's business was hit hard by the closure of the Canadian–American border and the shutdown of the travel industry.

cancelled, I contacted them and said, 'You can't even get into the province, so you've got to cancel.'"

Some future guests, mostly those from the US, were not aware of the restrictions and thought their trips were still possible. They weren't.

"June is a bust; it feels pretty awful," Suzan says. "I'm approaching hundreds of nights of cancellations right through to September."

It's devastating, but while Suzan worries about her own business, it's the larger picture that keeps her up at night. "I mean, for the economy, right? I'm such a small player in such a small piece of all this. Tourism is huge; there's bigger fish to fry in terms of the international border with the US. How do we stay safe? How do we make sure our guests are safe and feel safe?"

She is proud of the way her community has stepped up in terms of self-isolating and social distancing. "People have been very serious about it in this town. I have friends that go nowhere. They stay home and no one comes in. It's a little town; everything's closed, restaurants are closed," she says. "I miss having people come around—my friends, not paying guests."

For now, she sees the upside—at least in terms of the environment. "I think I'm seeing more stars at night. When you sit out here, it's unbelievable—no planes," she says. "I think Mother Nature is healing, and I think that's a wonderful thing for her."

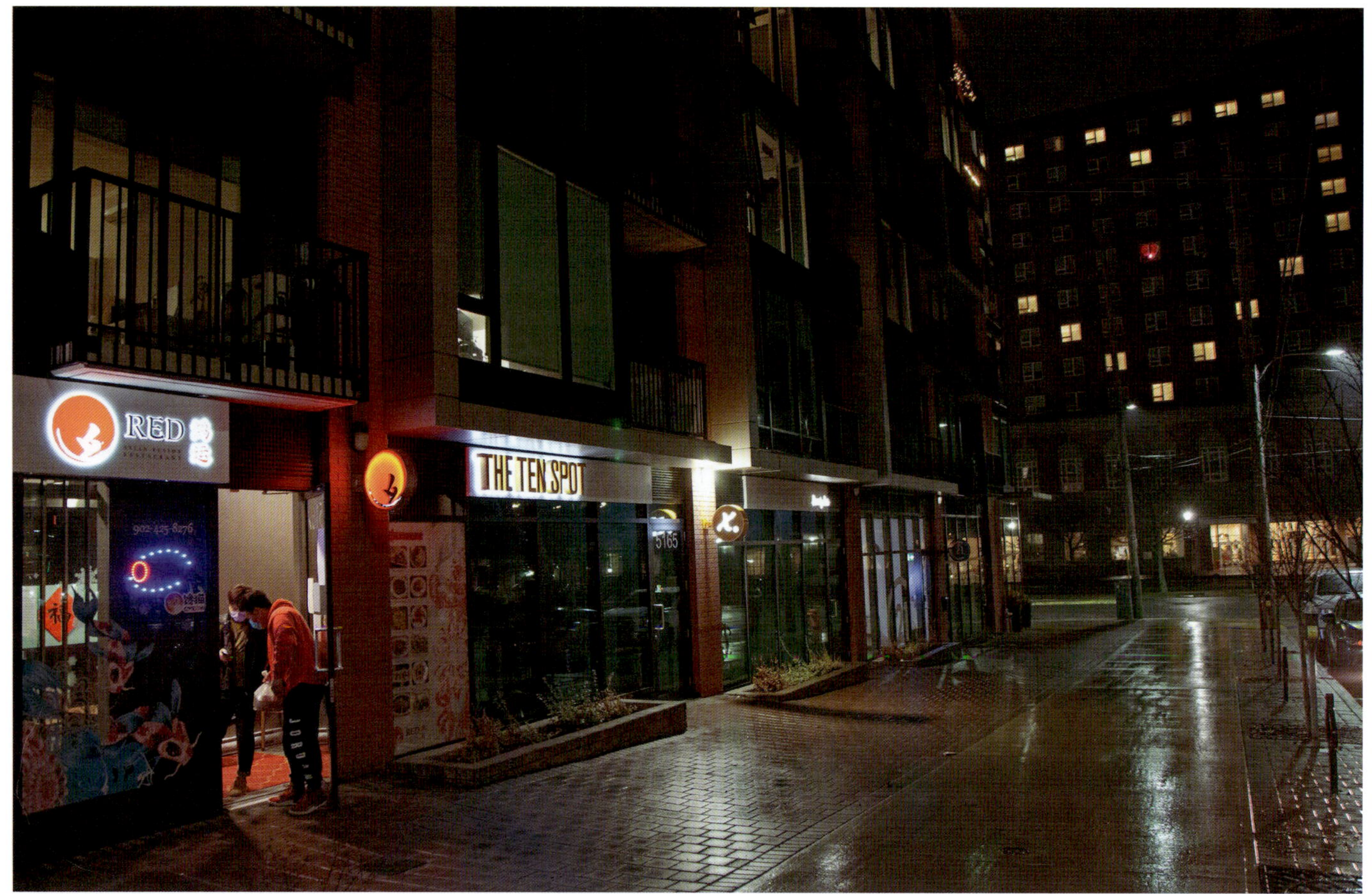

When the COVID-19 pandemic virtually stopped people from travelling, hotel occupancy rates in Canada dropped below 80 percent. To show support for health-care workers in Halifax, the Westin Hotel lit up its empty rooms so the windows formed the shape of a heart. (Tim Krochak)

BOOKS ON BIKES:
Bookmark

Behind locked doors a clockwork military-style operation is taking place: Erica Flake, kneeling, helmet in hand, goes over a map. Her backpack is stuffed with packages, their addresses in sequential order. The "general," Mike Hamm, stands behind a computer screen, a phone in his hand, while another co-worker unloads boxes in a corner.

This is not the bunker of a paramilitary operation; it's the Bookmark bookstore on Halifax's Spring Garden Rd. The shop has been closed to the public for weeks, but the rush inside makes it clear the business is very much open.

"We wanted to do the best that we could for our community because we knew that people would want books to read," says Mike, who manages the store.

As Nova Scotians' televisions and electronic devices delivered bad news day after day, the people at Bookmark soon realized that they could offer an escape—and that it could be just a phone call away. They decided to offer curbside pickup, shipping by mail, and even bicycle deliveries as a new way to reach customers. And business has been booming.

"The phones are ringing when we start our day, and the phones are ringing when we close. It's that type of intense support from the reading neighbourhood that we're getting," says Mike.

"We've been shipping to Newfoundland, we've been shipping to Ontario—rural Ontario, they can't get certain books where they are. Shipping is a whole

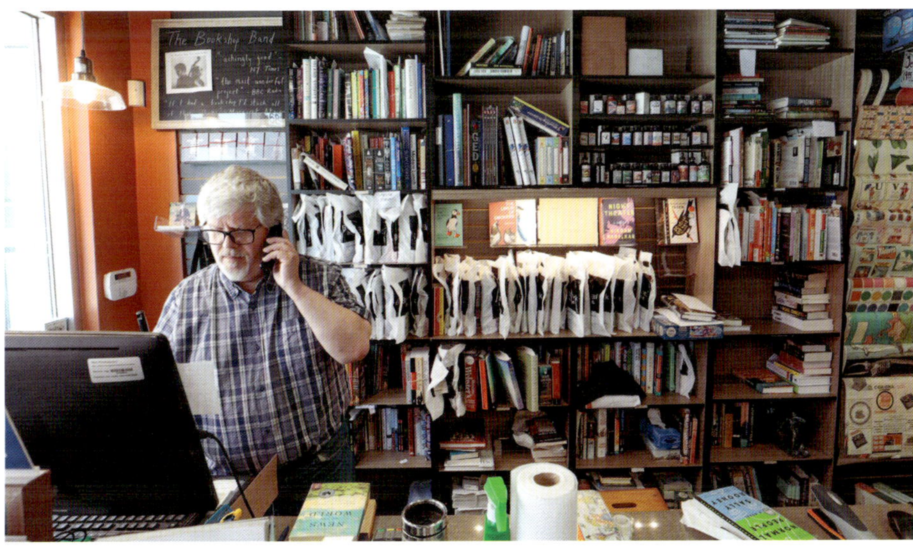

Manager Mike Hamm takes calls while organizing pickup orders at Bookmark on Spring Garden Rd. in Halifax.

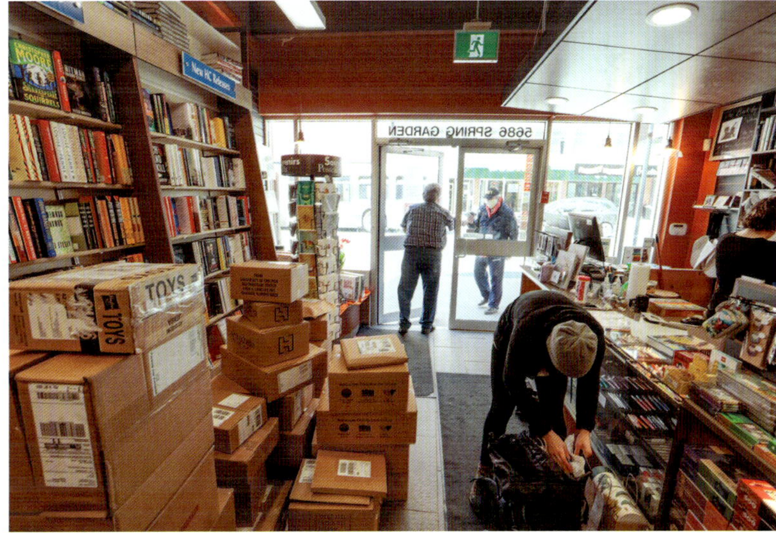

Erica Flake organizes her delivery route as she prepares for a day of delivering books on her bicycle.

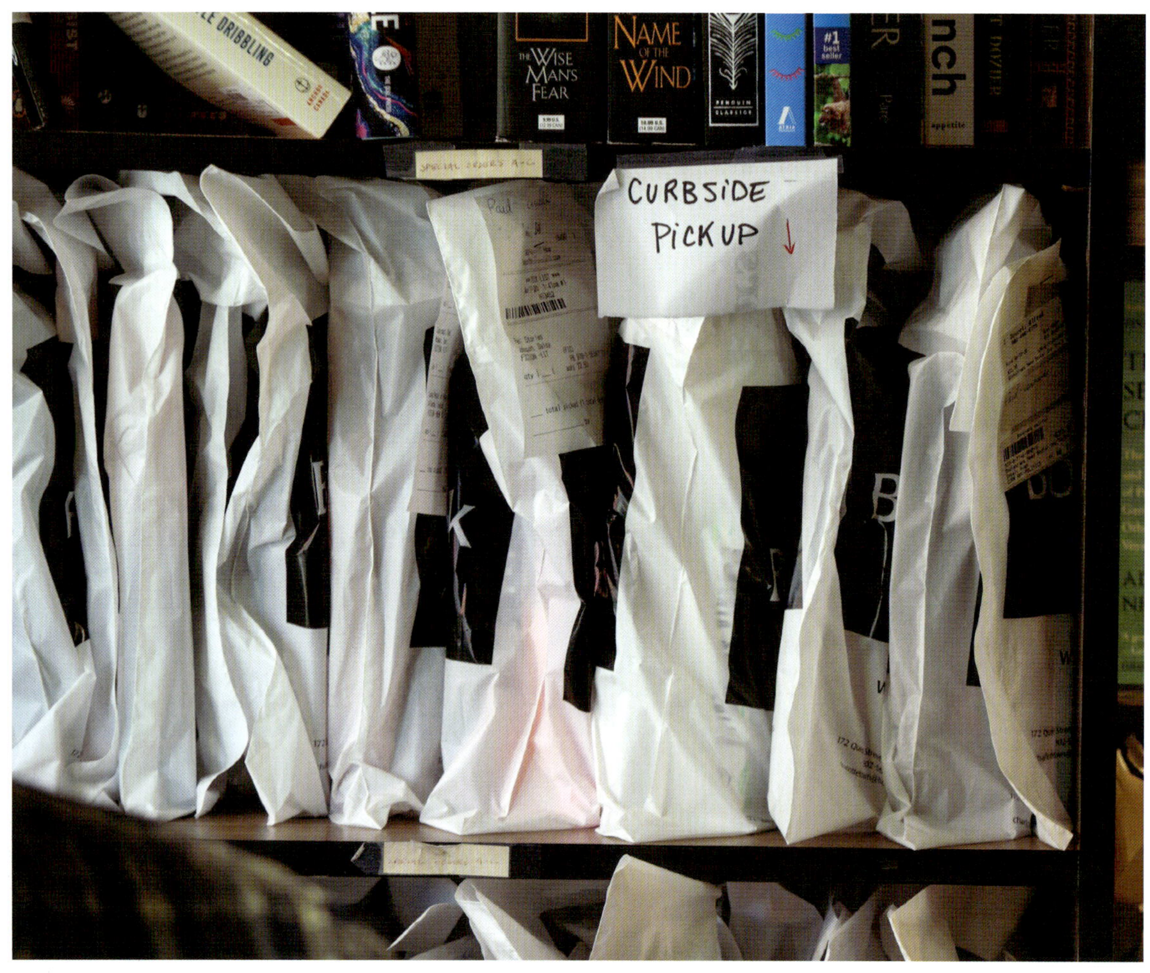

Books ready for curbside pickup at Bookmark in Halifax.

new avenue for us. Before the pandemic we had a web store for over two years. People used it marginally, but when this happened, it just exploded. We're really, really, gratefully surprised," he says.

He says people find solace in books. "It's the direct connection. It's the *holding* as book lovers. We understand it's the look of the book, it's the feel of the book, the smell of the ink on the book. It's all of these very tactile things that creates a very, very close bond. It's a personal, intimate connection that printed books make with people. And it's something you can do all by yourself and anywhere."

Mike has been working in bookstores for close to thirty years. "I could never think of a life without books. For people who I thought were maybe casual readers, [the pandemic has] brought the message home that they find them an essential thing—not necessarily like shelter, food, and clothing, but for mental health and for educational purposes."

The reading community has responded in kind to the services Bookmark has provided. Customers have been dropping off food and trays of sweets to show their appreciation for staff.

We just had a lady bring in a tin of baked cookies," says Mike.

"It's community-building, and that's what an independent bookstore does.... It just makes our job so fulfilling."

BURSTING THE BUBBLE

On May 15, the province introduced "the immediate family bubble," which allowed two immediate family households to come together without physical distancing. The change meant some families and friends within Atlantic Canada could finally come together—and hug.

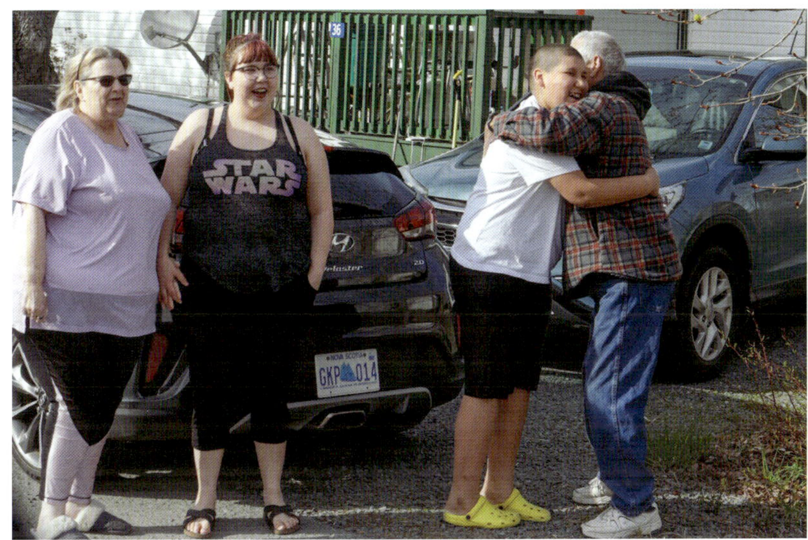

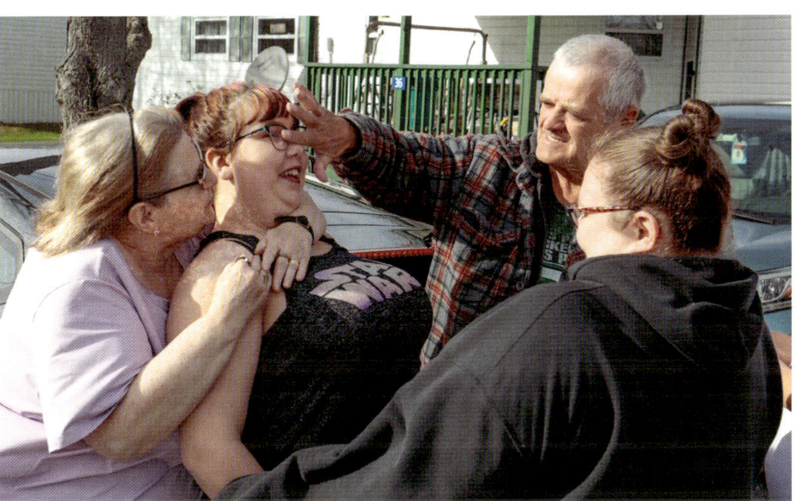

TOP LEFT: *Elijah Rayner-Paris gives his grandfather, Kendall Rayner, a hug as grandmother, Jayne (far left), and sister, Kendra, look on.*

BOTTOM LEFT: *Kendra Rayner gets a hug from her grandmother, Jayne Rayner (far left), as her grandfather, Kendall Rayner, has some fun with her. Her mom, Jean Rayner-Paris, looks on at right*

RIGHT: *The first sixty seconds after a sixty-day wait to share some hugs. Photographer Steve Wadden's parents reunite with him and his family on Sunday, May 17, after being physically separated for two months due to COVID-19 distancing restrictions. Pictured, clockwise from top left, are Steve Wadden's nephew Joseph MacDonald, ten, and his son William Wadden, three, painting a welcome sign on the window; Steve's parents, Wilma and Barry Wadden, greeting William (in the striped shirt) and Joseph; Steve's wife, Emily Wadden, hugging Barry as Wilma hugs Joseph; and Barry hugging William. (Steve Wadden)*

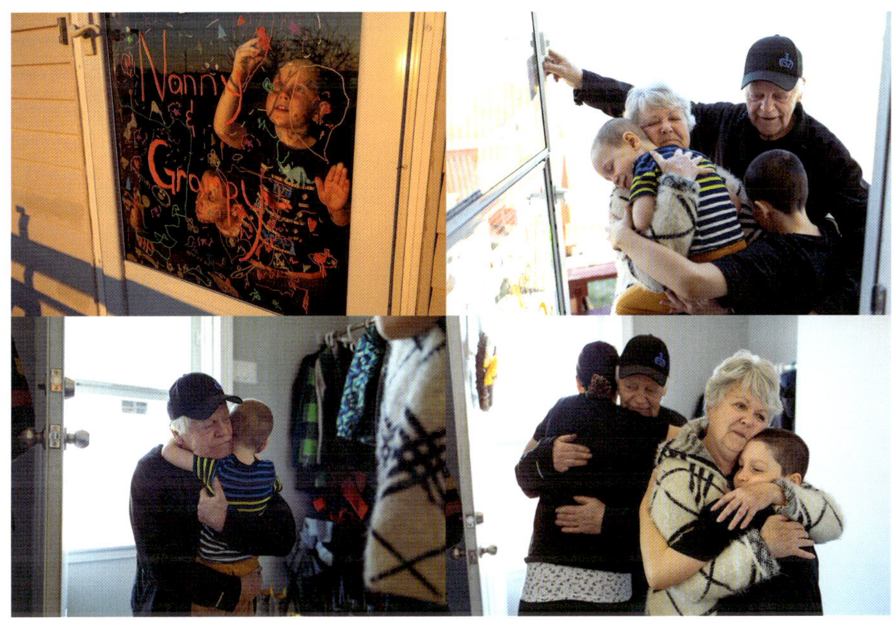

TAKING WINE ONLINE:
Lightfoot & Wolfville

As Michael Lightfoot talks, he gazes over the gently rolling lands his family has farmed for seven generations—the very farm in Upper Wolfville where he grew up as a child, learning bushcraft on his grandmother's property, and "living his boyhood dream."

Today, that dream means running a successful vineyard with his wife, Jocelyn, and his daughters Rachel, Kori, and Michaela (the couple also has a daughter, Meadow, who is too young to be involved in the business yet). The Lightfoot & Wolfville vineyard is currently a scraggly brown where winter has yet to give way to spring and the promise of a good season. Above, the blue sky is streaked with high clouds as the red cliffs of Blomidon shine in the distance.

But the usual Saturday flow of people enjoying a lunch from the giant stone pizza oven, or browsing over the display of their award-winning wines, is nowhere to be found.

The vineyard, like every other, has been shut down under the state of emergency. There is little traffic along Highway 1.

The Lightfoot team had spent all winter coming up with a new business plan to figure out how to draw more people and get more diverse events happening at the vineyard, but the pandemic threw a wrench into all that. "How are we going to take care of our large event business?" he wonders. "What are we going to do in 2020? What's 2021 look like? How are we going to pivot? How are we going to take advantage of all this traffic that comes through here? We worked our guts out all winter to come up with these beautiful plans, and then we went away on a nice vacation."

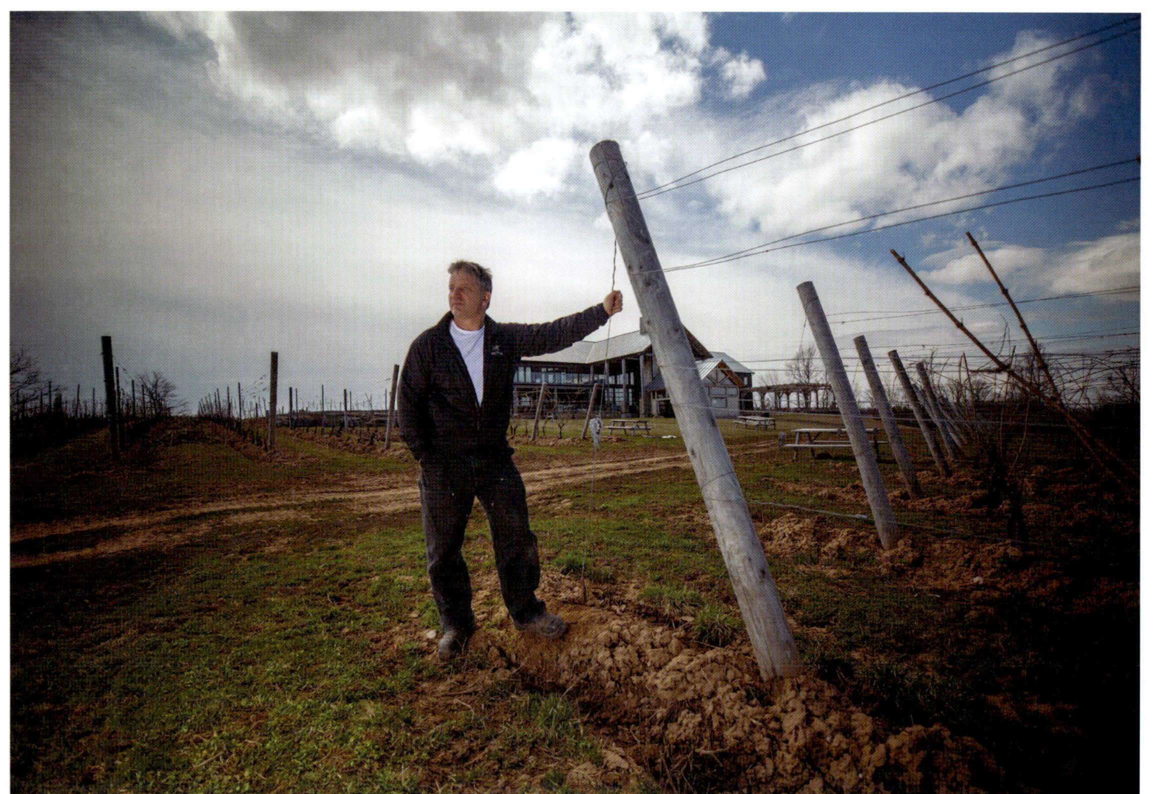

Michael Lightfoot surveys the land he grew up on, where his vineyard, Lightfoot & Wolfville, now stands. The company changed its business model to include delivery and online purchasing when it was forced to close its retail business and orders are now coming in from all across the country.

As they watched the early March sunsets over Taylor Bay in the Turks and Caicos, the pandemic was starting to get serious. "We were talking to some staff one evening and they were saying it was all a conspiracy, but then people started cancelling their reservations and airlines started restricting flights," says Michael. Messages from his daughters and friends urging them to return home began to sink in and they grabbed a flight home.

As government announced changes to the numbers of people who could gather, they knew the rules were going to have a serious effect on their operations. "It all unravelled. It was like, 'Holy shit!' All of the things we had talked about were out the window.... We had thirty weddings on the books this summer," he says.

"As time went on, I think both my wife and I realized that it was not just [going to affect] May. And even if [things] did open up a bit this summer, people aren't going to act the same way. They're not going to get in a room together. This is real, you know? This is real, and this is long-term."

The company had been working on its online presence before COVID-19 hit, but Jocelyn, Rachel, and Kori sensed that a shift to an online sales platform and contactless delivery could offer a big benefit. "Well, thank God they were taking the initiative to do this," says Michael.

"I've got to tell you, I get goosebumps. It has absolutely blown up. We have fifty-five, sixty-five orders a day coming in for cases of wine." Those orders are coming from across the country, with people ordering cases of wine from as far away as Alberta.

"We have pallets of wine going out with Canada Post right now, van-loads of wine going to Halifax and all over Nova Scotia. It's incredible," says Michael. What the business lost in event sales they have gained back—and more—in online sales.

"We're living in a historic moment," he says. "I watched my grandparents and my father lean into problems like this." He says during the wars there had been a complete breakdown of the supply chains; apples heading to Europe were rotting on the trees, and farmers were eking out a hardscrabble existence. His grandparents turned the apples to cider to quench the thirst of the returning soldiers—and managed to keep their farm from going under.

"They looked for opportunity, right? So even if we were internally fearful, we suppressed it and we said, 'We have to lean into this. We have to say it's going to be all right.'"

And it is. "People want something from home," says Michael. "That's what they're telling us: ... I just want to taste something from home.'"

BREWING UP BUSINESS:
Brightwood Brewery

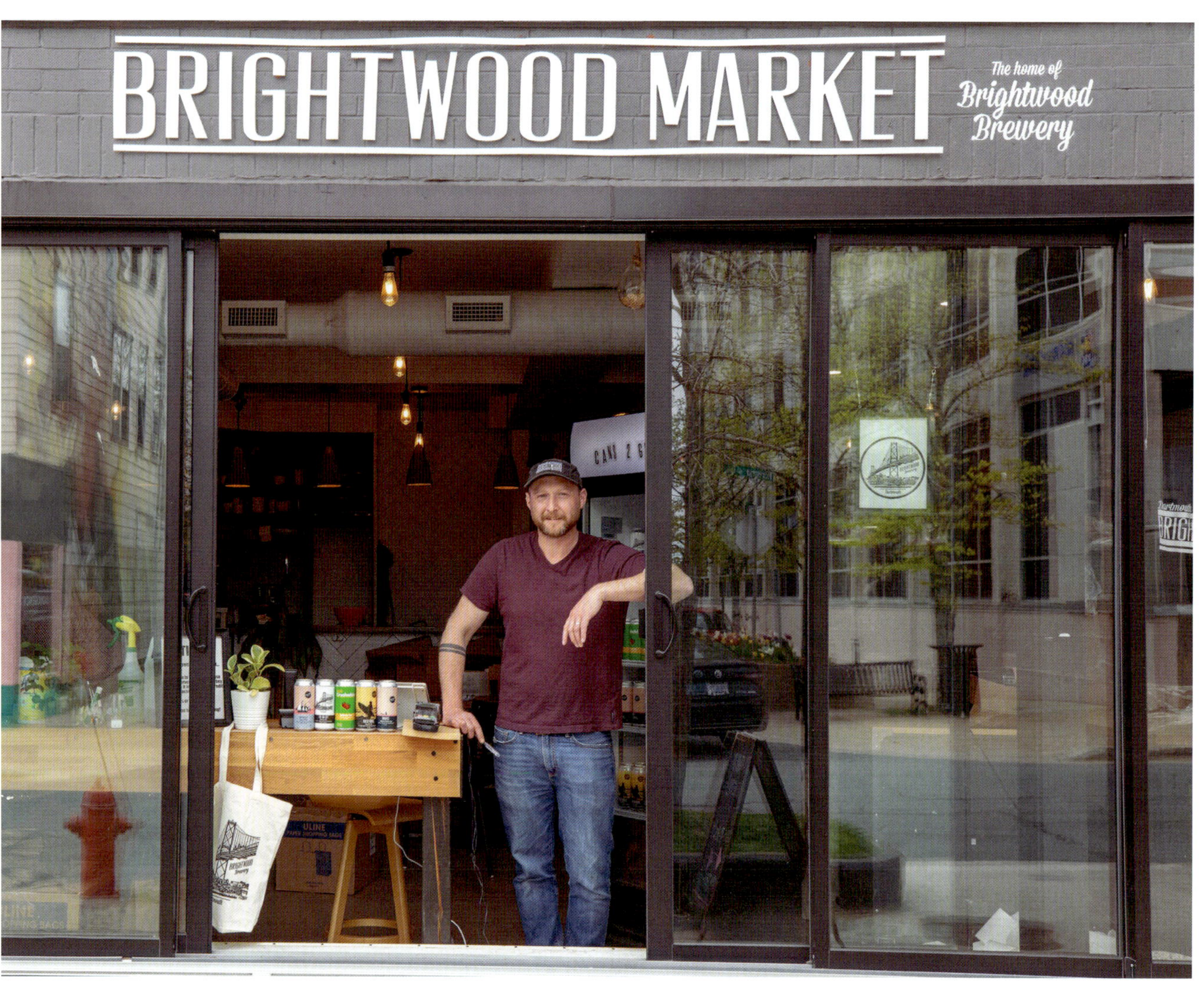

Ian Lawson kept Dartmouth's Brightwood Brewery in business by adapting to offer curbside pick-up and delivery.

Ian Lawson stands in the window at Brightwood Brewery on Portland St. in Dartmouth, watching as people step up to the window and order beer.

Not beer by the glass: take-out beer by the can and by the case. His taproom is closed, the chairs stacked up with the tables in a corner, most of his staff laid off.

"[The pandemic] completely turned our business plan upside down," says Ian, who co-owns the brewery with Matt McGrail. "We used to sell a lot of kegs to other restaurants and bars, pour glasses for clients inside, and all of that changed. Now we are 100 percent takeout."

Ian admits they did not see it coming. "Seeing COVID-19 kind of rear its head in China, we never thought that we would see the kind of lockdowns and closures we have

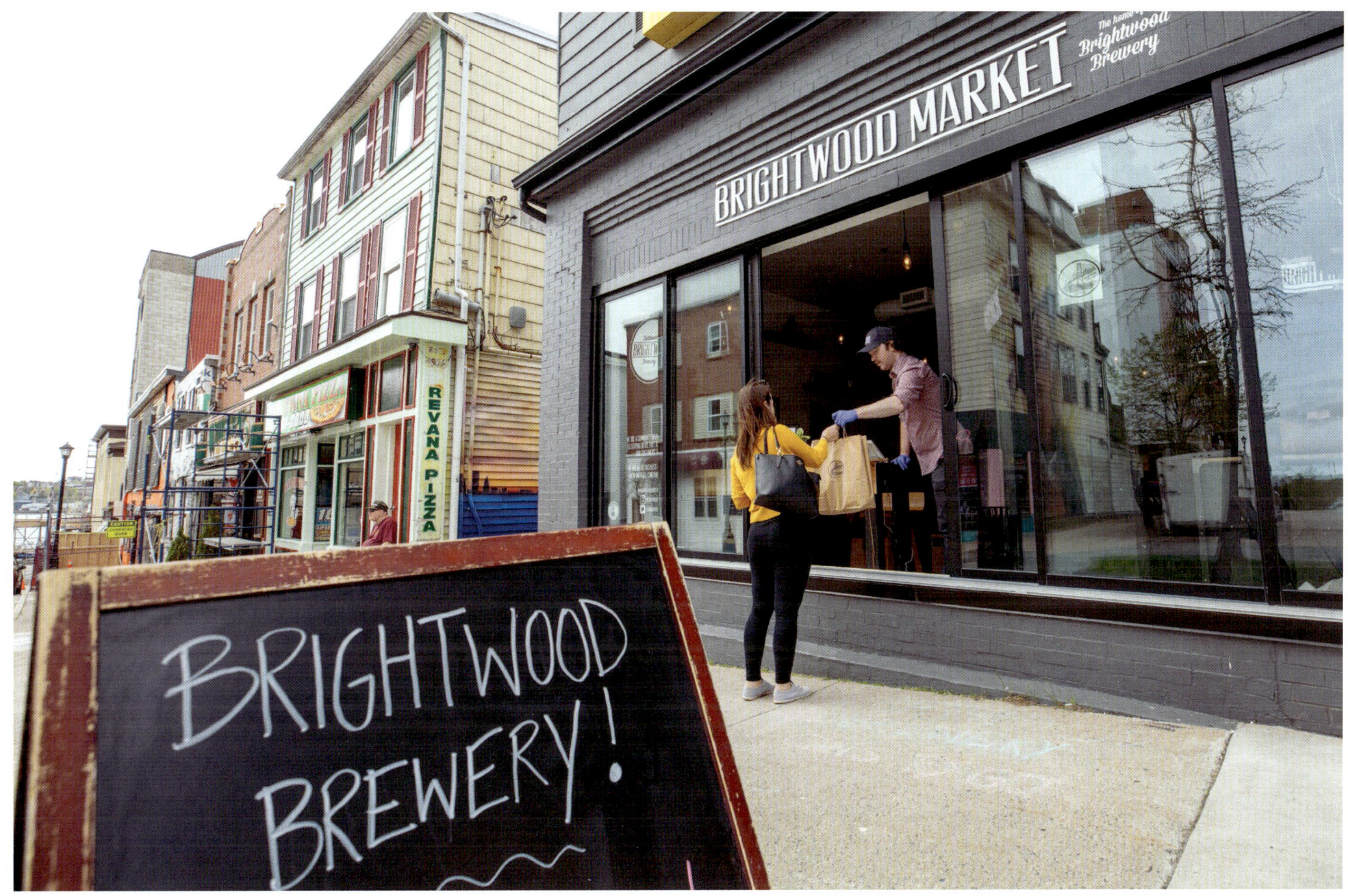

Sean Clancy fulfils a window order at the Brightwood Brewery taproom on Portland St. in Dartmouth

seen here. I guess in early March, when they started cancelling large gatherings, we [realized] things were going to be bad."

They closed the taproom, started a delivery service, and began doing takeout from she shop's front window. "I learned that we're super adaptable," says Ian, "because now everything we sell goes out in a can. I have learned that in business we need to be super frugal."

He also learned that the business was part of an incredibly supportive community. "A lot of people are reaching out and buying whatever they can to keep us afloat—to see us through this. That is an amazing feeling for a business."

The brewery reciprocated by launching an ale called Backyards Hazy Pale Ale.

"We are all at home, so enjoy it in your own backyard," says Ian.

After the mass shooting in Nova Scotia on the weekend of April 19, Ian and Matt decided to donate proceeds from sales of Backyards to the Mental Health Foundation of Nova Scotia.

"Whatever we could do to help," says Ian. The beer became one of their top sellers, and by the time the campaign ended on July 26, they had raised $5,394 for the foundation.

"It was our way of giving back," he says.

THE T-SHIRT THAT TOOK OFF:
My Home Apparel

It was mid-March, and Miriah Kearney was not having a good week.

In fact, she was not having a good two weeks. The founder and president of My Home Mercantile, a giftware company that sells curated Canadian-made and globally discovered giftware, and its sister company, My Home Apparel, which produces and creates Canadian-made and made-in-Nova Scotia clothing, had just closed both her Truro and Moncton stores. She'd had to make what she described as one of the hardest choices of her career and lay off thirteen of her staff.

She had spent the first two months of 2020 backpacking through Australia, Indonesia, Malaysia, and the Philippines with her family, and had returned home in early March to get ready for the coming season, she explains. As we chat, she leans against the counter in her shop and looks out toward the empty street in downtown Truro. The word "HOME," with the shape of the province of Nova Scotia in place of the letter "O," beams proudly from the wall behind her. "Within ten days of me returning, the entire world flipped upside down."

"Upside down" because of COVID-19 and the province-wide state of emergency that had been declared due to the pandemic. "Within four days we had to close down production, because not only did [our stores] close, but all the stores we supply cancelled their orders," she says.

"We all knew it was the right thing to do to flatten the curve, [but] the company lost a hundred thousand dollars right off the top. I panicked, because I thought, 'How I am ever going to make ends meet?'"

But fate had something unexpected in store for her. On Friday, April 3, she and her family were watching as Premier Stephen McNeil and Chief Medical Officer of Health Robert Strang presented their daily COVID-19 status update. Frustrated with Nova Scotians who were not obeying social distancing orders, the premier admonished citizens to "stay the blazes home" as the weekend approached. "I looked at my husband and said, 'That would make a really good T-shirt.'"

Within a few hours she had a rough drawing ready and sent it to her designer. Twenty-two hours later the T-shirt went live on her website. "I was thinking we would sell a hundred, maybe two hundred if we were lucky," she recalls. "I was at the kitchen table and my husband was in the living room and I hit refresh—and we had sold hundreds of T-shirts." Her eyes widen as she tells the story. "Every time I hit refresh, it was thousands more dollars. At 5:00 P.M. I came in to work and stared at the screen. I was paralyzed. I was in shock, just watching it go."

By Sunday morning she and her staff were ecstatic. "I don't think the three of us had slept because we were just so happy. We were also panicked because—what were we going to do?"

The company had shut down production and now had to figure out how to fulfill the huge number of orders rolling in. It took Kearney and her staff just twenty-four hours to get suppliers organized and to figure out how they could bring some staff back safely while adhering to social distancing regulations.

"On Monday night we re-launched again, and we sold out again!" she says. "We realized that the messaging of staying home was resonating across the country."

She enlisted her mom and her husband, who had been laid off from his job as a carpenter (he had been working on projects for Bird Construction in China until January 2020, when he'd left to join the family on their vacation), to help out. "This basically has revitalized the company. Not only did people buy the 'Blazes' T-shirt, they started buying other items off the website. That's how I'm keeping the lights on and people employed."

My Home Apparel has always donated 5 percent of all its profits to initiatives aiming to end homelessness in Canada, but Kearney decided early on that 100 percent of the money she made from the T-shirts would go to charity—despite the fact that she was worried her company would not survive the pandemic. "In my heart, I knew if I was going down I wanted to go down doing something great. I've always been in business to make an impact. I have to pay my bills and support my family, but I've always

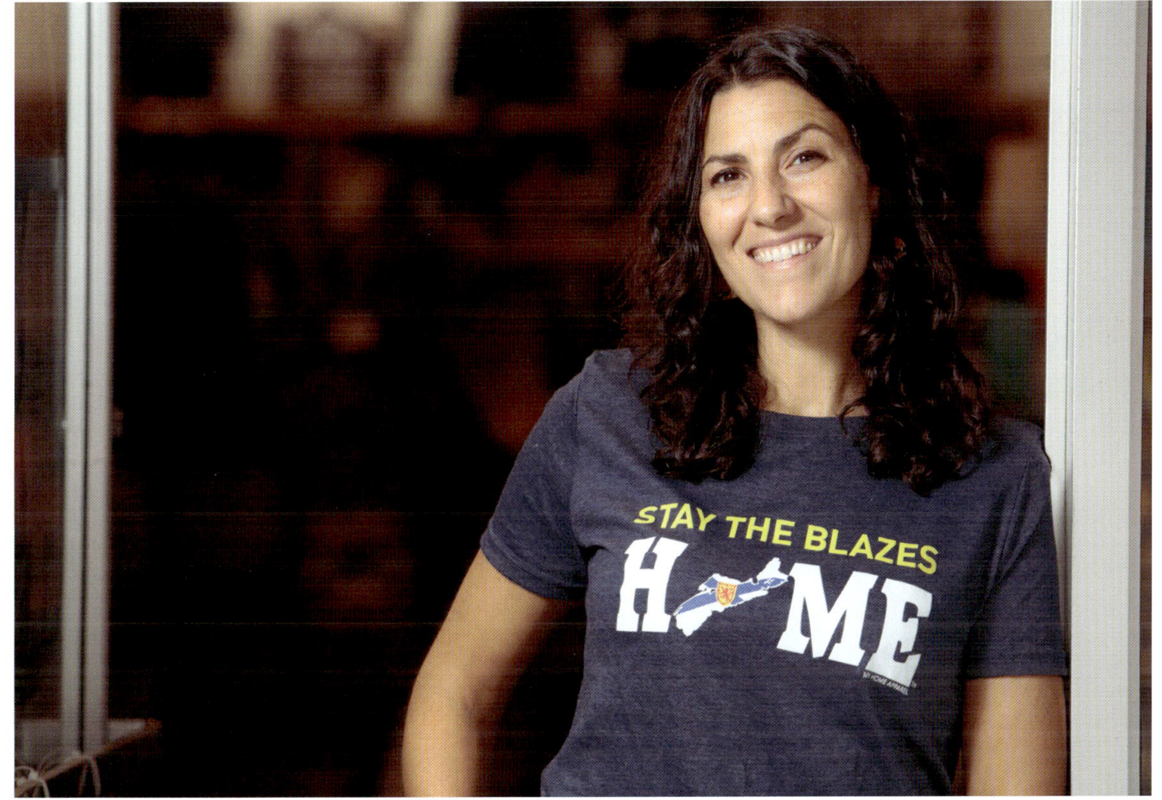

Miriah Kearney, owner of My Home Apparel, created this "Stay The Blazes Home" T-shirt in response to Premier Stephen McNeil's admonition to Nova Scotians. Sales of the shirt took off; Miriah donated 100 percent of the profits to charity.

wanted to be 'people over profits,'" she says. "If I'm going down, let's do something great in the process, and that will be my legacy—not that another business went under, but that we made it and did something amazing along the way."

Kearney has lived up to her word. More than a hundred thousand dollars from her T-shirt sales has been divided among Shelter Nova Scotia, Feed Nova Scotia, Adsum House, the QEII Health Science Centre's COVID-19 relief fund, the Canada Helps COVID-19 relief fund, and Food Banks Canada. "I'm never surprised by the compassion of Maritimers," she says, "but for the support that Canadians have shown for our business during this time, I'll be forever grateful." And the spinoff online business has helped keep her company alive.

She knows her small gesture will have a place in the history books. "I tip my hat to the premier. We were able to act fast and think quickly and do something impactful. I'll always remember this experience on different levels: the hardship, what my staff went through," she says.

"In my personal life I've had some incredible moments: being a mother, being married, travelling around the world. But in the midst of the pandemic, in the darkest time for many people, this has been the most amazing moment in my business—the most impactful, exciting, emotional." She looks to the stairway and listens to the bustle upstairs as the "Stay the Blazes Home" T-shirt crew works away.

"In the darkest times, we had the greatest light."

AFTERWORD:

Q&A with The Honourable Stephen McNeil

Given the title of this book, we thought it was only fitting to ask Stephen McNeil, premier of the province of Nova Scotia, to share his thoughts on what it's been like to govern through the COVID-19 pandemic. In the summer of 2020, Nimbus Publishing reached out by email, and Premier McNeil kindly agreed to contribute his thoughts for this book. Shortly after we received his responses, Premier McNeil announced he would be stepping down. Our questions and his answers appear below.

Q. *Can you tell us when you started to get a sense that Nova Scotia was not going to escape the COVID-19 pandemic and how you responded?*

A. I understood from Public Health that the coronavirus was going to come here; I just didn't know the extent. When it arrived, we needed to drastically reduce the direct contact between individuals, even though it meant hurting the economy. We also knew our senior citizens were particularly vulnerable, so long-term care facilities were closed to visitors. These were critical decisions that were made with Public Health. We basically shut down the service economy early on.

We also knew it would be important for Public Health to keep people informed, as this was an ever-changing situation. And we needed to get people ollowing Public Health protocols.

Q. *This book is called* Stay the Blazes Home: Dispatches from Nova Scotia during the COVID-19 Pandemic, *which is clearly a nod to the phrase you coined during one of your coronavirus updates with Dr. Strang. Can you tell us what was going through your mind when you told Nova Scotians to "Stay the blazes home"? And why do you think the phrase resonated so much with Nova Scotians?*

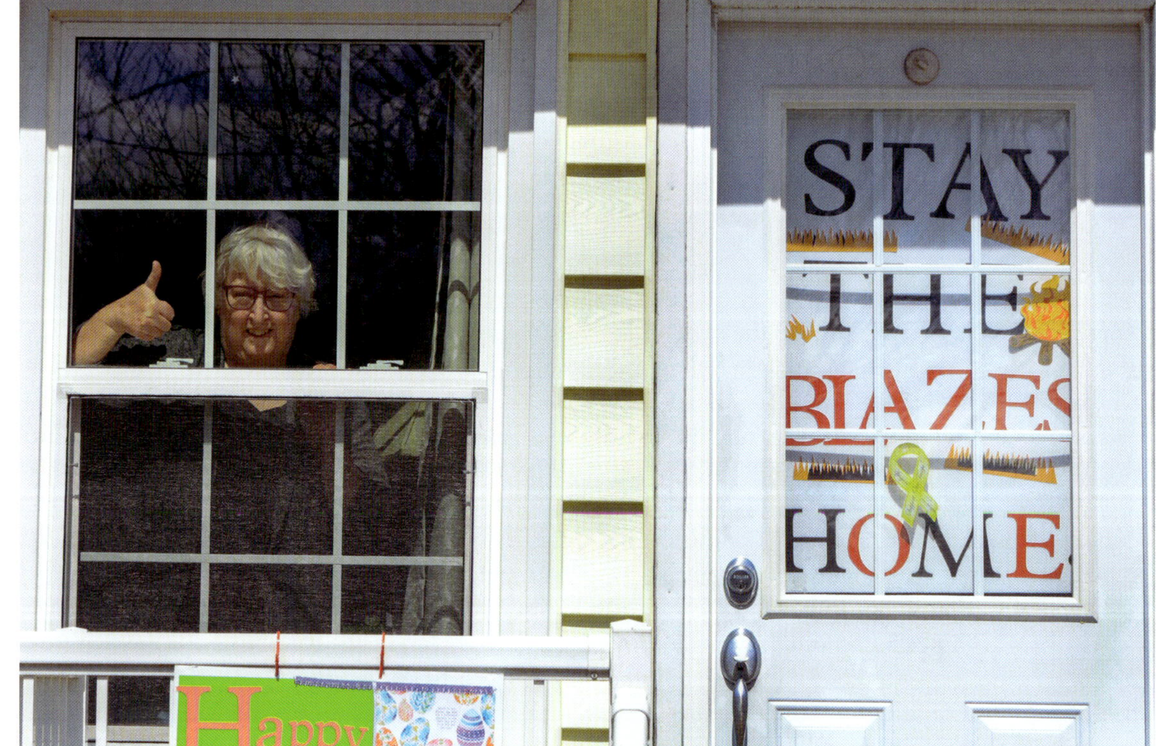

Phyllis Murray of Cloverdale Rd. in Halifax had a message to people passing in her neighbourhood.

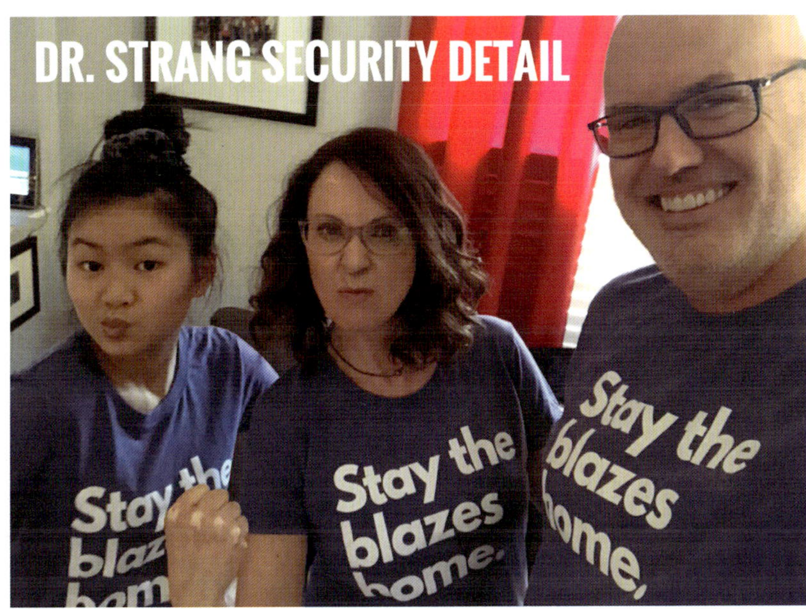

Leanne Andrecyk of Halifax says she and her family had a lot of fun posing as Dr. Strang's "Security Detail."

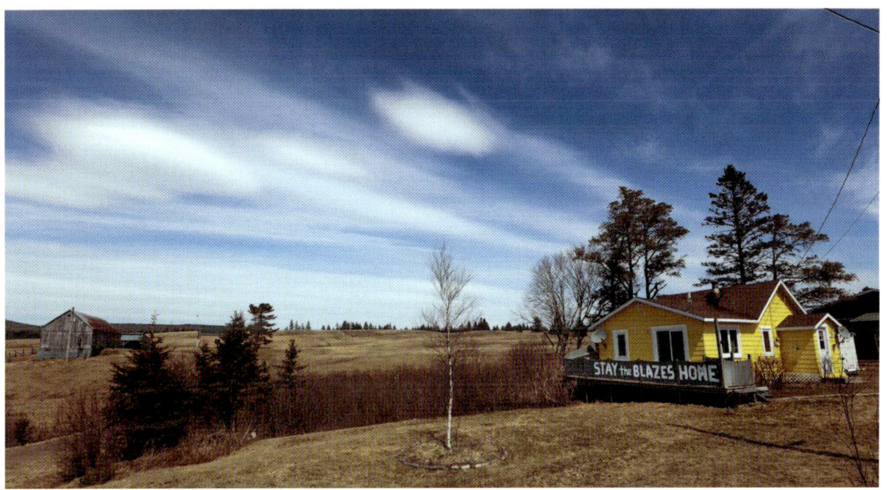

"I was going to paint my fence [to read] 'Stay Home,' as I felt society was not following the state of emergency in Nova Scotia," says Kimberley Deuville, owner of the property in Nuttby, NS, pictured here. "So when Premier Stephen McNeil was getting frustrated with Nova Scotians not staying home, and he showed his frustration by saying, 'Stay the Blazes Home,'—and where I already had the paint out anyway—it just seemed right to paint his quote and maybe educate people driving by."

A. Early on, some people were not following Public Health protocols, which was frustrating, both for me and the majority of Nova Scotians who were taking the proper steps to keep themselves and others safe. Working with people in my office, we came up with the phrase. It seemed to fit.

I think it resonated because many of us could hear our parents or grandparents emphasizing the importance of their advice in a similar way, and it underlined the seriousness of COVID. It's an old-fashioned saying that connected during this modern day pandemic.

It also seemed to resonate across the country. We had lots of calls and feedback from across Canada.

Q. *What have you learned (personally and professionally) through the course of this pandemic?*

A. The importance of communicating directly with Nova Scotians, clearly telling them all you know when you know it.

On a personal level: the importance of being kind through successes and difficulties, and how kindness toward others goes a long way toward helping everyone.

Q. *This book will come out in October 2020. If there's one thing you'd like to say to the people of Nova Scotia about the pandemic, what would it be?*

A. How critical it is you follow and practice the advice of Public Health, even when you feel invincible yourself. Following the advice of Public Health goes a long way to not only protect you, but to protect everyone, in this pandemic or others. It's how we stop the spread and keep people safe.

As we work through this and we know the virus will still be here, we still need to follow the protocols—wash your hands, keep social distance, wear a mask.

And I would urge people to continue being kind and supportive, and to look out for each other.

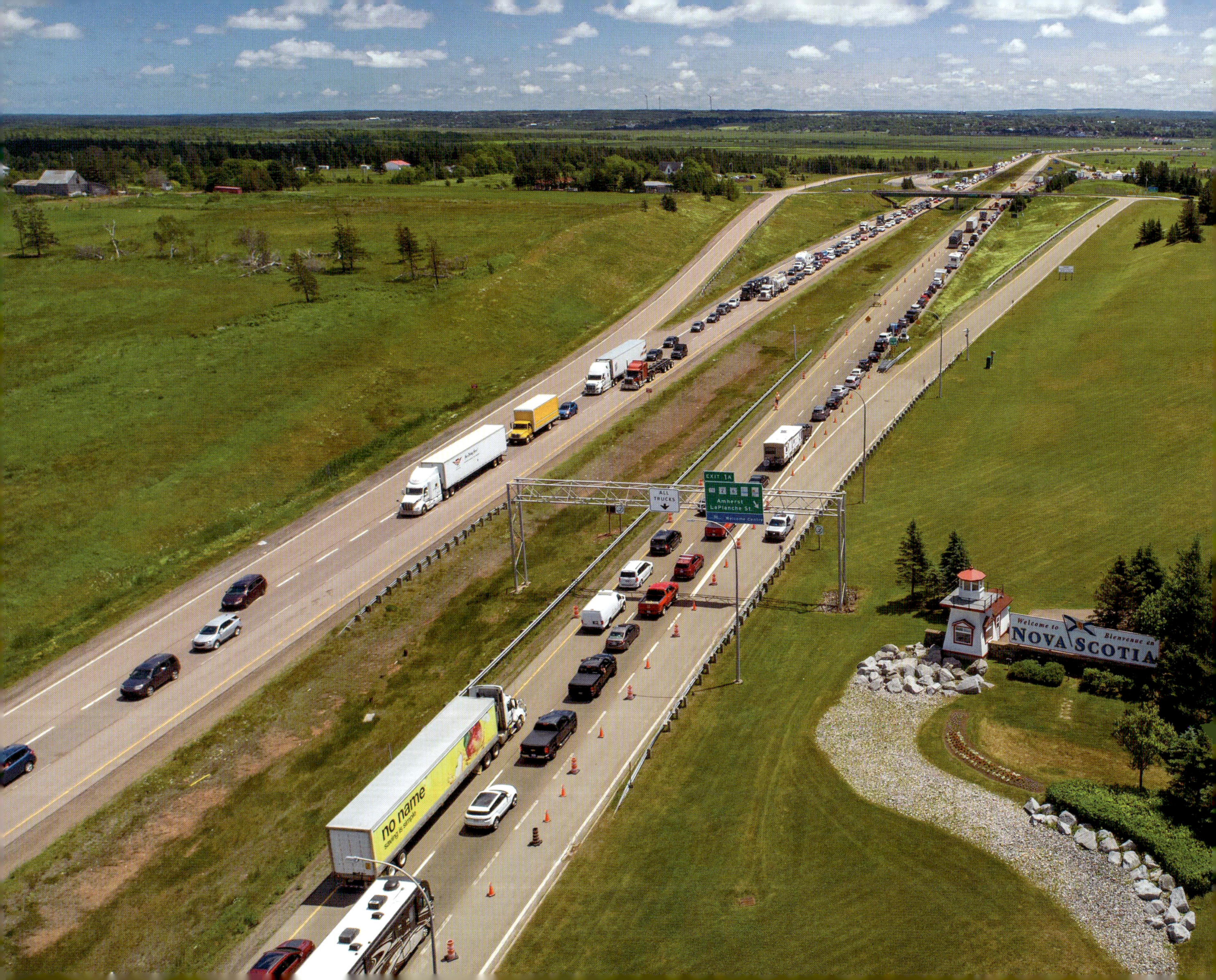
ALL TRUCKS
EXIT 1A
Amherst
LaPlanche St.
Welcome Centre
Welcome to
NOVA SCOTIA
Bienvenue en
no name

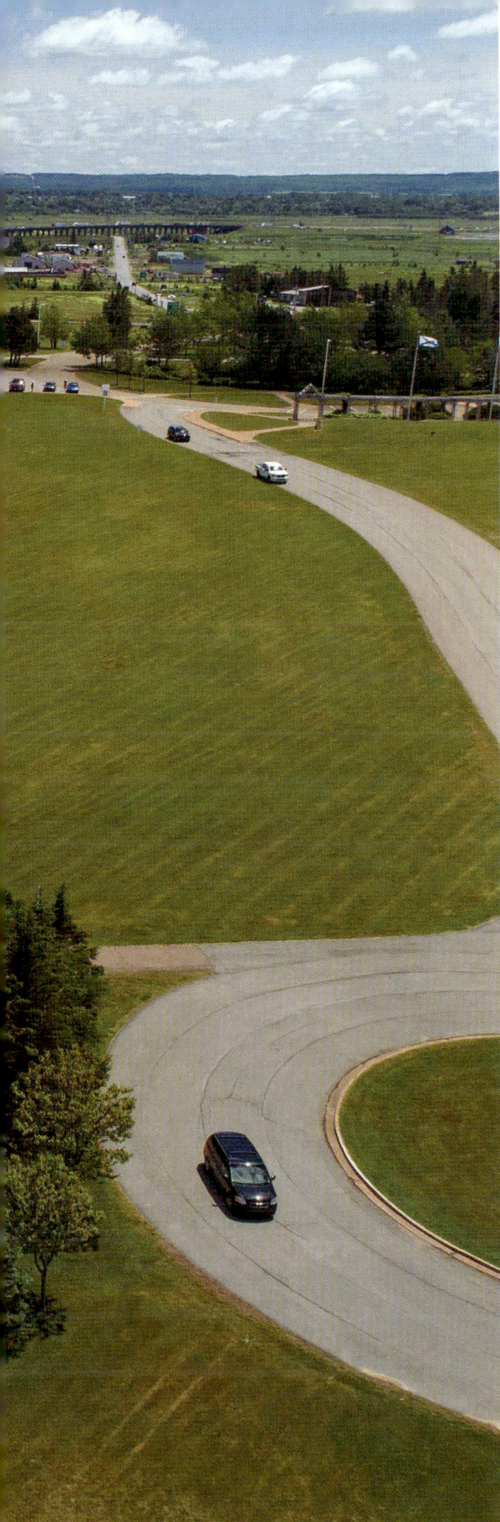

ACKNOWLEDGEMENTS

Creating this book has been a humbling experience.

So many people opened up about their fears, hopes, and sorrows during this pandemic; I am lucky to have been able to include their stories on these pages. To everyone who let me into their life—thank you!

To photographer Paul Darrow for his support during this project and for contributing many images: thank you! Also, to photographers Steve Wadden, Nicola Davison, Tim Krochak, and Christian Laforce, who contributed images as well: thank you for your storytelling work. This book could not have been done without you. And thanks to all of you for agreeing to allow a portion of the royalties to go to the Mental Health Association of Nova Scotia.

When the market for books had fallen through the floor because of the pandemic and publishers were struggling to keep afloat, Terrilee Bulger, general manager and co-owner of Nimbus Publishing, ran with the idea to create this book. Thank you. (Hope it works!)

Words are not my forte and everything you read in this book has Angela Mombourquette's fingerprints all over it. She is an amazing editor and I hope she doesn't turn her back on editing after she finishes this project (ha)! Any errors on these pages are my own.

To all who contributed snapshots from their lives to help us tell this story—thank you so much. It was inspiring to witness how we navigated the pandemic separately but together.

Suppertime in my home during the lockdown was a mixture of classroom talk and story ideas. Thanks to Sandy Wagg for all your help during the long/short/long process of getting this book done within the deadline, kinda.

And to all of the readers who buy this book: I hope it becomes a memento of what it was like to live through the spring of 2020. Thanks to all of you.

Len Wagg
August 2020
len@lenwagg.com

On June 24, the Council of Atlantic Premiers announced that interprovincial travel in Atlantic Canada, for Atlantic Canadian residents only, would be permitted without the requirement to self-isolate. On July 3 the "Atlantic Bubble" came into being. The long line of traffic at the border between Nova Scotia and New Brunswick is evidence of just how eager Maritimers were to take advantage of the relaxed travel restrictions.

MORE BOOKS FROM LEN WAGG

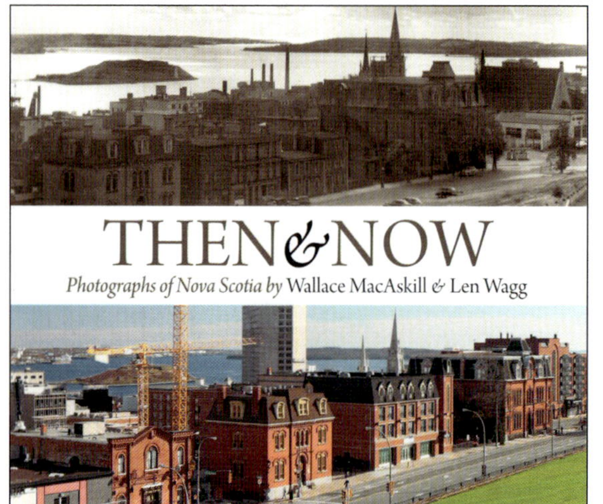

Then & Now
(978-1-77108-340-9)

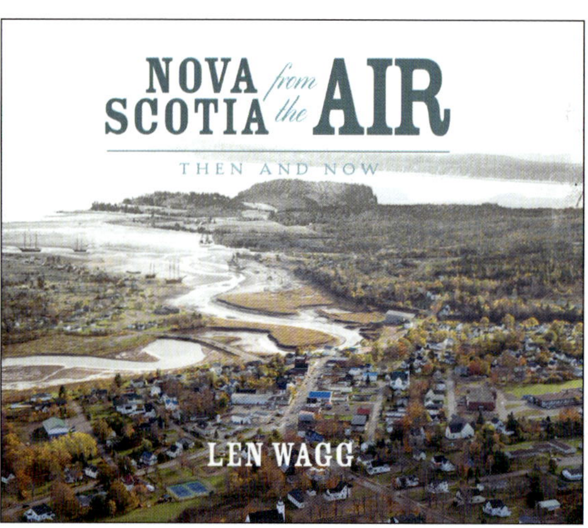

Nova Scotia from the Air
(978-1-77108-745-2)

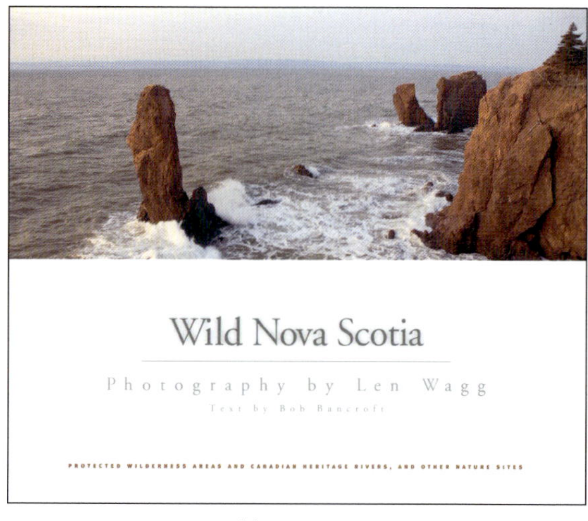

Wild Nova Scotia
(978-1-55109-945-3)

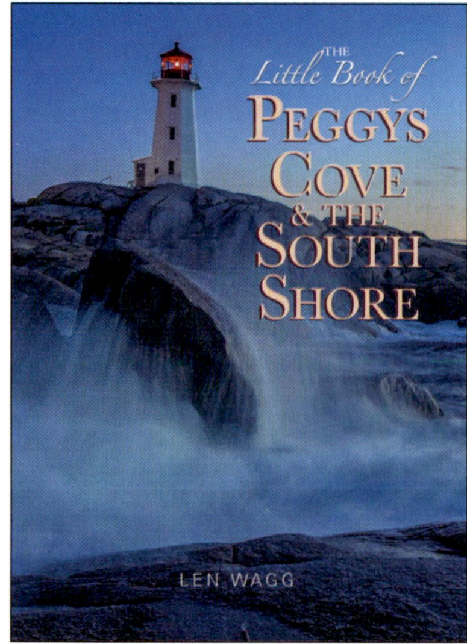

The Little Book of Peggys Cove and the South Shore
(978-1-77108-821-3)

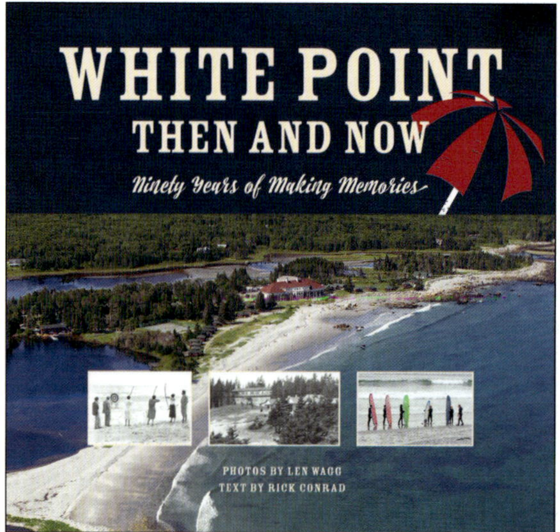

White Point Then & Now
(978-1-77108-612-7)

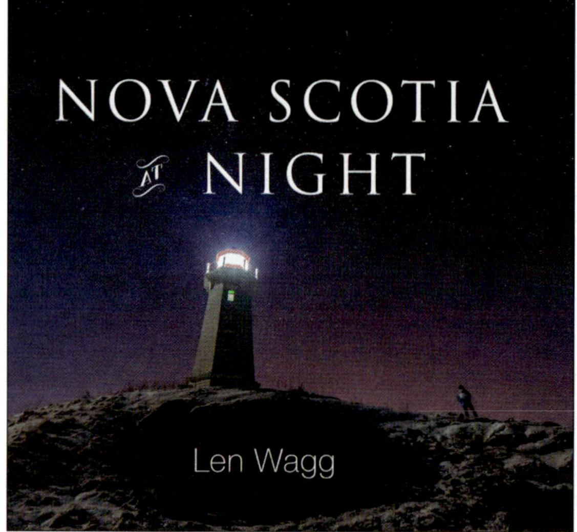

Nova Scotia at Night
(978-1-77108-522-9)